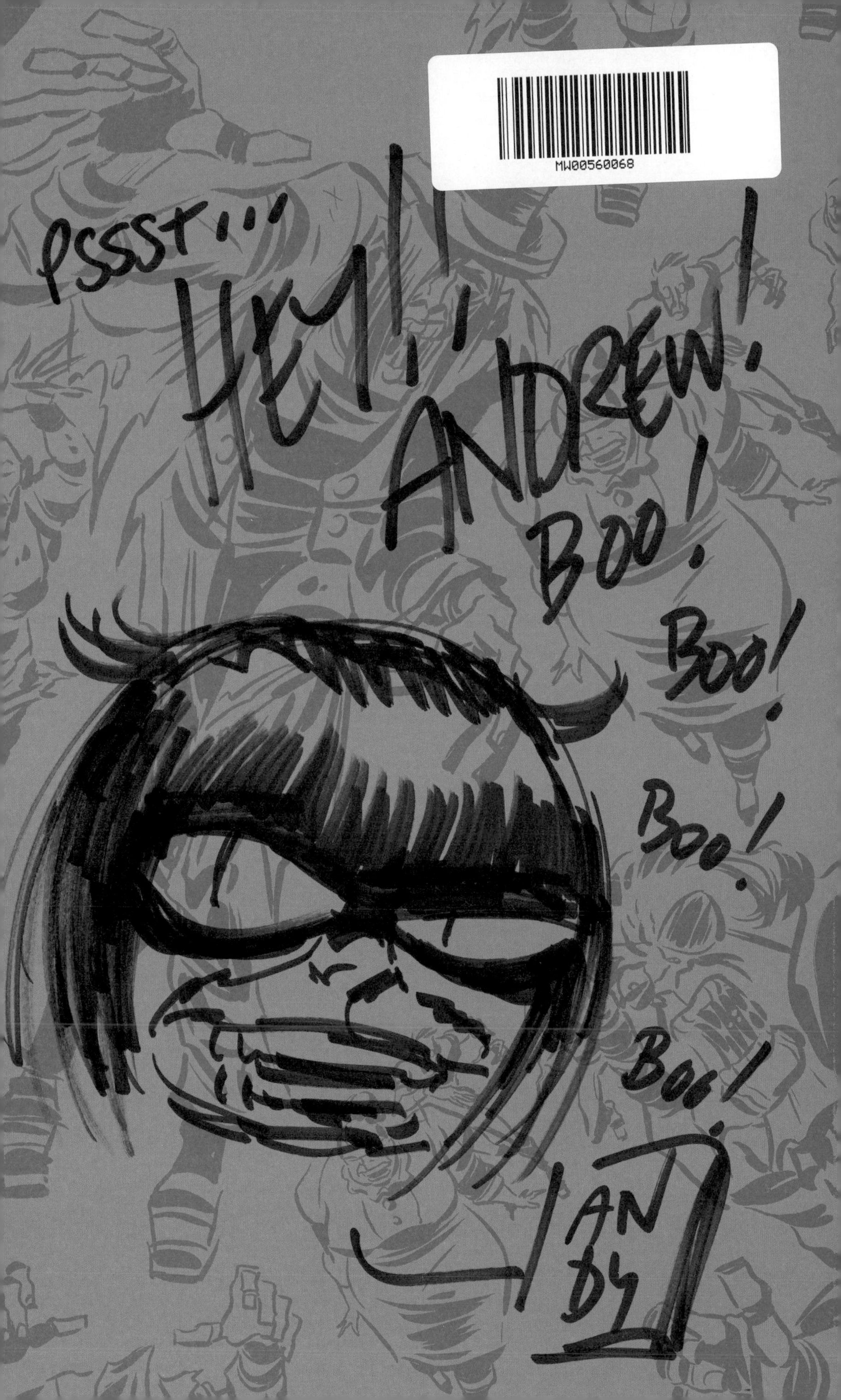
PSSST...
HEY!!
ANDREW!
BOO!
BOO!
BOO!
BOO!

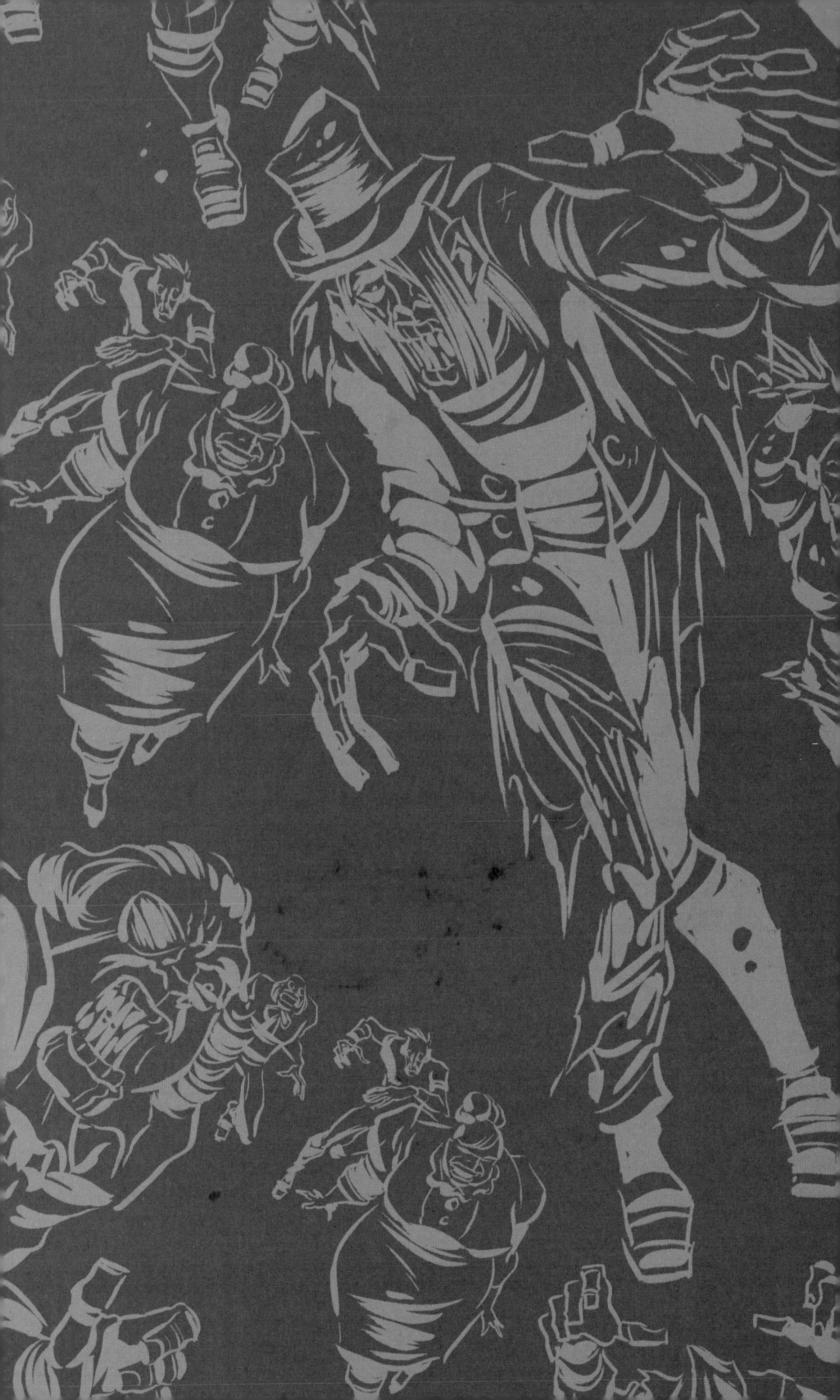

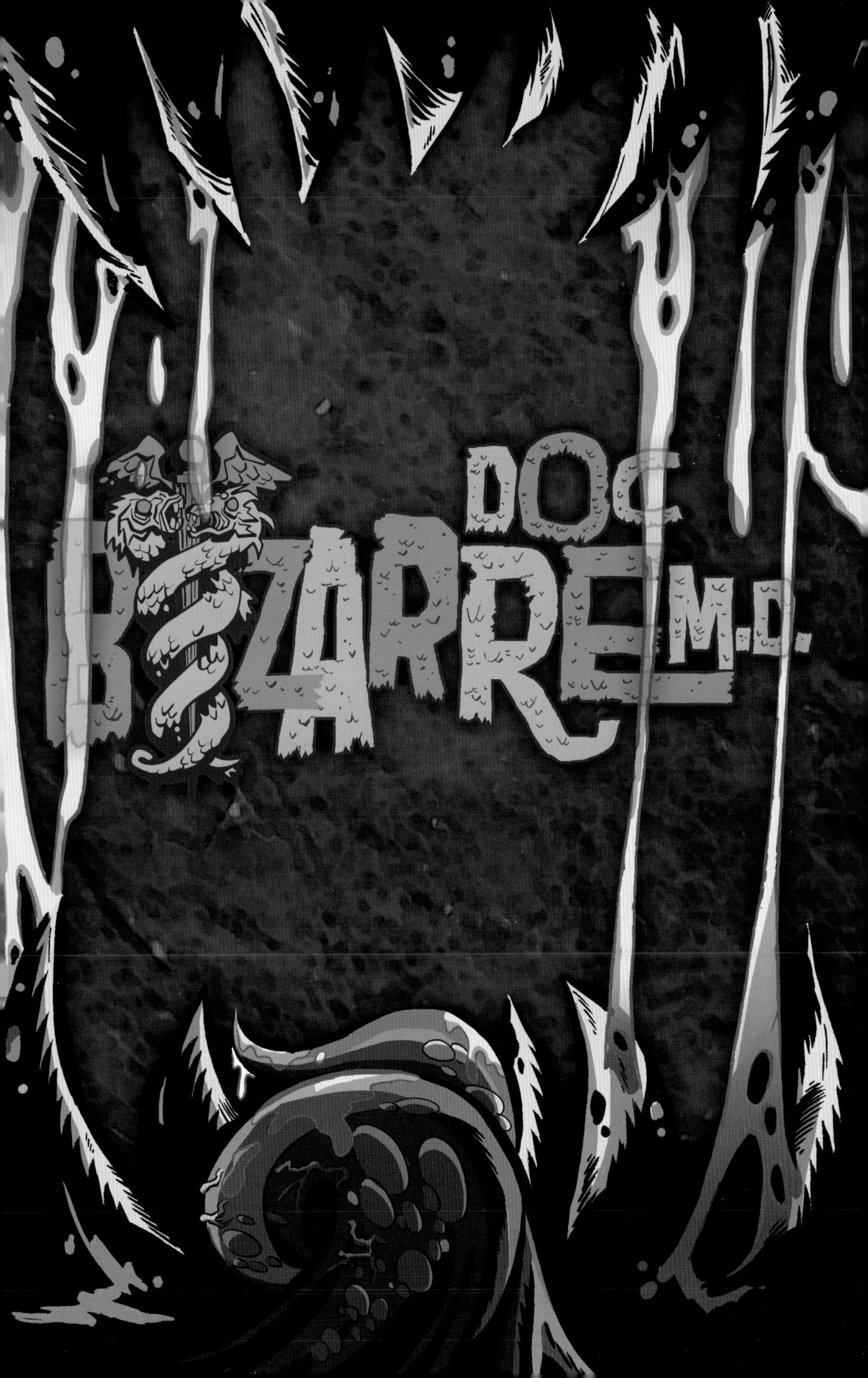
DOC
BIZARRE M.D.

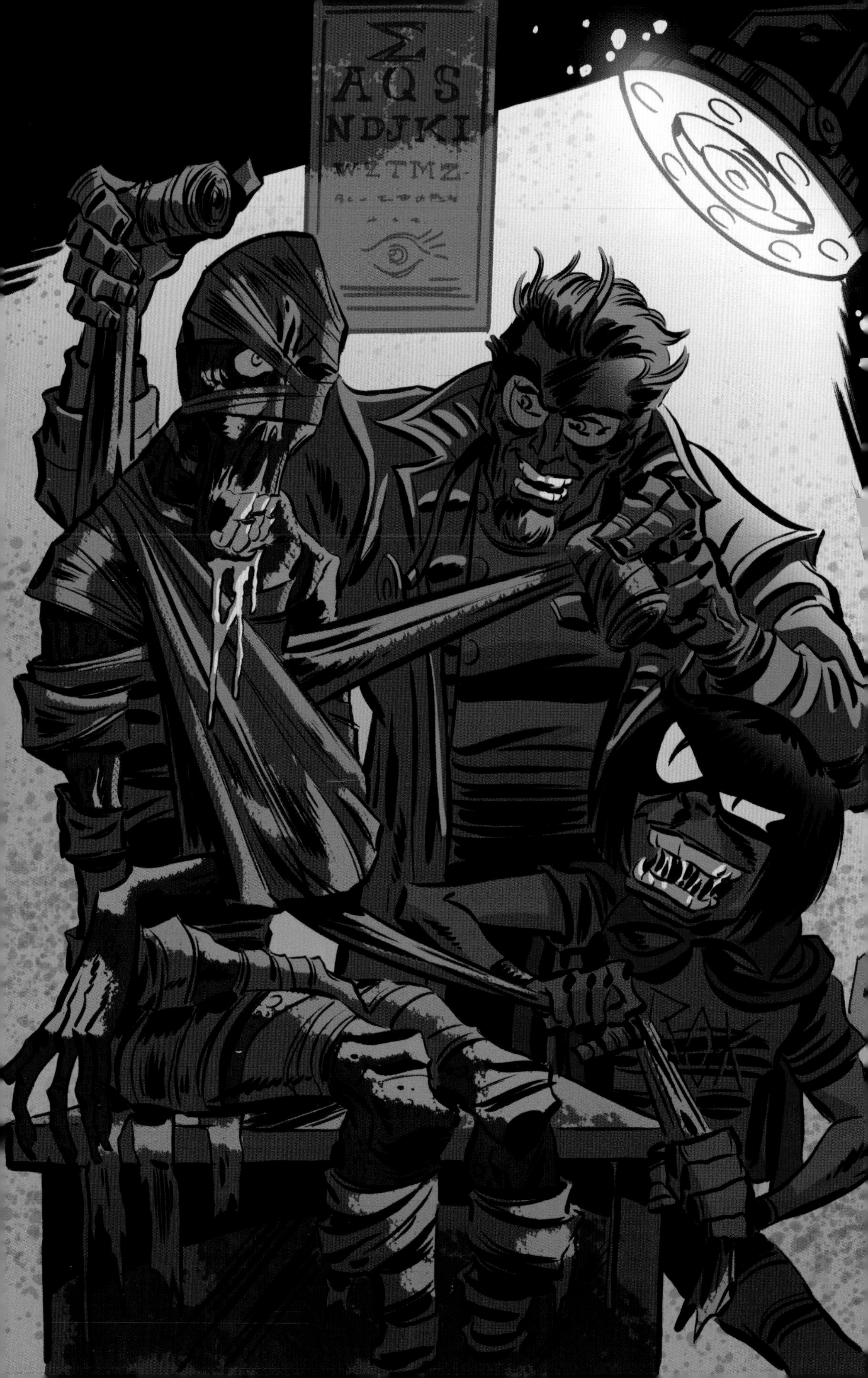
AQS
NDJKI
WZTMZ

CO-CREATORS

JOE CASEY
WRITER

ANDY SURIANO
ART & COLORS

LETTERING
RUS WOOTON

BOOK DESIGN
DREW GILL

LOGO DESIGN
PETER GIRARDI

SPECIAL THANKS TO
MARC LETZMANN

MAN OF
action
STUDIOS

WWW.MANOFACTION.TV

DOC BIZARRE, M.D.

First Printing. October 2011.
Published by Image Comics, Inc.

Office of publication:
2134 Allston Way, Second Floor,
Berkeley, California 94704.

International Rights Representative:
Christine Meyer — christine@gfloystudio.com

Printed in Korea.

ISBN: 978-1-60706-455-8

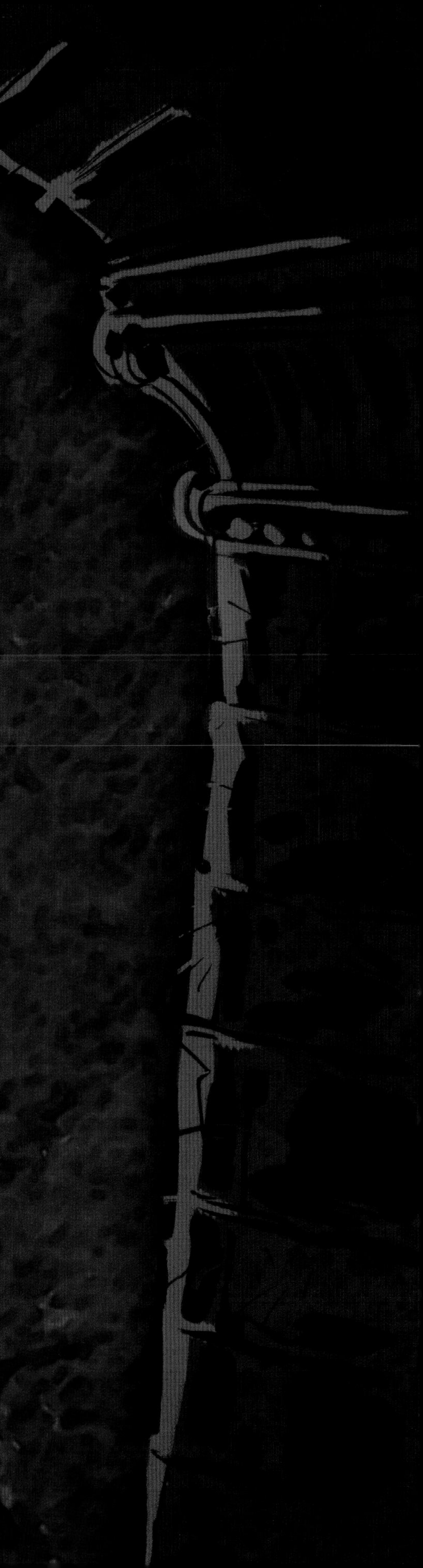

IMAGE COMICS, INC.

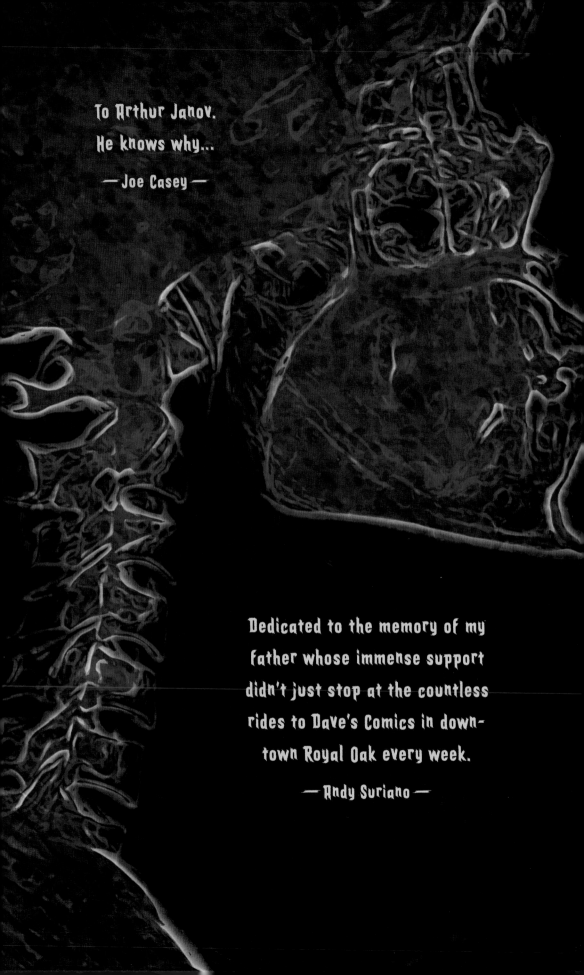

To Arthur Janov.
He knows why...

—Joe Casey—

Dedicated to the memory of my
father whose immense support
didn't just stop at the countless
rides to Dave's Comics in down-
town Royal Oak every week.

—Andy Suriano—

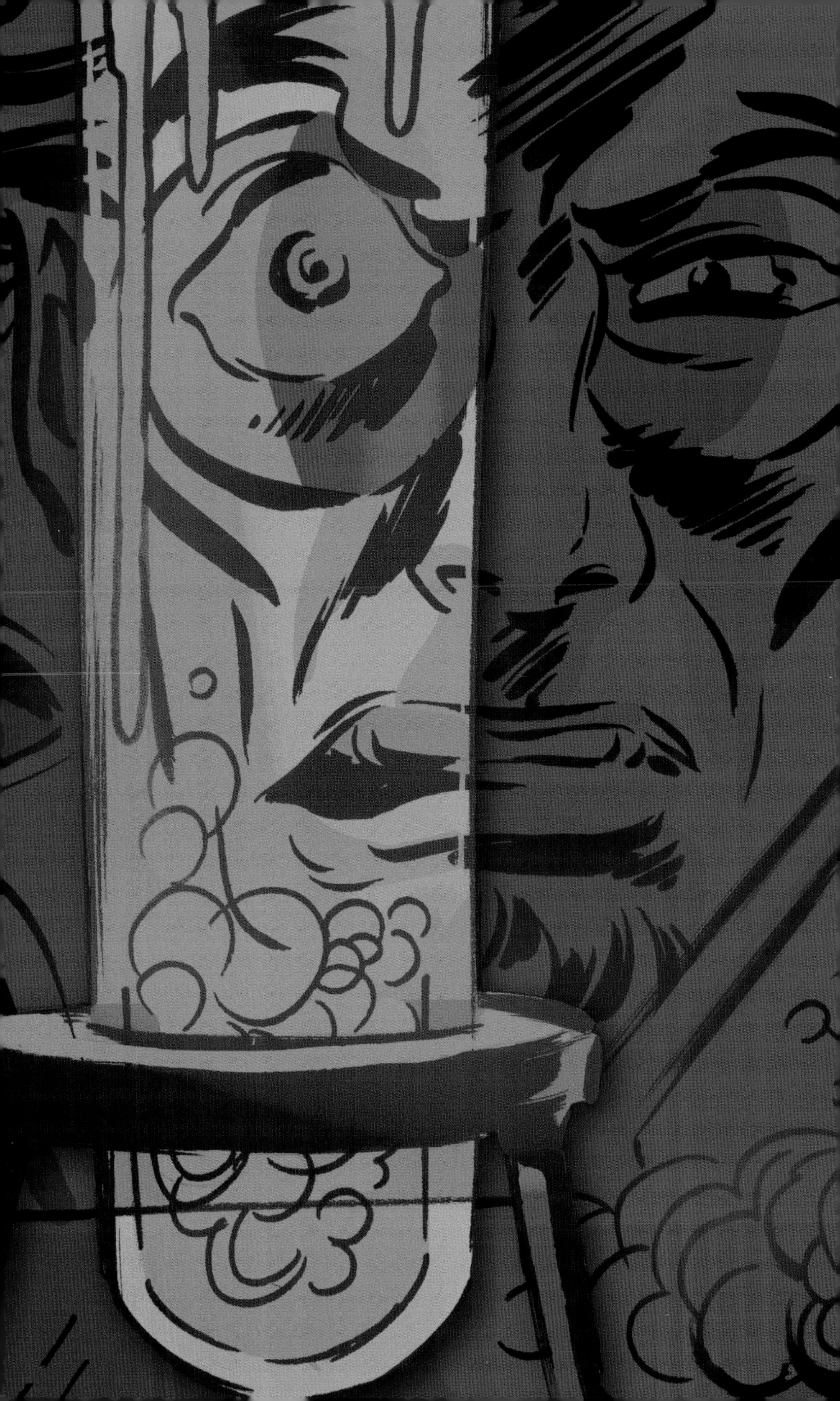

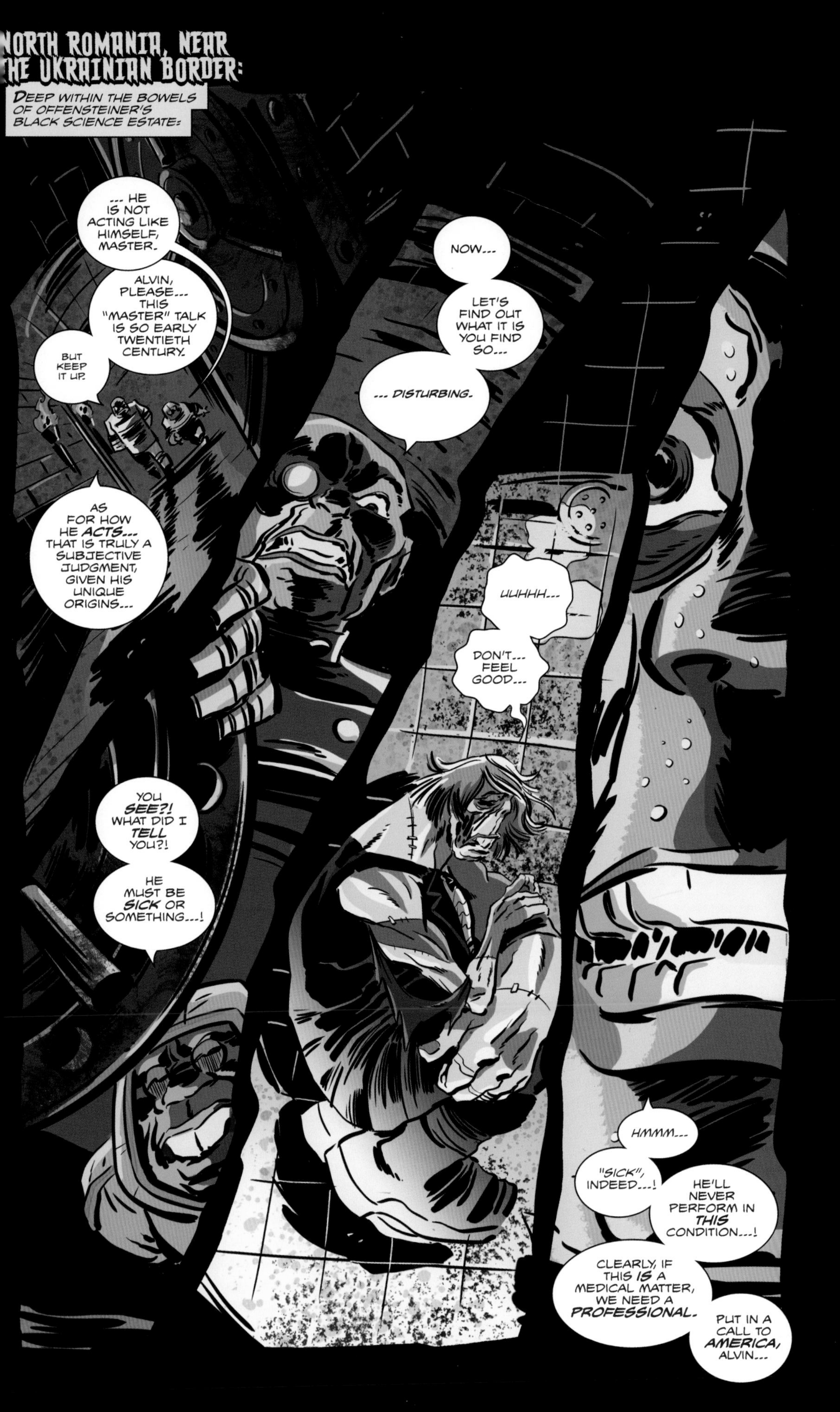
NORTH ROMANIA, NEAR THE UKRAINIAN BORDER:
DEEP WITHIN THE BOWELS OF OFFENSTEINER'S BLACK SCIENCE ESTATE:
... HE IS NOT ACTING LIKE HIMSELF, MASTER.
ALVIN, PLEASE... THIS "MASTER" TALK IS SO EARLY TWENTIETH CENTURY.
BUT KEEP IT UP.
AS FOR HOW HE ACTS... THAT IS TRULY A SUBJECTIVE JUDGMENT, GIVEN HIS UNIQUE ORIGINS...
NOW...
LET'S FIND OUT WHAT IT IS YOU FIND SO...
... DISTURBING.
UUHHH...
DON'T... FEEL GOOD...
YOU SEE?! WHAT DID I TELL YOU?!
HE MUST BE SICK OR SOMETHING...!
HMMM...
"SICK", INDEED...!
HE'LL NEVER PERFORM IN THIS CONDITION...!
CLEARLY, IF THIS IS A MEDICAL MATTER, WE NEED A PROFESSIONAL.
PUT IN A CALL TO AMERICA, ALVIN...

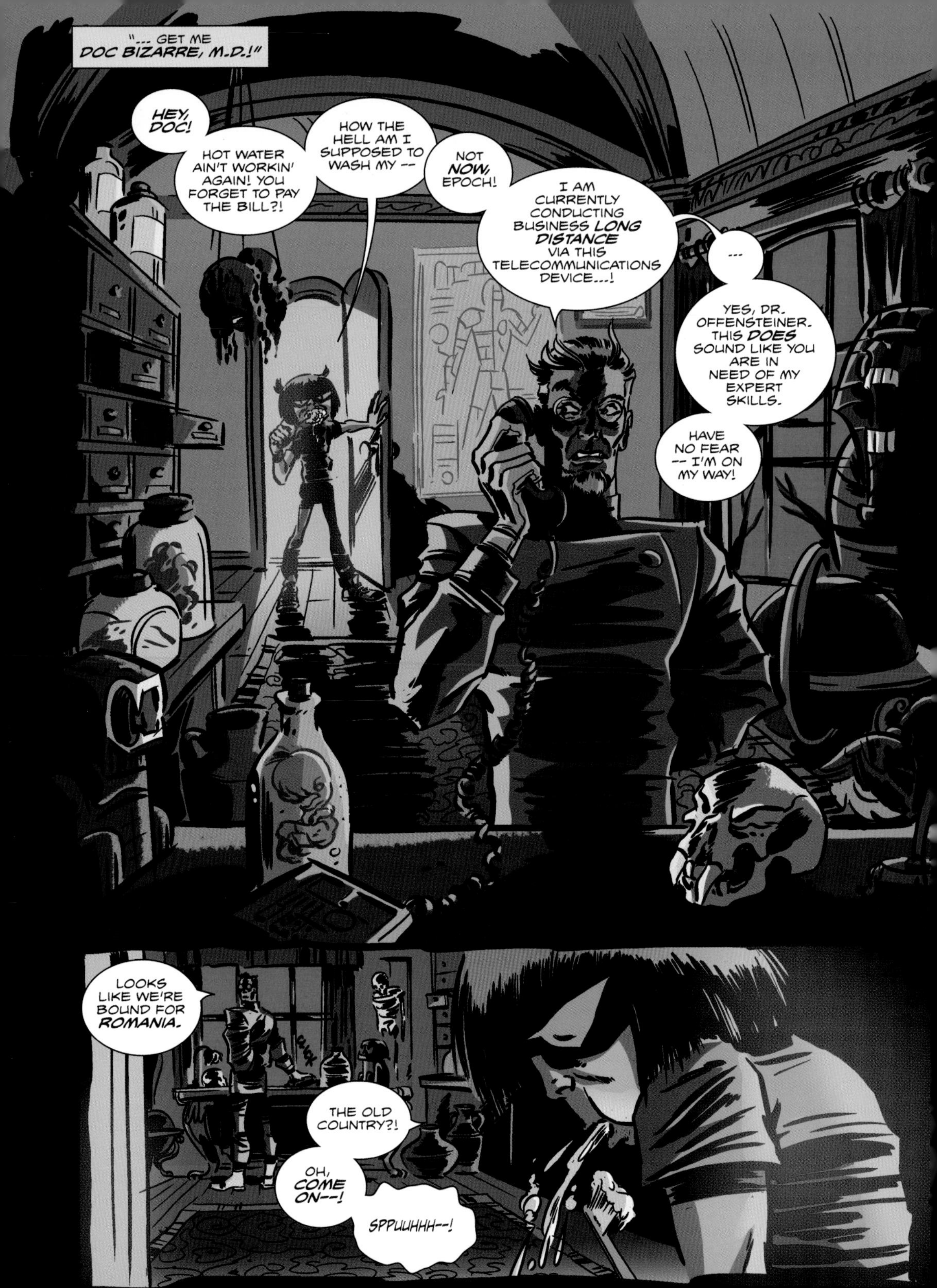
"... GET ME DOC BIZARRE, M.D.!"
HEY, DOC!
HOT WATER AIN'T WORKIN' AGAIN! YOU FORGET TO PAY THE BILL?!
HOW THE HELL AM I SUPPOSED TO WASH MY --
NOT NOW, EPOCH!
I AM CURRENTLY CONDUCTING BUSINESS LONG DISTANCE VIA THIS TELECOMMUNICATIONS DEVICE...!
...
YES, DR. OFFENSTEINER. THIS DOES SOUND LIKE YOU ARE IN NEED OF MY EXPERT SKILLS.
HAVE NO FEAR -- I'M ON MY WAY!
LOOKS LIKE WE'RE BOUND FOR ROMANIA.
CLICK
THE OLD COUNTRY?!
OH, COME ON--!
SPPUUHHH--!

DOC BIZARRE M.D.™

JOE CASEY: Writer
ANDY SURIANO: Artist
RUS WOOTON: Letterer

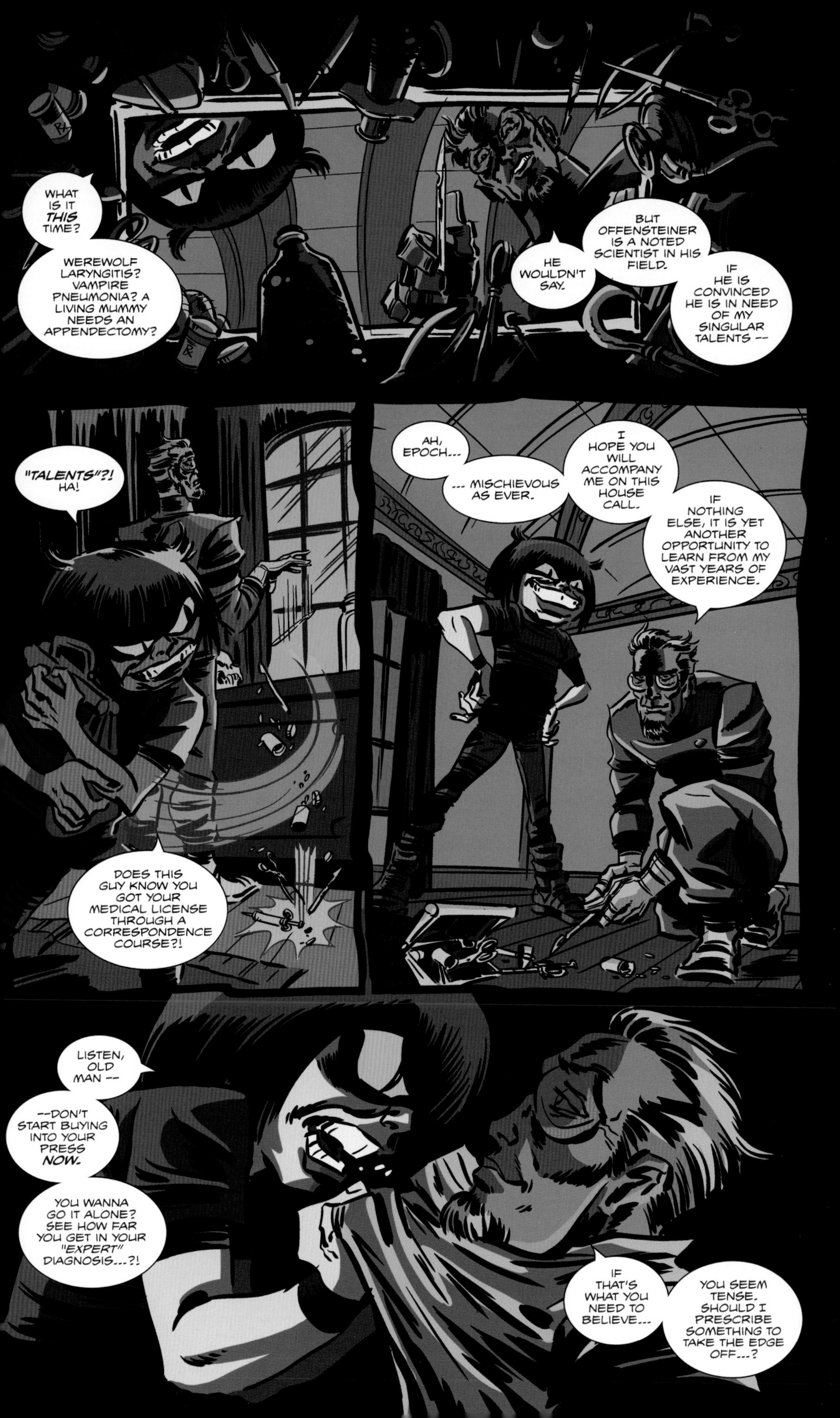
WHAT IS IT *THIS* TIME?
WEREWOLF LARYNGITIS? VAMPIRE PNEUMONIA? A LIVING MUMMY NEEDS AN APPENDECTOMY?
HE WOULDN'T SAY.
BUT OFFENSTEINER IS A NOTED SCIENTIST IN HIS FIELD.
IF HE IS CONVINCED HE IS IN NEED OF MY SINGULAR TALENTS --
"TALENTS"?! HA!
DOES THIS GUY KNOW YOU GOT YOUR MEDICAL LICENSE THROUGH A CORRESPONDENCE COURSE?!
AH, EPOCH...
... MISCHIEVOUS AS EVER.
I HOPE YOU WILL ACCOMPANY ME ON THIS HOUSE CALL.
IF NOTHING ELSE, IT IS YET ANOTHER OPPORTUNITY TO LEARN FROM MY VAST YEARS OF EXPERIENCE.
LISTEN, OLD MAN --
--DON'T START BUYING INTO YOUR PRESS *NOW.*
YOU WANNA GO IT ALONE? SEE HOW FAR YOU GET IN YOUR *"EXPERT"* DIAGNOSIS...?!
IF THAT'S WHAT YOU NEED TO BELIEVE...
YOU SEEM TENSE. SHOULD I PRESCRIBE SOMETHING TO TAKE THE EDGE OFF...?

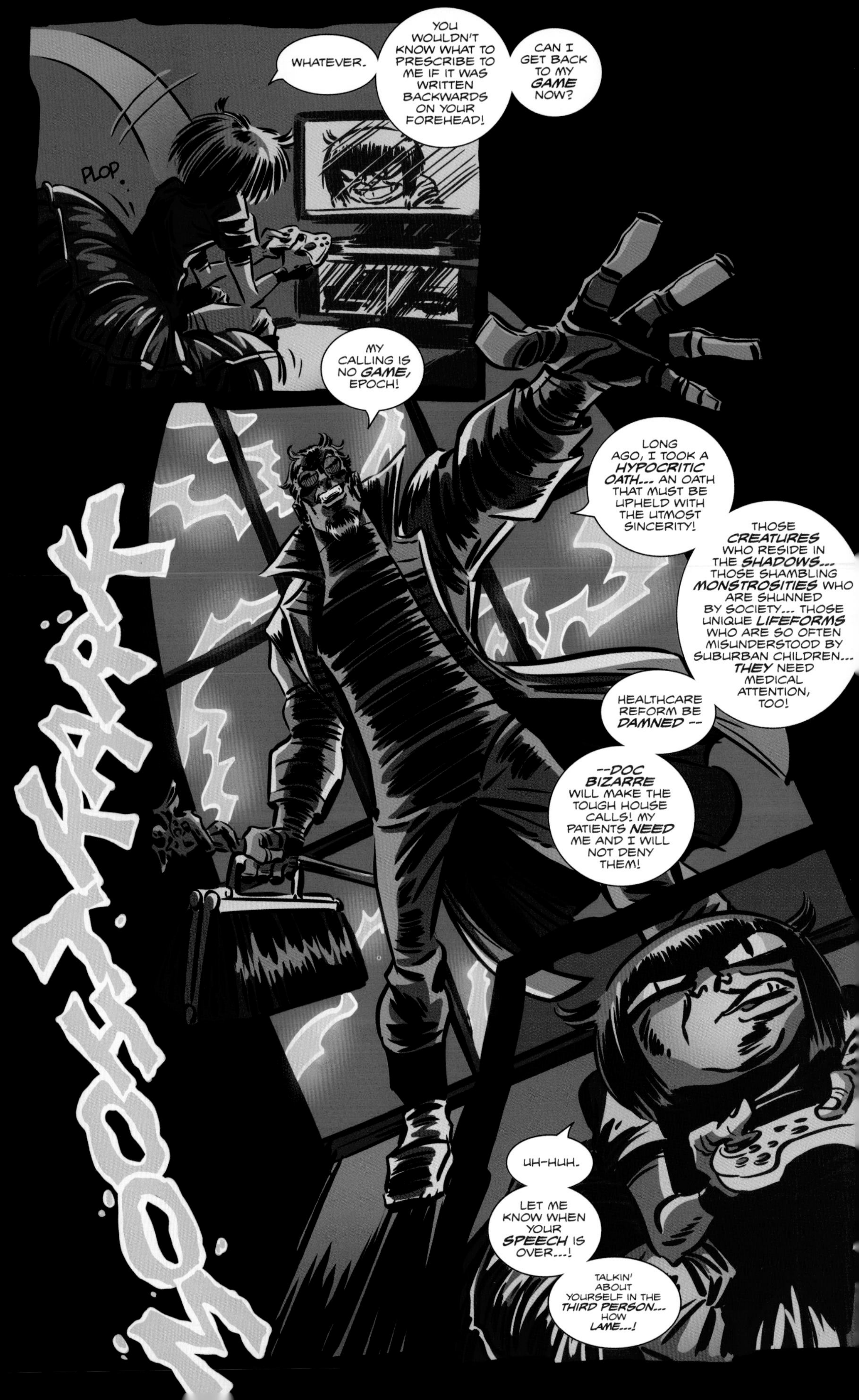
PLOP.
WHATEVER.
YOU WOULDN'T KNOW WHAT TO PRESCRIBE TO ME IF IT WAS WRITTEN BACKWARDS ON YOUR FOREHEAD!
CAN I GET BACK TO MY GAME NOW?
MY CALLING IS NO GAME, EPOCH!
WOOSHFARK
LONG AGO, I TOOK A HYPOCRITIC OATH... AN OATH THAT MUST BE UPHELD WITH THE UTMOST SINCERITY!
THOSE CREATURES WHO RESIDE IN THE SHADOWS... THOSE SHAMBLING MONSTROSITIES WHO ARE SHUNNED BY SOCIETY... THOSE UNIQUE LIFEFORMS WHO ARE SO OFTEN MISUNDERSTOOD BY SUBURBAN CHILDREN... THEY NEED MEDICAL ATTENTION, TOO!
HEALTHCARE REFORM BE DAMNED --
--DOC BIZARRE WILL MAKE THE TOUGH HOUSE CALLS! MY PATIENTS NEED ME AND I WILL NOT DENY THEM!
UH-HUH.
LET ME KNOW WHEN YOUR SPEECH IS OVER...!
TALKIN' ABOUT YOURSELF IN THE THIRD PERSON... HOW LAME...!

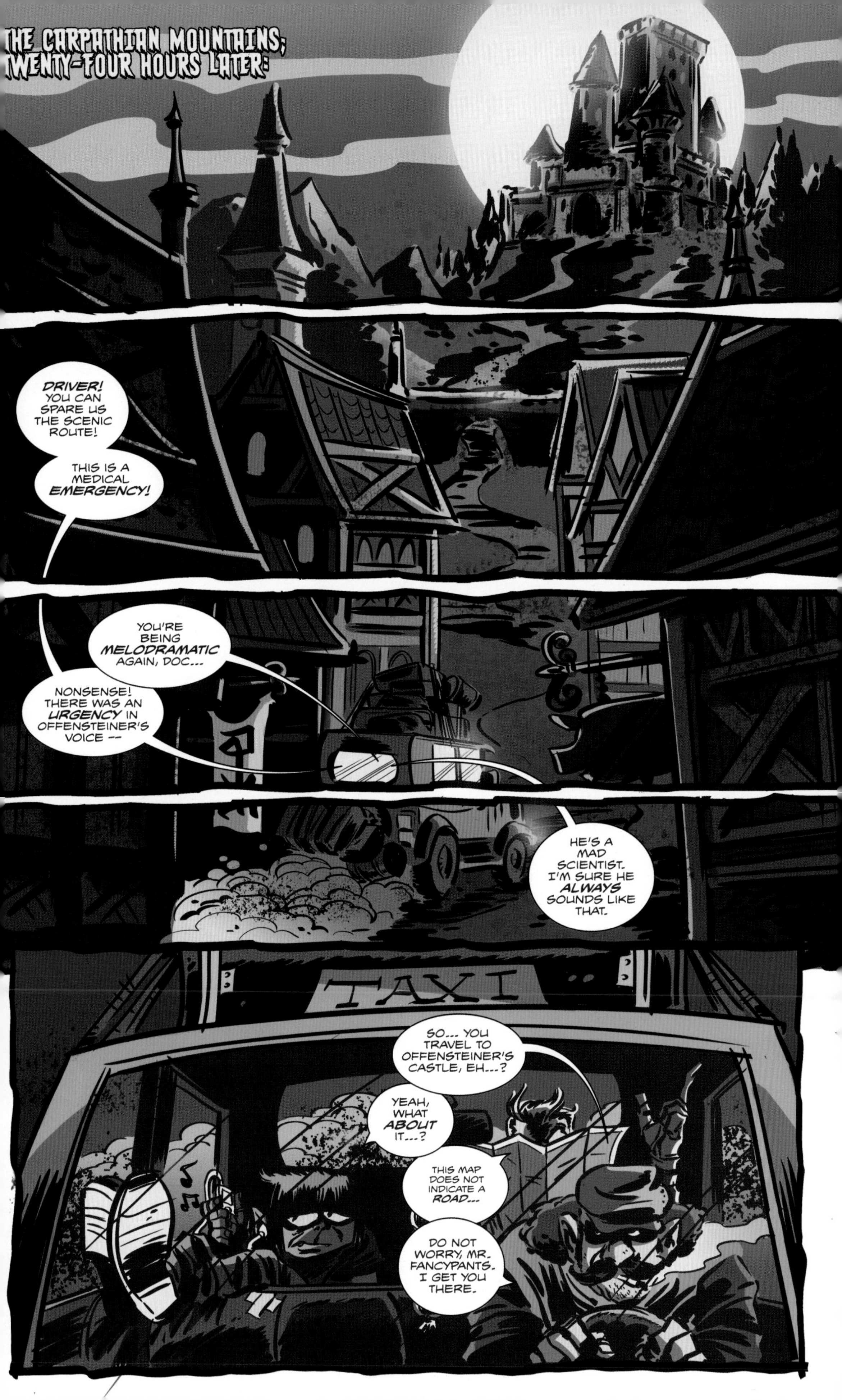
THE CARPATHIAN MOUNTAINS; TWENTY-FOUR HOURS LATER:
DRIVER! YOU CAN SPARE US THE SCENIC ROUTE!
THIS IS A MEDICAL EMERGENCY!
YOU'RE BEING MELODRAMATIC AGAIN, DOC...
NONSENSE! THERE WAS AN URGENCY IN OFFENSTEINER'S VOICE --
HE'S A MAD SCIENTIST. I'M SURE HE ALWAYS SOUNDS LIKE THAT.
TAXI
SO... YOU TRAVEL TO OFFENSTEINER'S CASTLE, EH...?
YEAH, WHAT ABOUT IT...?
THIS MAP DOES NOT INDICATE A ROAD...
DO NOT WORRY, MR. FANCYPANTS. I GET YOU THERE.

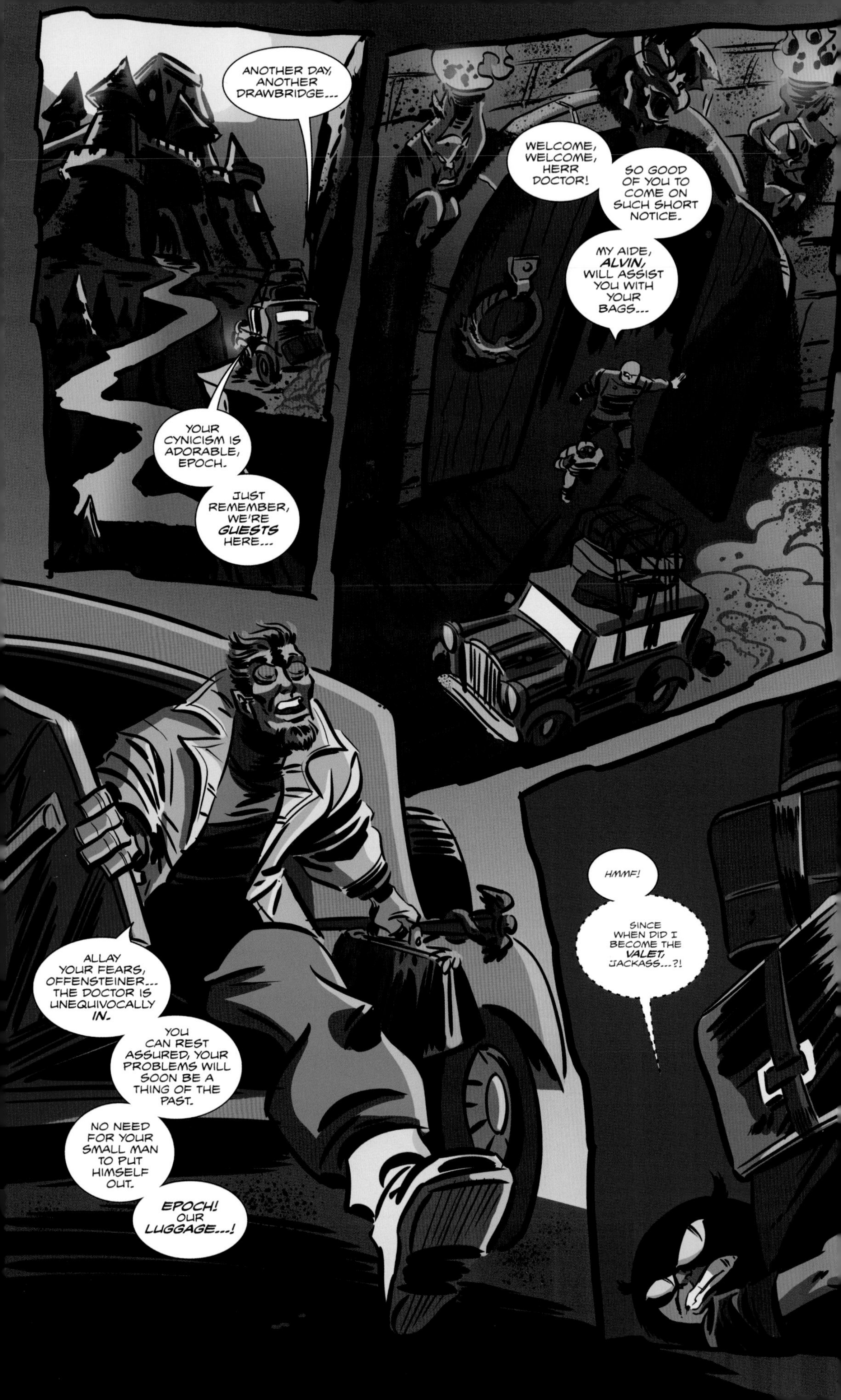
ANOTHER DAY, ANOTHER DRAWBRIDGE...
YOUR CYNICISM IS ADORABLE, EPOCH.
JUST REMEMBER, WE'RE *GUESTS* HERE...
WELCOME, WELCOME, HERR DOCTOR!
SO GOOD OF YOU TO COME ON SUCH SHORT NOTICE.
MY AIDE, *ALVIN,* WILL ASSIST YOU WITH YOUR BAGS...
ALLAY YOUR FEARS, OFFENSTEINER... THE DOCTOR IS UNEQUIVOCALLY *IN.*
YOU CAN REST ASSURED, YOUR PROBLEMS WILL SOON BE A THING OF THE PAST.
NO NEED FOR YOUR SMALL MAN TO PUT HIMSELF OUT.
EPOCH! OUR *LUGGAGE...!*
HMMF!
SINCE WHEN DID I BECOME THE *VALET,* JACKASS...?!

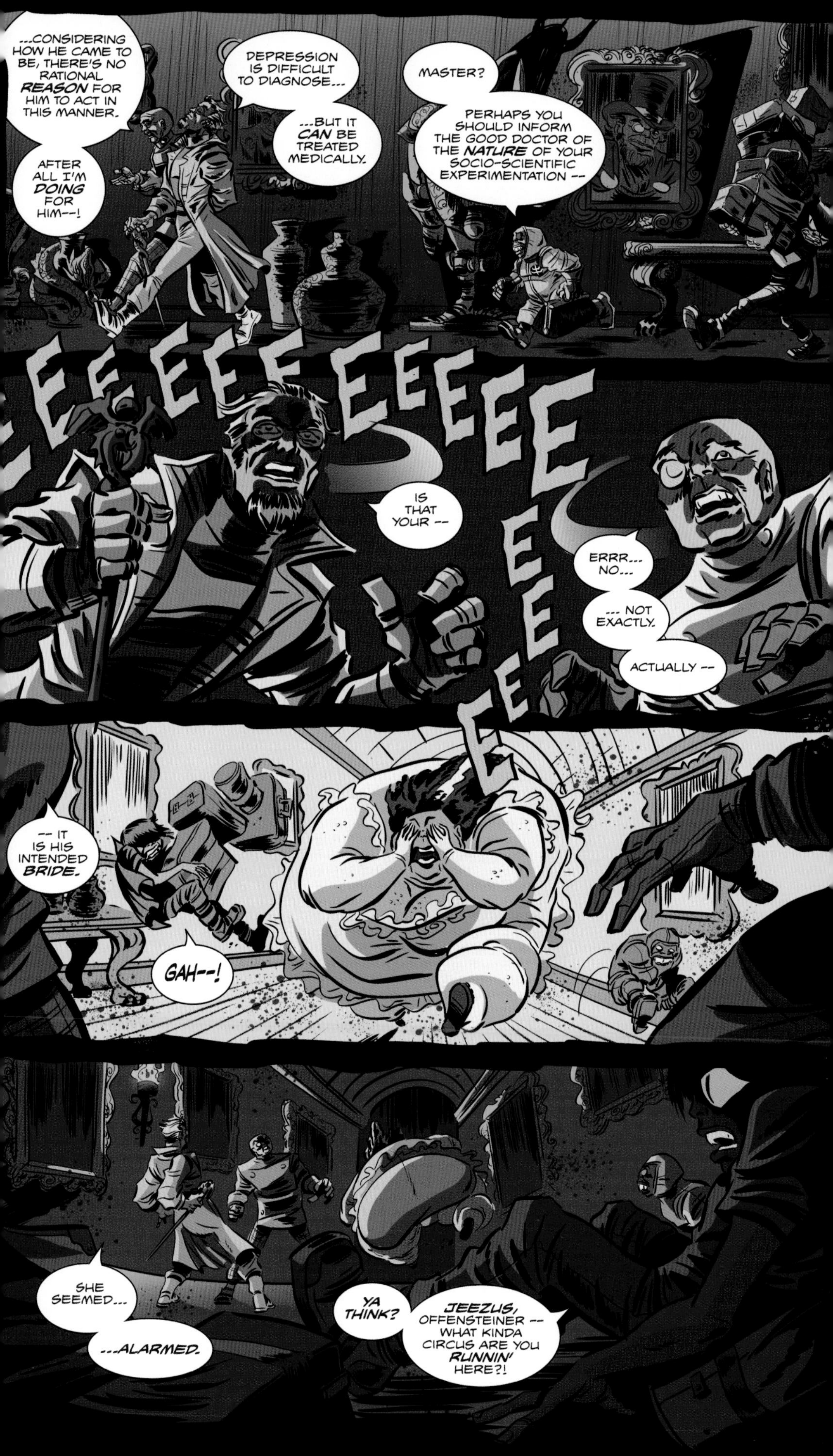
...CONSIDERING HOW HE CAME TO BE, THERE'S NO RATIONAL REASON FOR HIM TO ACT IN THIS MANNER.
AFTER ALL I'M DOING FOR HIM--!
DEPRESSION IS DIFFICULT TO DIAGNOSE...
...BUT IT CAN BE TREATED MEDICALLY.
MASTER?
PERHAPS YOU SHOULD INFORM THE GOOD DOCTOR OF THE NATURE OF YOUR SOCIO-SCIENTIFIC EXPERIMENTATION --
EEEEEEEEEEEEEEEE
IS THAT YOUR --
ERRR... NO...
... NOT EXACTLY.
ACTUALLY --
-- IT IS HIS INTENDED BRIDE.
GAH--!
SHE SEEMED...
...ALARMED.
YA THINK?
JEEZUS, OFFENSTEINER -- WHAT KINDA CIRCUS ARE YOU RUNNIN' HERE?!

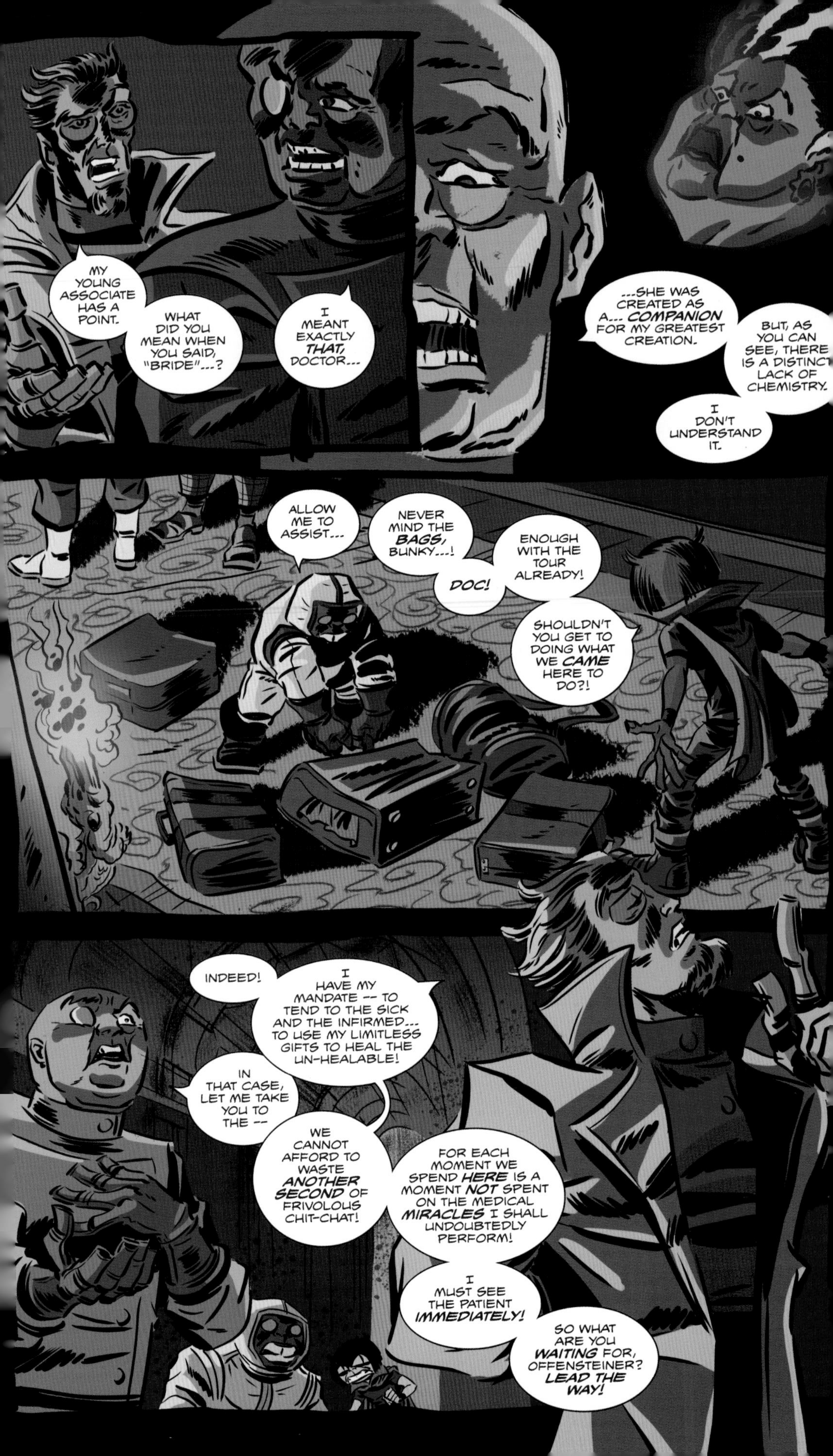
MY YOUNG ASSOCIATE HAS A POINT.
WHAT DID YOU MEAN WHEN YOU SAID, "BRIDE"...?
I MEANT EXACTLY *THAT,* DOCTOR...
...SHE WAS CREATED AS A... *COMPANION* FOR MY GREATEST CREATION.
BUT, AS YOU CAN SEE, THERE IS A DISTINCT LACK OF CHEMISTRY.
I DON'T UNDERSTAND IT.
ALLOW ME TO ASSIST...
NEVER MIND THE *BAGS,* BUNKY...!
DOC!
ENOUGH WITH THE TOUR ALREADY!
SHOULDN'T YOU GET TO DOING WHAT WE *CAME* HERE TO DO?!
INDEED!
I HAVE MY MANDATE -- TO TEND TO THE SICK AND THE INFIRMED... TO USE MY LIMITLESS GIFTS TO HEAL THE UN-HEALABLE!
IN THAT CASE, LET ME TAKE YOU TO THE --
WE CANNOT AFFORD TO WASTE *ANOTHER SECOND* OF FRIVOLOUS CHIT-CHAT!
FOR EACH MOMENT WE SPEND *HERE* IS A MOMENT *NOT* SPENT ON THE MEDICAL *MIRACLES* I SHALL UNDOUBTEDLY PERFORM!
I MUST SEE THE PATIENT *IMMEDIATELY!*
SO WHAT ARE YOU *WAITING* FOR, OFFENSTEINER? *LEAD THE WAY!*

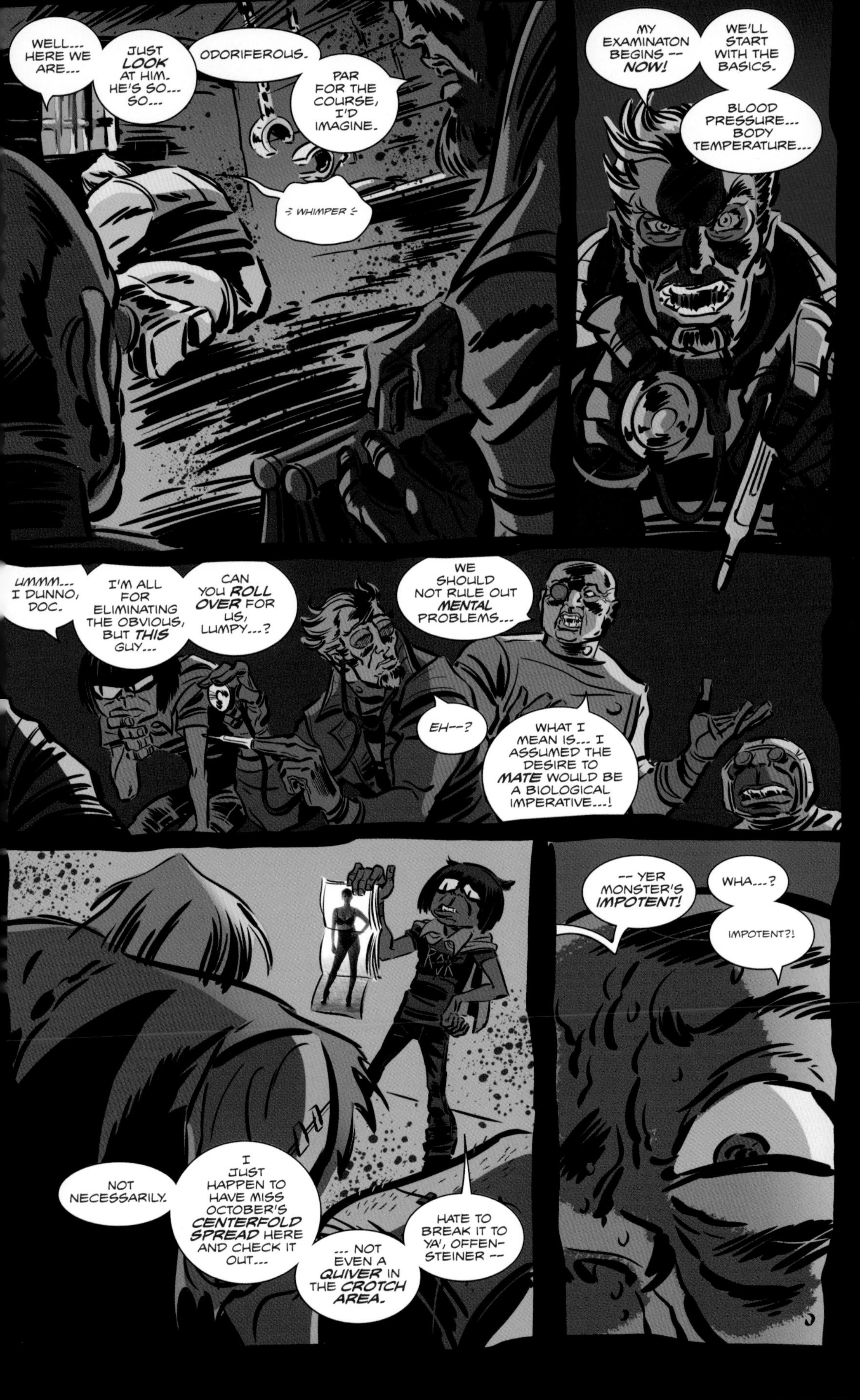

WELL... HERE WE ARE...
JUST LOOK AT HIM. HE'S SO... SO...
ODORIFEROUS.
PAR FOR THE COURSE, I'D IMAGINE.
WHIMPER
MY EXAMINATON BEGINS -- NOW!
WE'LL START WITH THE BASICS.
BLOOD PRESSURE... BODY TEMPERATURE...
UMMM... I DUNNO, DOC.
I'M ALL FOR ELIMINATING THE OBVIOUS, BUT THIS GUY...
CAN YOU ROLL OVER FOR US, LUMPY...?
WE SHOULD NOT RULE OUT MENTAL PROBLEMS...
EH--?
WHAT I MEAN IS... I ASSUMED THE DESIRE TO MATE WOULD BE A BIOLOGICAL IMPERATIVE...!
NOT NECESSARILY.
I JUST HAPPEN TO HAVE MISS OCTOBER'S CENTERFOLD SPREAD HERE AND CHECK IT OUT...
... NOT EVEN A QUIVER IN THE CROTCH AREA.
HATE TO BREAK IT TO YA', OFFEN-STEINER --
-- YER MONSTER'S IMPOTENT!
WHA...?
IMPOTENT?!

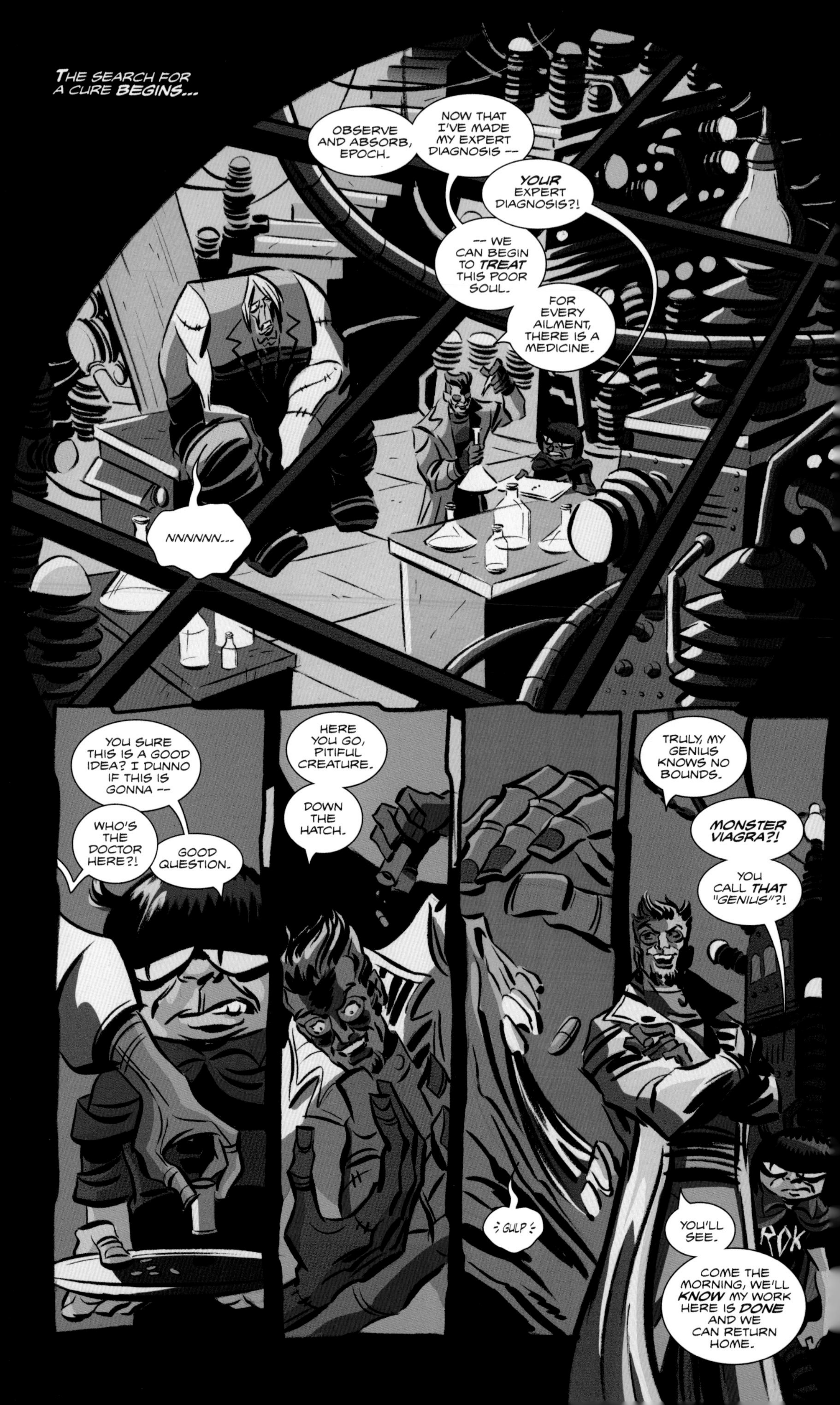

THE SEARCH FOR A CURE BEGINS...
OBSERVE AND ABSORB, EPOCH.
NOW THAT I'VE MADE MY EXPERT DIAGNOSIS --
YOUR EXPERT DIAGNOSIS?!
-- WE CAN BEGIN TO TREAT THIS POOR SOUL.
FOR EVERY AILMENT, THERE IS A MEDICINE.
NNNNNN...
YOU SURE THIS IS A GOOD IDEA? I DUNNO IF THIS IS GONNA --
WHO'S THE DOCTOR HERE?!
GOOD QUESTION.
HERE YOU GO, PITIFUL CREATURE.
DOWN THE HATCH.
GULP
TRULY, MY GENIUS KNOWS NO BOUNDS.
MONSTER VIAGRA?!
YOU CALL THAT "GENIUS"?!
YOU'LL SEE.
COME THE MORNING, WE'LL KNOW MY WORK HERE IS DONE AND WE CAN RETURN HOME.

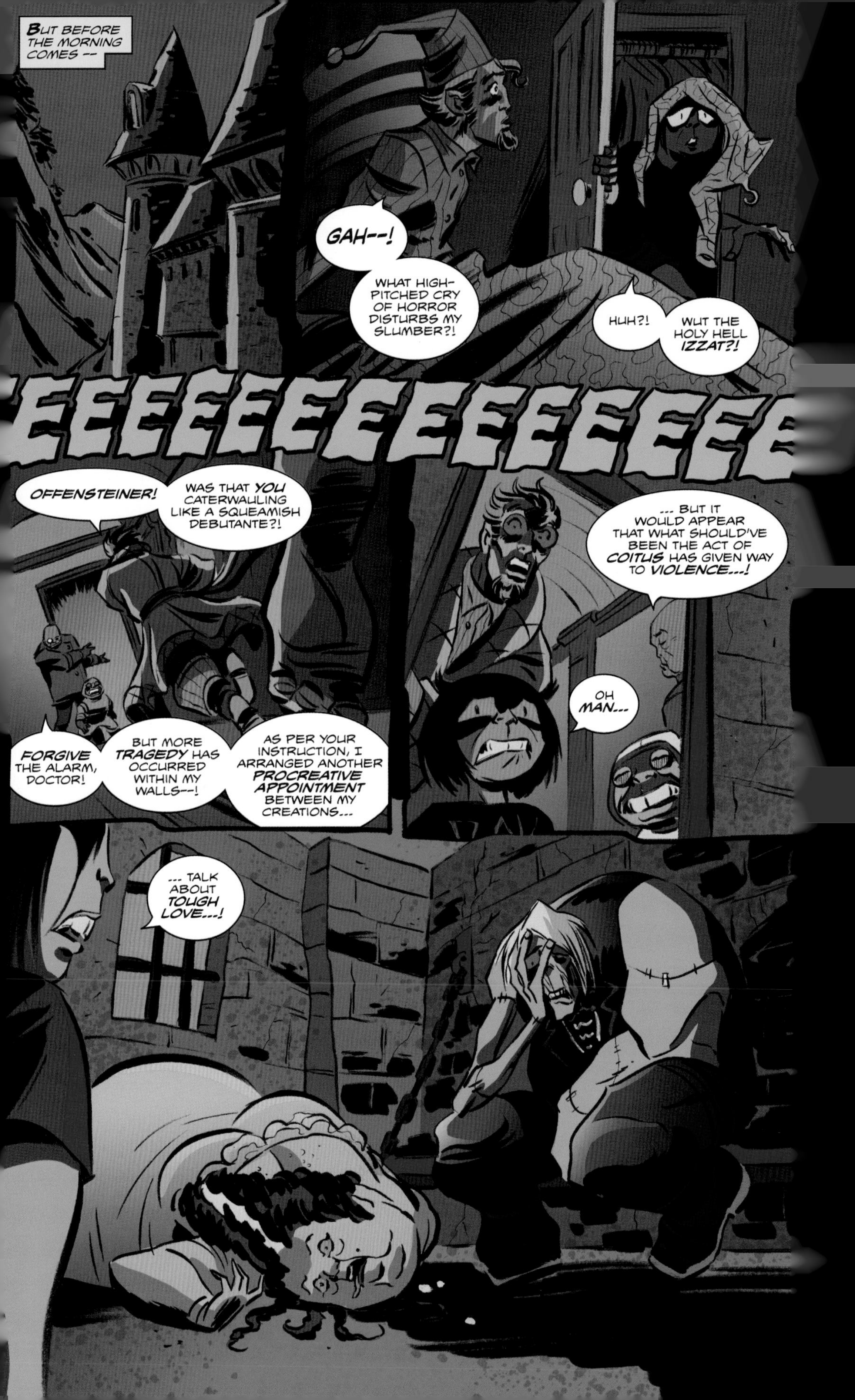
BUT BEFORE THE MORNING COMES --
GAH--!
WHAT HIGH-PITCHED CRY OF HORROR DISTURBS MY SLUMBER?!
HUH?!
WUT THE HOLY HELL IZZAT?!
EEEEEEEEEEEEEEEE
OFFENSTEINER!
WAS THAT YOU CATERWAULING LIKE A SQUEAMISH DEBUTANTE?!
FORGIVE THE ALARM, DOCTOR!
BUT MORE TRAGEDY HAS OCCURRED WITHIN MY WALLS--!
AS PER YOUR INSTRUCTION, I ARRANGED ANOTHER PROCREATIVE APPOINTMENT BETWEEN MY CREATIONS...
... BUT IT WOULD APPEAR THAT WHAT SHOULD'VE BEEN THE ACT OF COITUS HAS GIVEN WAY TO VIOLENCE...!
OH MAN...
... TALK ABOUT TOUGH LOVE...!

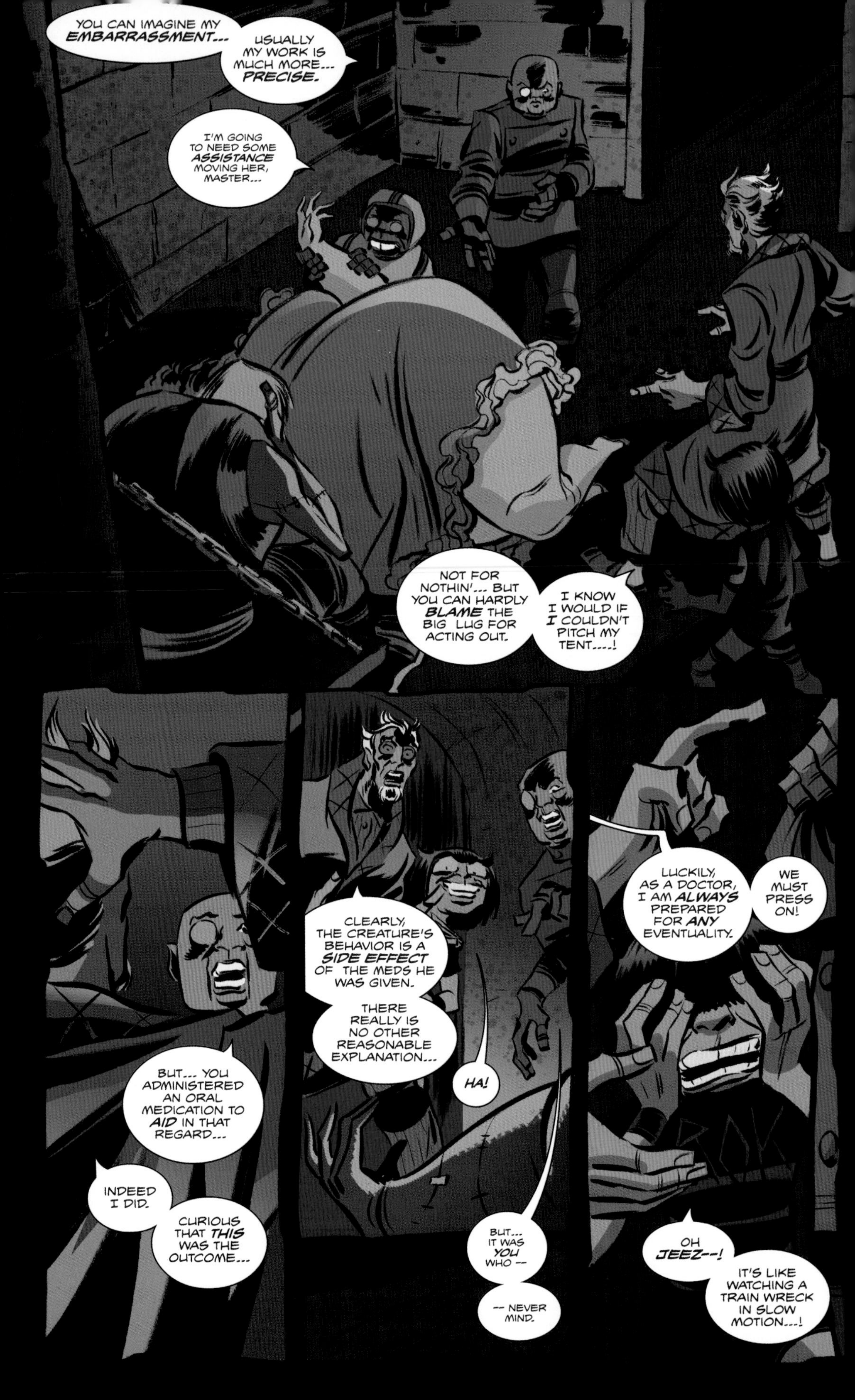
YOU CAN IMAGINE MY EMBARRASSMENT...
USUALLY MY WORK IS MUCH MORE... PRECISE.
I'M GOING TO NEED SOME ASSISTANCE MOVING HER, MASTER...
NOT FOR NOTHIN'... BUT YOU CAN HARDLY BLAME THE BIG LUG FOR ACTING OUT.
I KNOW I WOULD IF I COULDN'T PITCH MY TENT....!
BUT... YOU ADMINISTERED AN ORAL MEDICATION TO AID IN THAT REGARD...
INDEED I DID.
CURIOUS THAT THIS WAS THE OUTCOME...
CLEARLY, THE CREATURE'S BEHAVIOR IS A SIDE EFFECT OF THE MEDS HE WAS GIVEN.
THERE REALLY IS NO OTHER REASONABLE EXPLANATION...
HA!
BUT... IT WAS YOU WHO --
-- NEVER MIND.
LUCKILY, AS A DOCTOR, I AM ALWAYS PREPARED FOR ANY EVENTUALITY.
WE MUST PRESS ON!
OH JEEZ--!
IT'S LIKE WATCHING A TRAIN WRECK IN SLOW MOTION...!

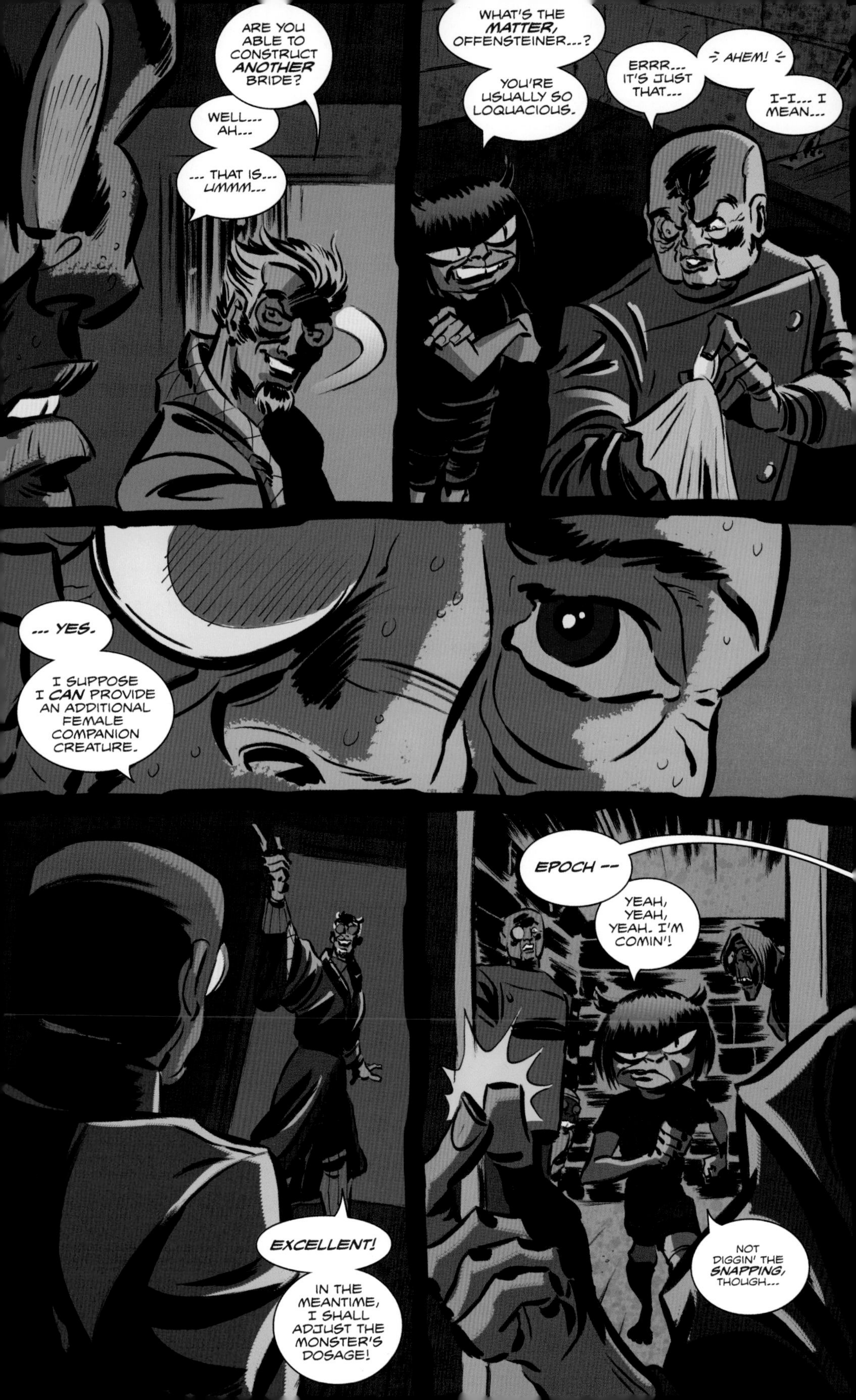

ARE YOU ABLE TO CONSTRUCT ANOTHER BRIDE?
WELL... AH...
... THAT IS... UMMM...
WHAT'S THE MATTER, OFFENSTEINER...?
YOU'RE USUALLY SO LOQUACIOUS.
ERRR... IT'S JUST THAT...
AHEM!
I-I... I MEAN...
... YES.
I SUPPOSE I CAN PROVIDE AN ADDITIONAL FEMALE COMPANION CREATURE.
EXCELLENT!
IN THE MEANTIME, I SHALL ADJUST THE MONSTER'S DOSAGE!
EPOCH --
YEAH, YEAH, YEAH. I'M COMIN'!
NOT DIGGIN' THE SNAPPING, THOUGH...

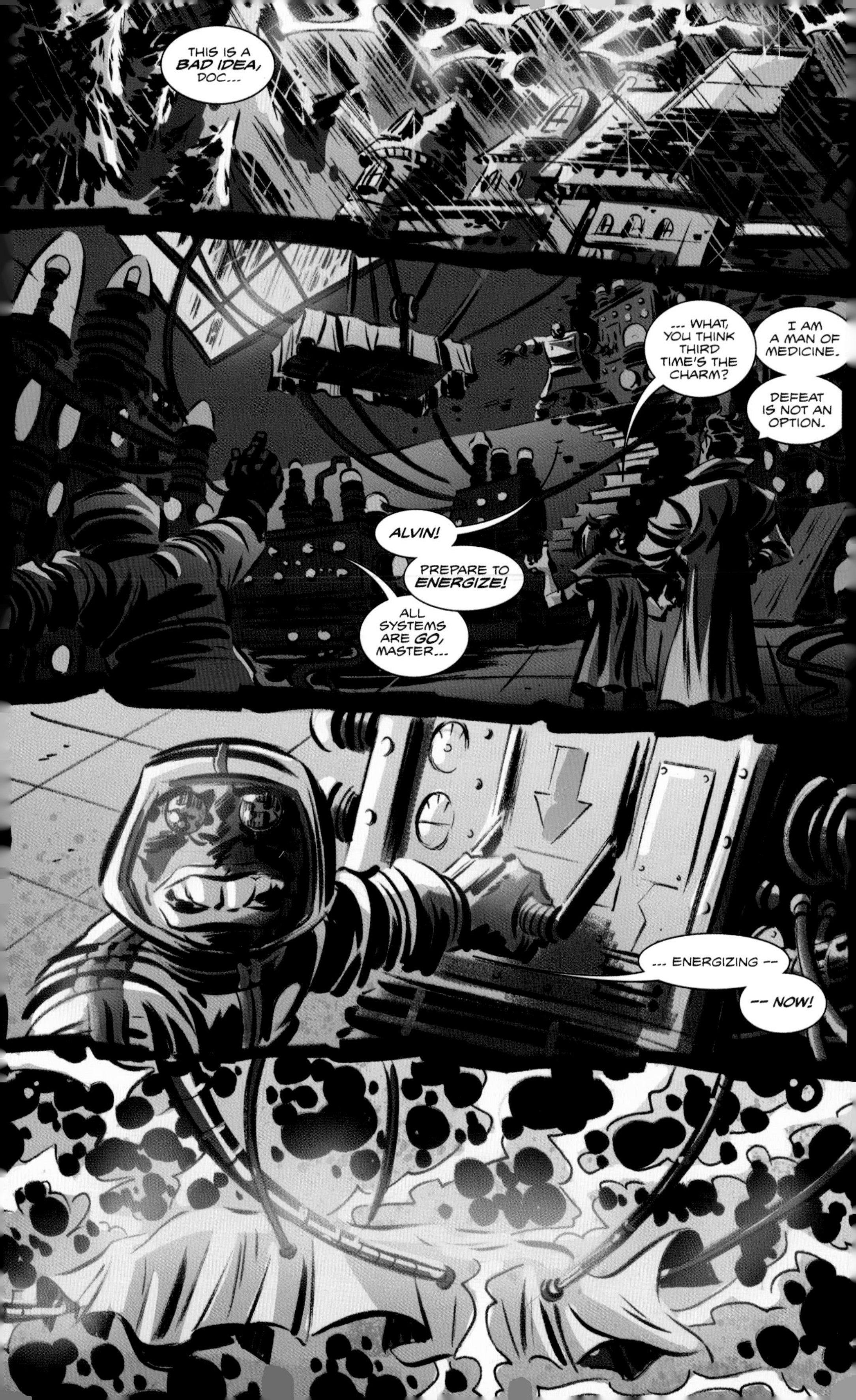
THIS IS A BAD IDEA, DOC...
... WHAT, YOU THINK THIRD TIME'S THE CHARM?
I AM A MAN OF MEDICINE.
DEFEAT IS NOT AN OPTION.
ALVIN!
PREPARE TO ENERGIZE!
ALL SYSTEMS ARE GO, MASTER...
... ENERGIZING --
-- NOW!

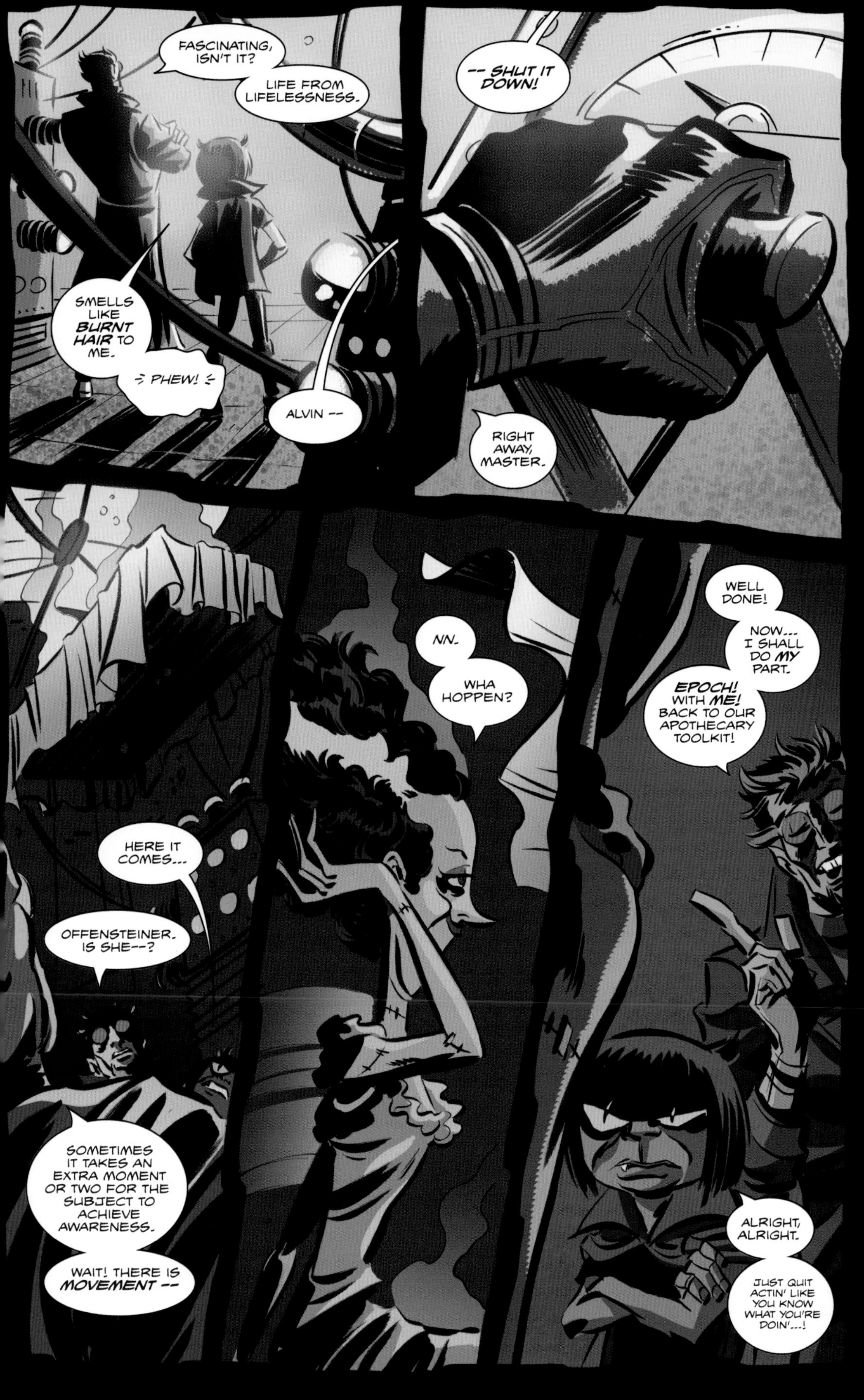
FASCINATING, ISN'T IT?
LIFE FROM LIFELESSNESS.
SMELLS LIKE BURNT HAIR TO ME.
PHEW!
ALVIN --
-- SHUT IT DOWN!
RIGHT AWAY, MASTER.
HERE IT COMES...
OFFENSTEINER. IS SHE--?
SOMETIMES IT TAKES AN EXTRA MOMENT OR TWO FOR THE SUBJECT TO ACHIEVE AWARENESS.
WAIT! THERE IS MOVEMENT --
NN.
WHA HOPPEN?
WELL DONE!
NOW... I SHALL DO MY PART.
EPOCH! WITH ME! BACK TO OUR APOTHECARY TOOLKIT!
ALRIGHT, ALRIGHT.
JUST QUIT ACTIN' LIKE YOU KNOW WHAT YOU'RE DOIN'...!

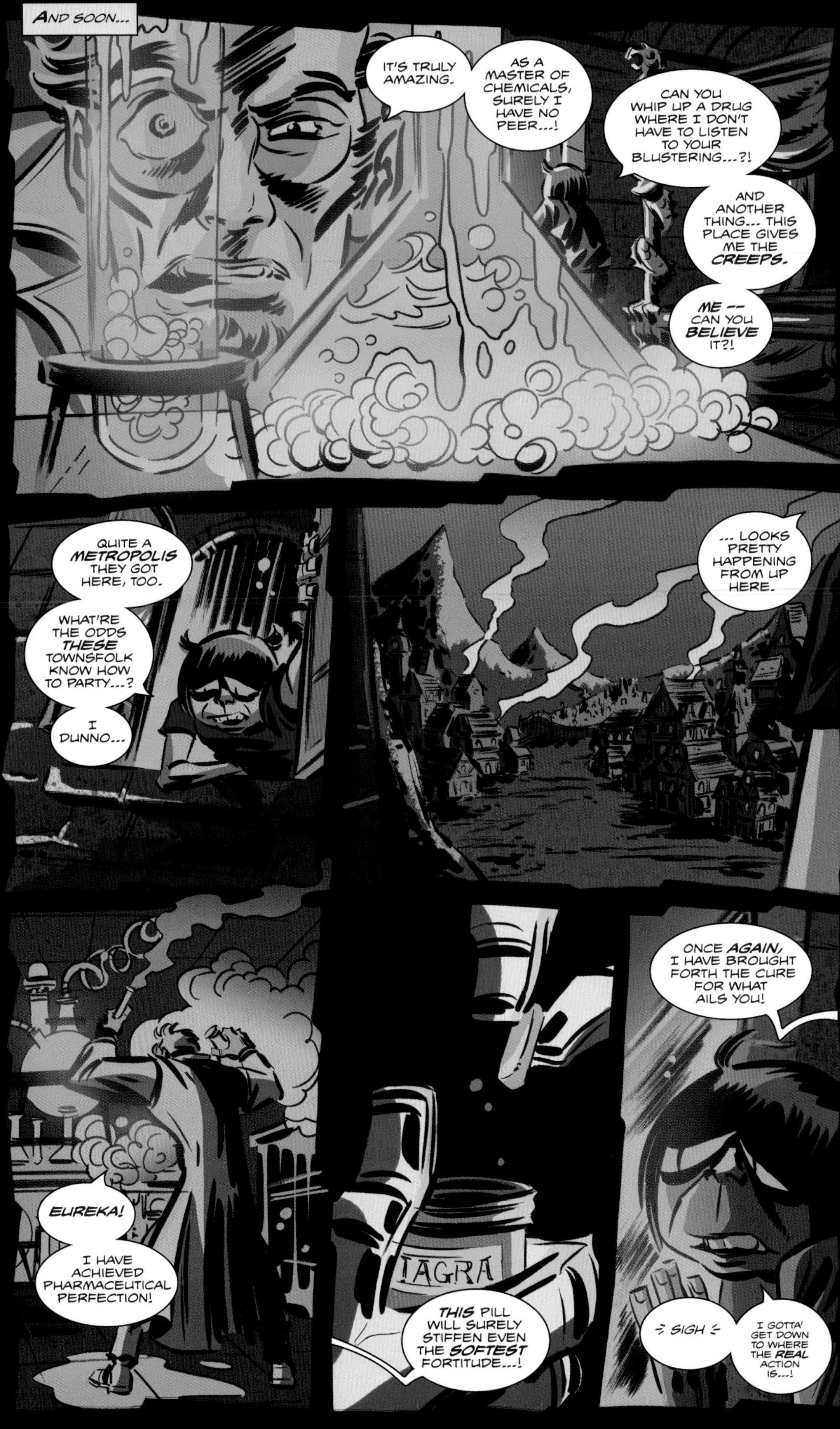
AND SOON...
IT'S TRULY AMAZING.
AS A MASTER OF CHEMICALS, SURELY I HAVE NO PEER...!
CAN YOU WHIP UP A DRUG WHERE I DON'T HAVE TO LISTEN TO YOUR BLUSTERING...?!
AND ANOTHER THING... THIS PLACE GIVES ME THE CREEPS.
ME -- CAN YOU BELIEVE IT?!
QUITE A METROPOLIS THEY GOT HERE, TOO.
WHAT'RE THE ODDS THESE TOWNSFOLK KNOW HOW TO PARTY...?
I DUNNO...
... LOOKS PRETTY HAPPENING FROM UP HERE.
EUREKA!
I HAVE ACHIEVED PHARMACEUTICAL PERFECTION!
IAGRA
THIS PILL WILL SURELY STIFFEN EVEN THE SOFTEST FORTITUDE...!
ONCE AGAIN, I HAVE BROUGHT FORTH THE CURE FOR WHAT AILS YOU!
SIGH
I GOTTA' GET DOWN TO WHERE THE REAL ACTION IS...!

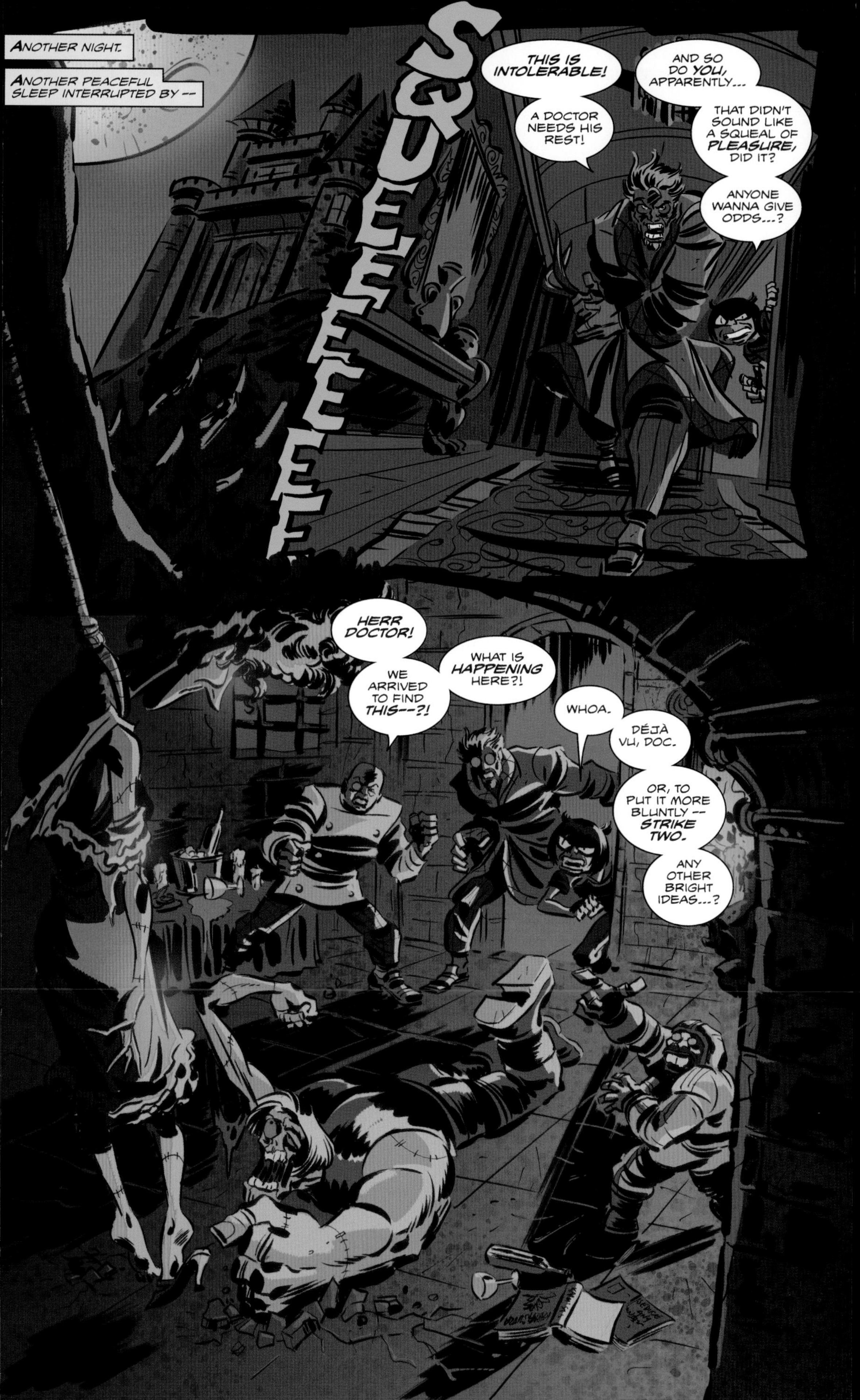

ANOTHER NIGHT.
ANOTHER PEACEFUL SLEEP INTERRUPTED BY --
SQUEEEEEEEE
THIS IS INTOLERABLE!
A DOCTOR NEEDS HIS REST!
AND SO DO YOU, APPARENTLY...
THAT DIDN'T SOUND LIKE A SQUEAL OF PLEASURE, DID IT?
ANYONE WANNA GIVE ODDS...?
HERR DOCTOR!
WE ARRIVED TO FIND THIS--?!
WHAT IS HAPPENING HERE?!
WHOA.
DÉJÀ VU, DOC.
OR, TO PUT IT MORE BLUNTLY -- STRIKE TWO.
ANY OTHER BRIGHT IDEAS...?

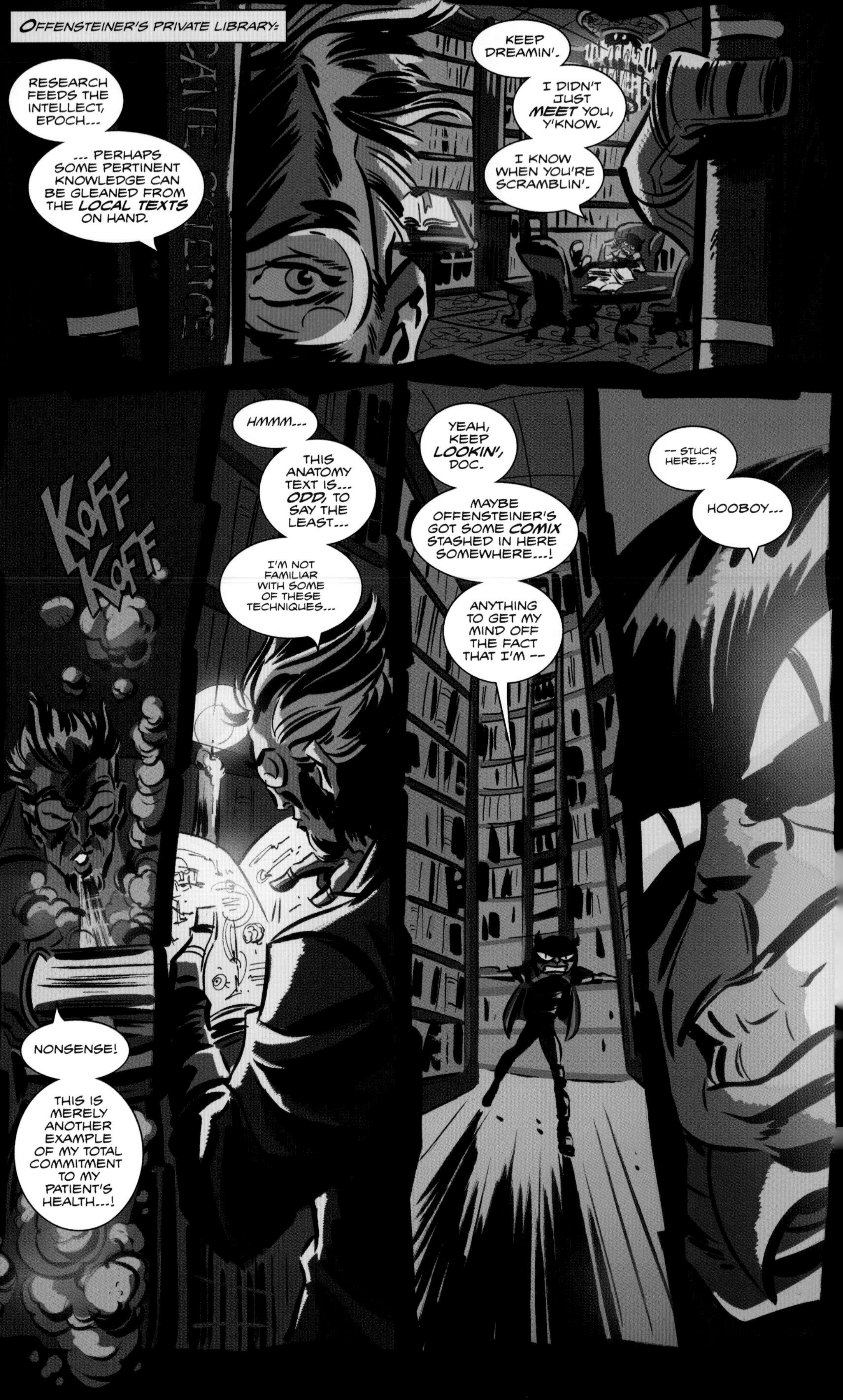

OFFENSTEINER'S PRIVATE LIBRARY:
RESEARCH FEEDS THE INTELLECT, EPOCH...
... PERHAPS SOME PERTINENT KNOWLEDGE CAN BE GLEANED FROM THE LOCAL TEXTS ON HAND.
KEEP DREAMIN'.
I DIDN'T JUST MEET YOU, Y'KNOW.
I KNOW WHEN YOU'RE SCRAMBLIN'.
KOFF KOFF
NONSENSE!
THIS IS MERELY ANOTHER EXAMPLE OF MY TOTAL COMMITMENT TO MY PATIENT'S HEALTH...!
HMMM...
THIS ANATOMY TEXT IS... ODD, TO SAY THE LEAST...
I'M NOT FAMILIAR WITH SOME OF THESE TECHNIQUES...
YEAH, KEEP LOOKIN', DOC.
MAYBE OFFENSTEINER'S GOT SOME COMIX STASHED IN HERE SOMEWHERE...!
ANYTHING TO GET MY MIND OFF THE FACT THAT I'M --
-- STUCK HERE...?
HOOBOY...

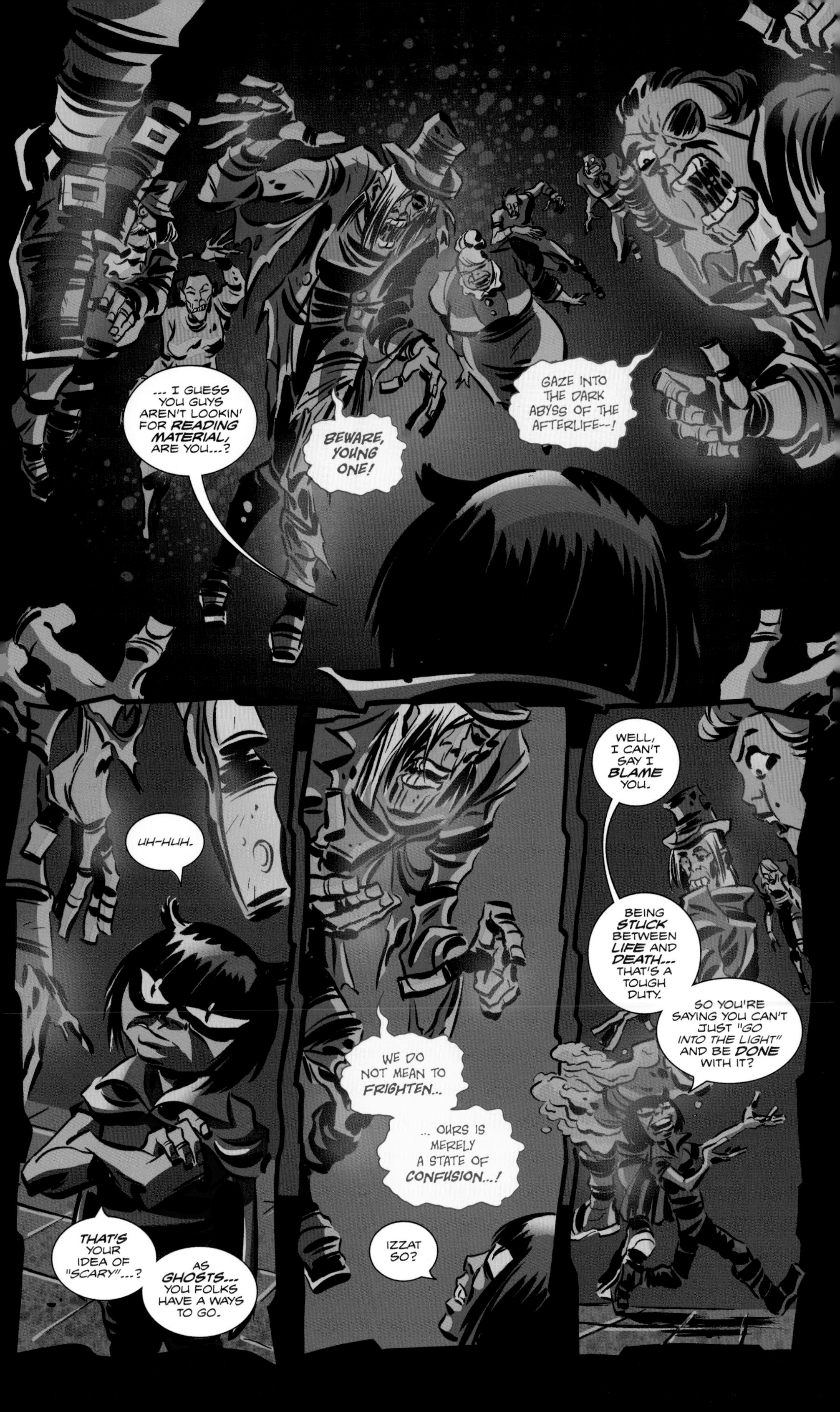
... I GUESS YOU GUYS AREN'T LOOKIN' FOR READING MATERIAL, ARE YOU...?
BEWARE, YOUNG ONE!
GAZE INTO THE DARK ABYSS OF THE AFTERLIFE--!
UH-HUH.
THAT'S YOUR IDEA OF "SCARY"...?
AS GHOSTS... YOU FOLKS HAVE A WAYS TO GO.
WE DO NOT MEAN TO FRIGHTEN...
... OURS IS MERELY A STATE OF CONFUSION...!
IZZAT SO?
WELL, I CAN'T SAY I BLAME YOU.
BEING STUCK BETWEEN LIFE AND DEATH... THAT'S A TOUGH DUTY.
SO YOU'RE SAYING YOU CAN'T JUST "GO INTO THE LIGHT" AND BE DONE WITH IT?

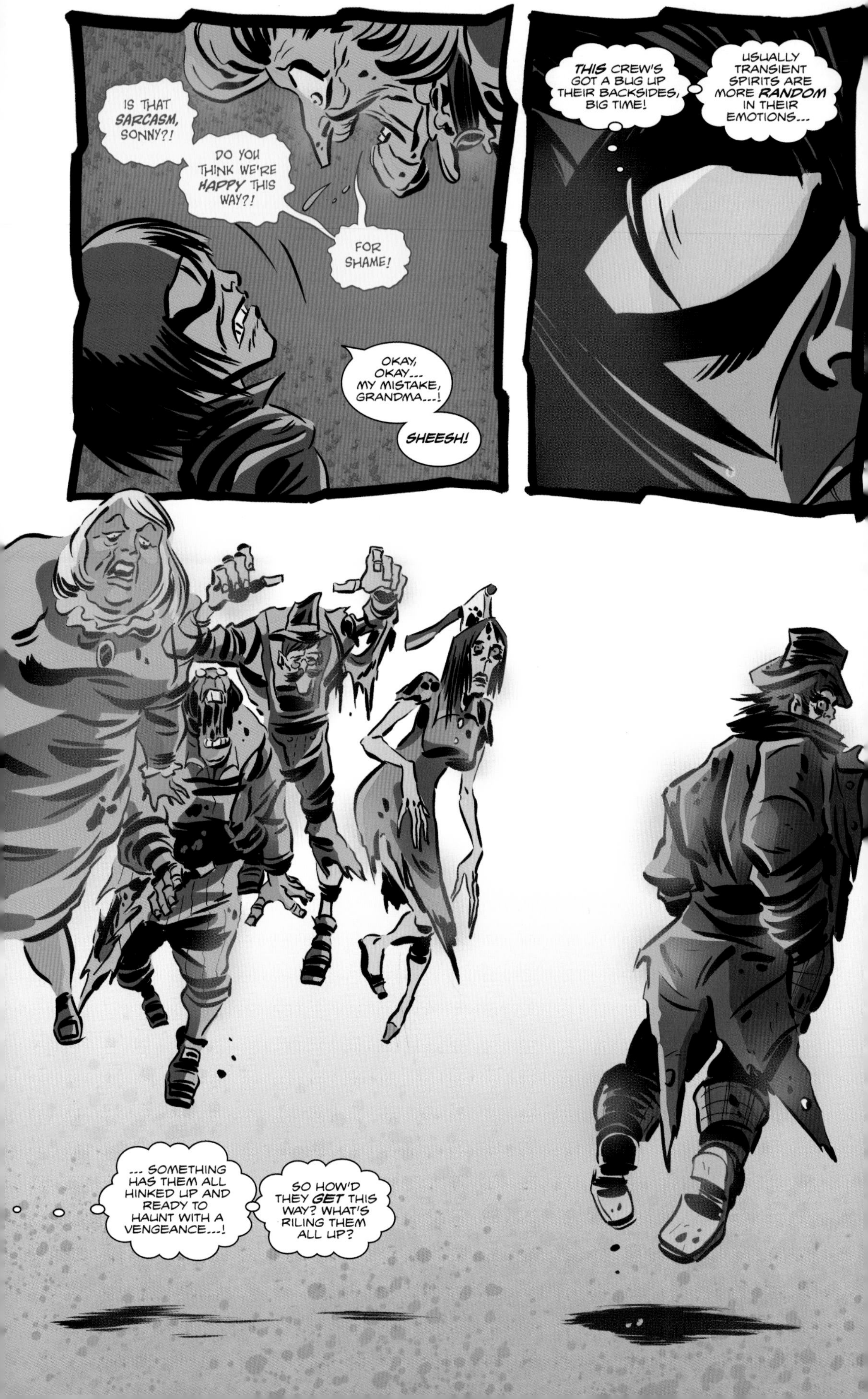
IS THAT SARCASM, SONNY?!
DO YOU THINK WE'RE HAPPY THIS WAY?!
FOR SHAME!
OKAY, OKAY... MY MISTAKE, GRANDMA...!
SHEESH!
THIS CREW'S GOT A BUG UP THEIR BACKSIDES, BIG TIME!
USUALLY TRANSIENT SPIRITS ARE MORE RANDOM IN THEIR EMOTIONS...
... SOMETHING HAS THEM ALL HINKED UP AND READY TO HAUNT WITH A VENGEANCE...!
SO HOW'D THEY GET THIS WAY? WHAT'S RILING THEM ALL UP?

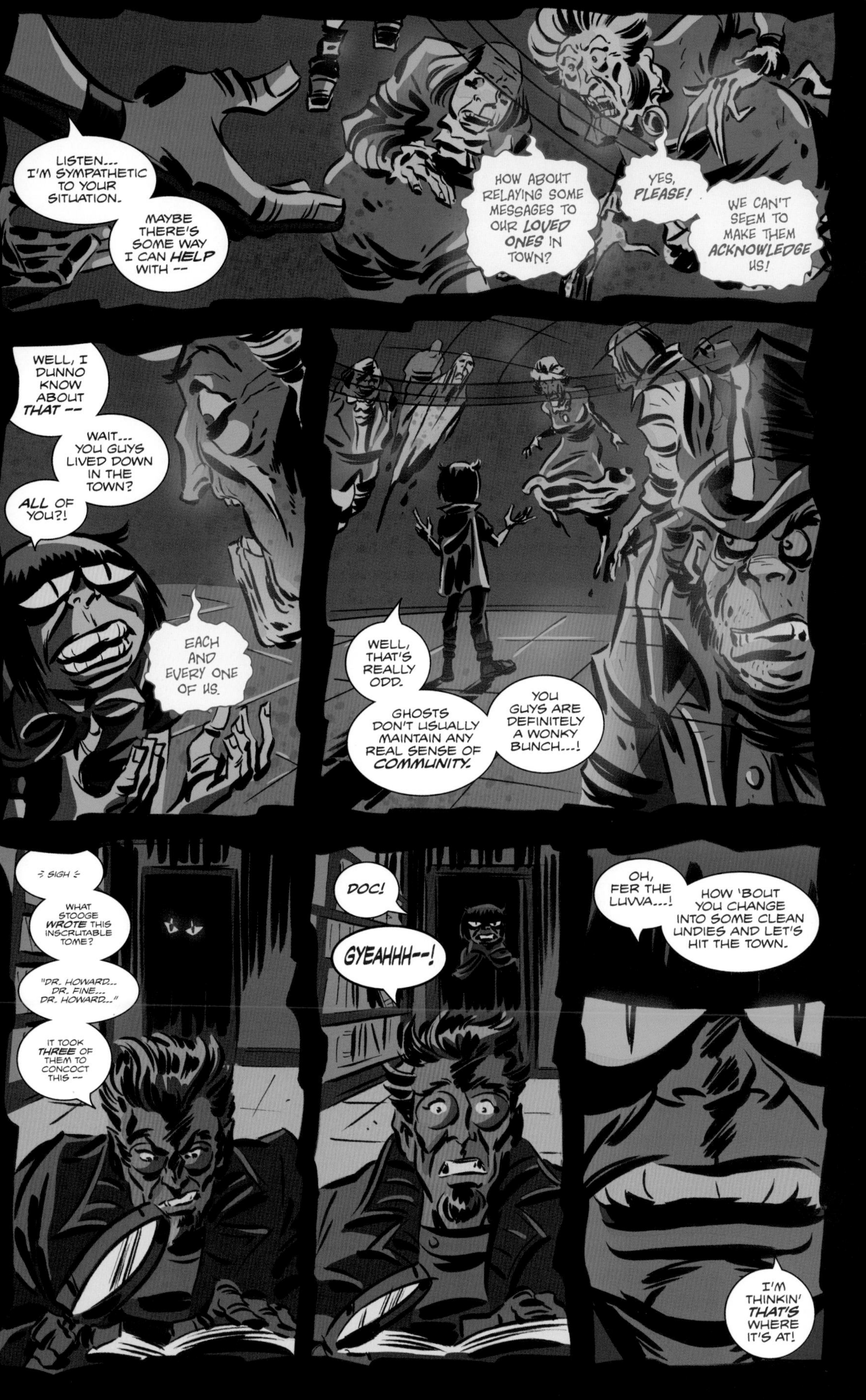
LISTEN... I'M SYMPATHETIC TO YOUR SITUATION.
MAYBE THERE'S SOME WAY I CAN HELP WITH --
HOW ABOUT RELAYING SOME MESSAGES TO OUR LOVED ONES IN TOWN?
YES, PLEASE!
WE CAN'T SEEM TO MAKE THEM ACKNOWLEDGE US!
WELL, I DUNNO KNOW ABOUT THAT --
WAIT... YOU GUYS LIVED DOWN IN THE TOWN?
ALL OF YOU?!
EACH AND EVERY ONE OF US.
WELL, THAT'S REALLY ODD.
GHOSTS DON'T USUALLY MAINTAIN ANY REAL SENSE OF COMMUNITY.
YOU GUYS ARE DEFINITELY A WONKY BUNCH...!
SIGH
WHAT STOOGE WROTE THIS INSCRUTABLE TOME?
"DR. HOWARD... DR. FINE... DR. HOWARD..."
IT TOOK THREE OF THEM TO CONCOCT THIS --
DOC!
GYEAHHH--!
OH, FER THE LUVVA...!
HOW 'BOUT YOU CHANGE INTO SOME CLEAN UNDIES AND LET'S HIT THE TOWN.
I'M THINKIN' THAT'S WHERE IT'S AT!

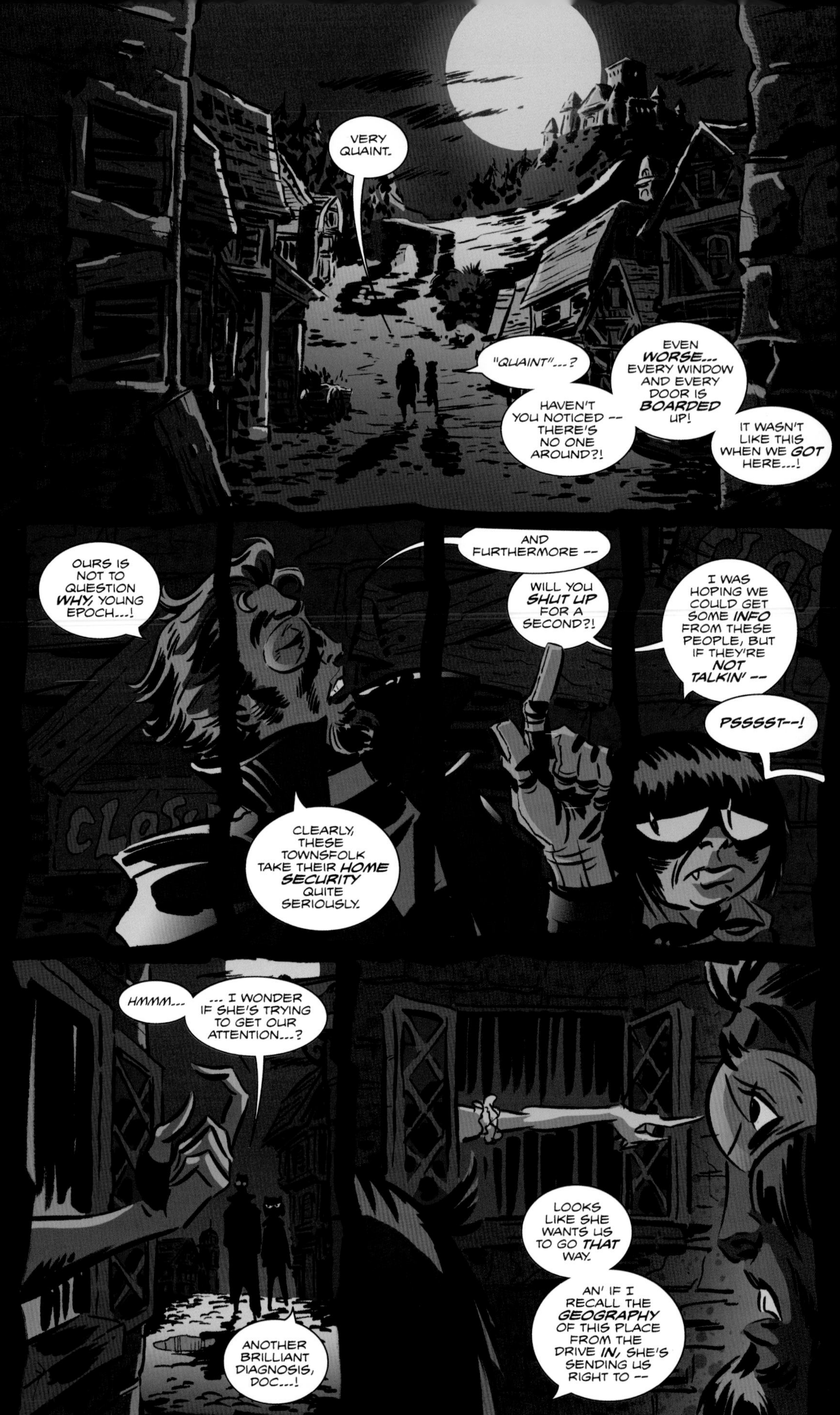
VERY QUAINT.
"QUAINT"...?
HAVEN'T YOU NOTICED -- THERE'S NO ONE AROUND?!
EVEN WORSE... EVERY WINDOW AND EVERY DOOR IS BOARDED UP!
IT WASN'T LIKE THIS WHEN WE GOT HERE...!
OURS IS NOT TO QUESTION WHY, YOUNG EPOCH...!
CLEARLY, THESE TOWNSFOLK TAKE THEIR HOME SECURITY QUITE SERIOUSLY.
AND FURTHERMORE --
WILL YOU SHUT UP FOR A SECOND?!
I WAS HOPING WE COULD GET SOME INFO FROM THESE PEOPLE, BUT IF THEY'RE NOT TALKIN' --
PSSSST--!
CLOSED
HMMM...
... I WONDER IF SHE'S TRYING TO GET OUR ATTENTION...?
ANOTHER BRILLIANT DIAGNOSIS, DOC...!
LOOKS LIKE SHE WANTS US TO GO THAT WAY.
AN' IF I RECALL THE GEOGRAPHY OF THIS PLACE FROM THE DRIVE IN, SHE'S SENDING US RIGHT TO --

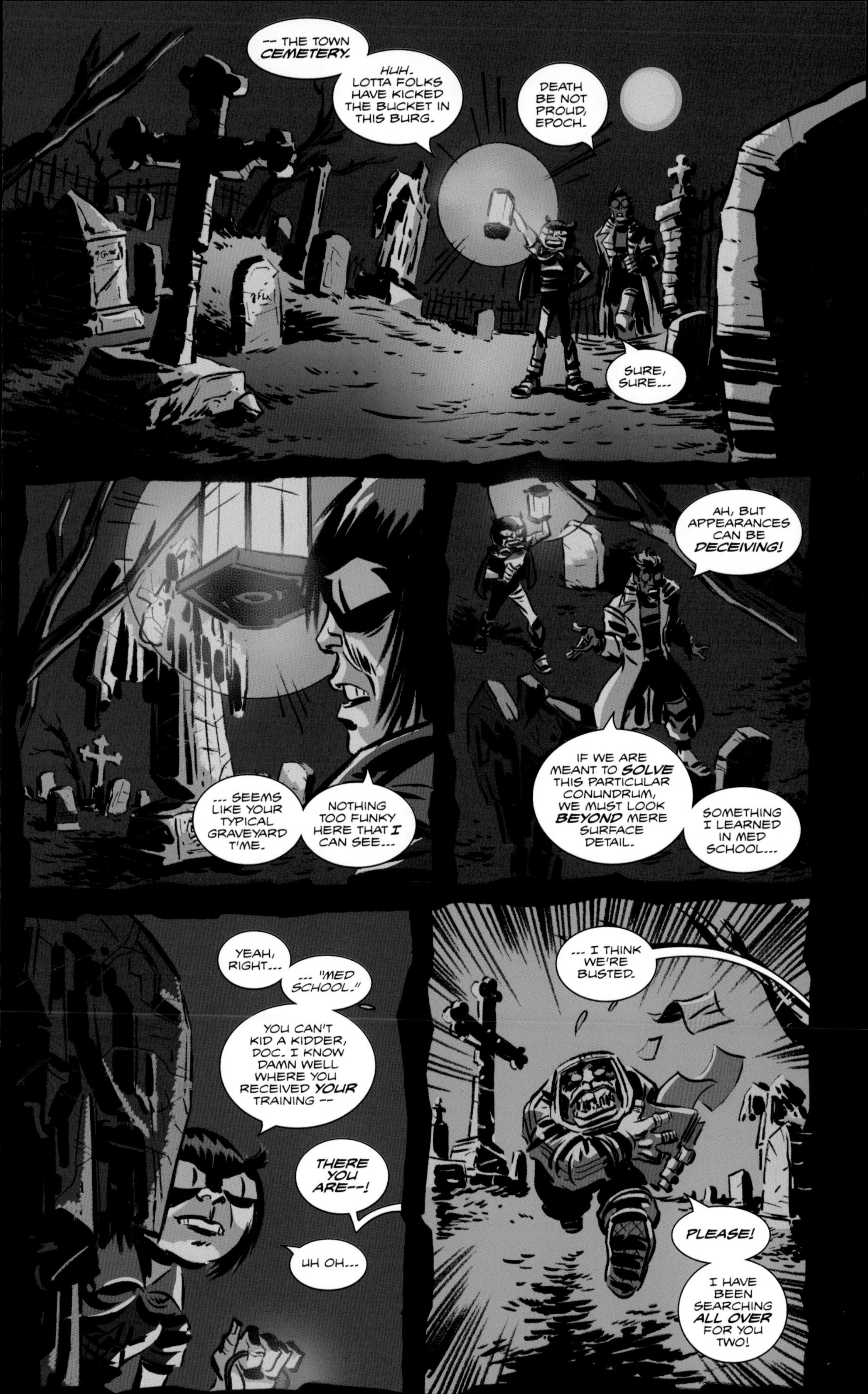
-- THE TOWN CEMETERY.
HUH. LOTTA FOLKS HAVE KICKED THE BUCKET IN THIS BURG.
DEATH BE NOT PROUD, EPOCH.
SURE, SURE...
... SEEMS LIKE YOUR TYPICAL GRAVEYARD T'ME.
NOTHING TOO FUNKY HERE THAT I CAN SEE...
AH, BUT APPEARANCES CAN BE DECEIVING!
IF WE ARE MEANT TO SOLVE THIS PARTICULAR CONUNDRUM, WE MUST LOOK BEYOND MERE SURFACE DETAIL.
SOMETHING I LEARNED IN MED SCHOOL...
YEAH, RIGHT...
... "MED SCHOOL."
YOU CAN'T KID A KIDDER, DOC. I KNOW DAMN WELL WHERE YOU RECEIVED YOUR TRAINING --
THERE YOU ARE--!
UH OH...
... I THINK WE'RE BUSTED.
PLEASE!
I HAVE BEEN SEARCHING ALL OVER FOR YOU TWO!

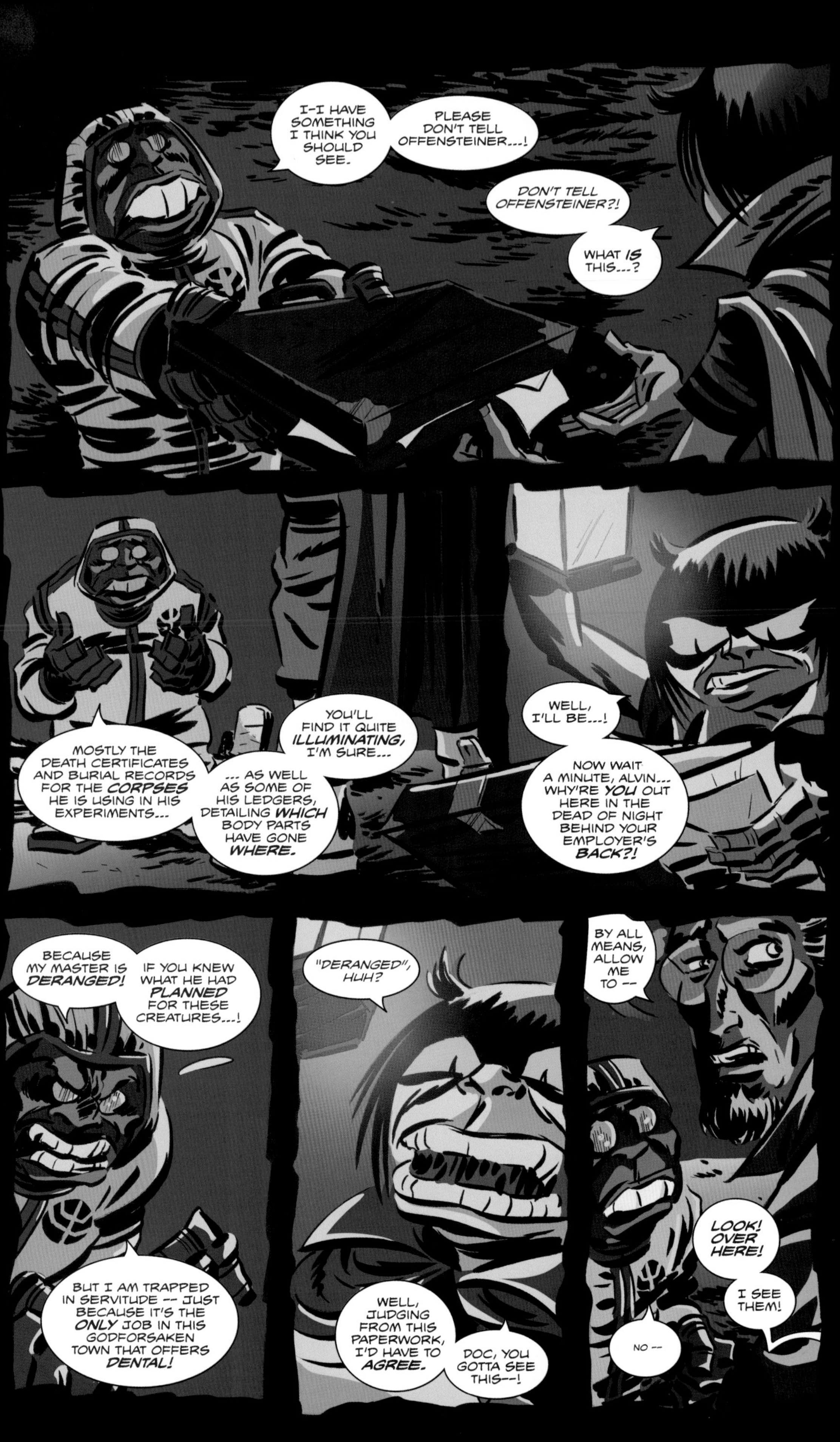
I-I HAVE SOMETHING I THINK YOU SHOULD SEE.
PLEASE DON'T TELL OFFENSTEINER...!
DON'T TELL OFFENSTEINER?!
WHAT IS THIS...?
YOU'LL FIND IT QUITE ILLUMINATING, I'M SURE...
MOSTLY THE DEATH CERTIFICATES AND BURIAL RECORDS FOR THE CORPSES HE IS USING IN HIS EXPERIMENTS...
... AS WELL AS SOME OF HIS LEDGERS, DETAILING WHICH BODY PARTS HAVE GONE WHERE.
WELL, I'LL BE...!
NOW WAIT A MINUTE, ALVIN... WHY'RE YOU OUT HERE IN THE DEAD OF NIGHT BEHIND YOUR EMPLOYER'S BACK?!
BECAUSE MY MASTER IS DERANGED!
IF YOU KNEW WHAT HE HAD PLANNED FOR THESE CREATURES...!
BUT I AM TRAPPED IN SERVITUDE -- JUST BECAUSE IT'S THE ONLY JOB IN THIS GODFORSAKEN TOWN THAT OFFERS DENTAL!
"DERANGED", HUH?
WELL, JUDGING FROM THIS PAPERWORK, I'D HAVE TO AGREE.
DOC, YOU GOTTA SEE THIS--!
BY ALL MEANS, ALLOW ME TO --
LOOK! OVER HERE!
I SEE THEM!
NO --

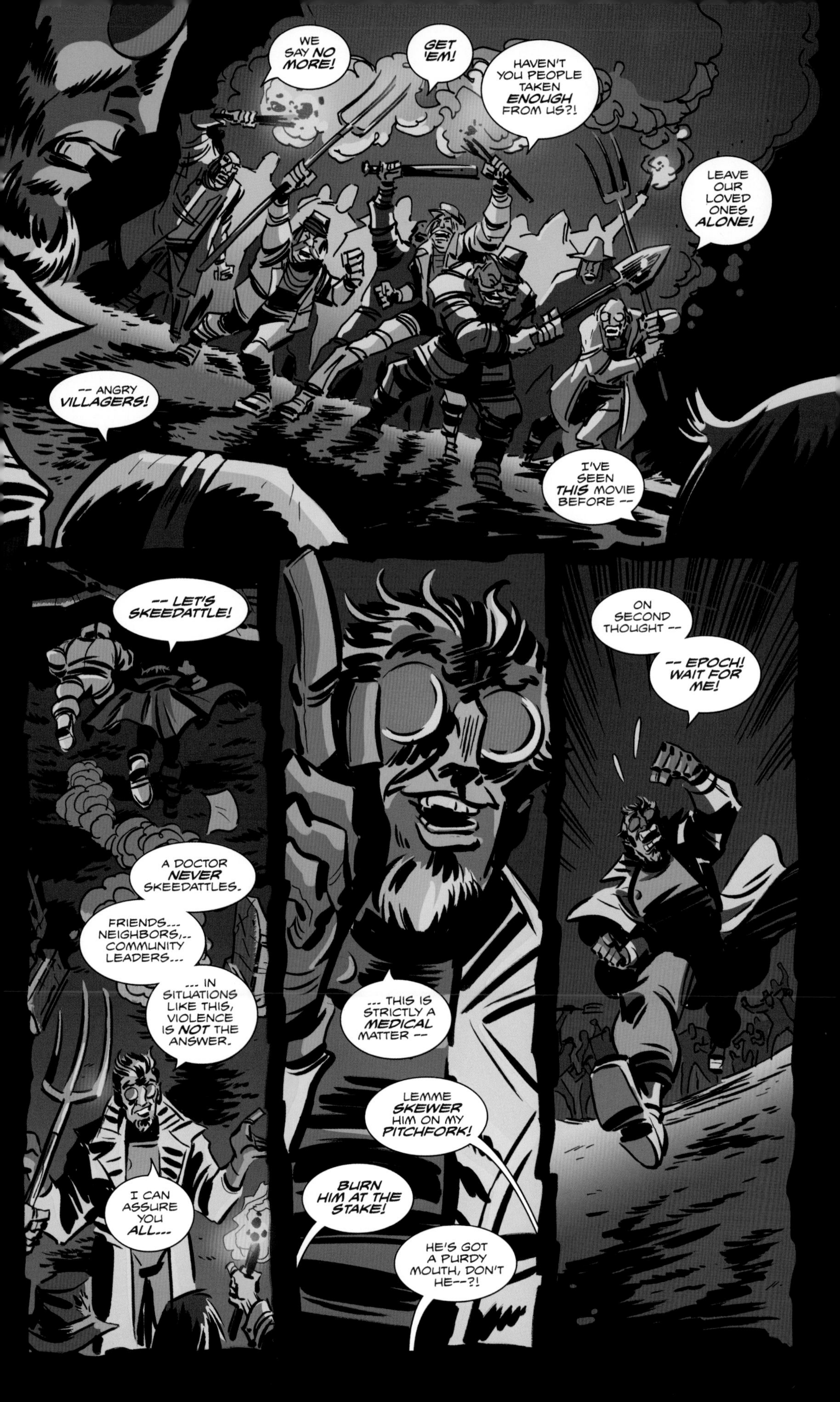
WE SAY NO MORE!
GET 'EM!
HAVEN'T YOU PEOPLE TAKEN ENOUGH FROM US?!
LEAVE OUR LOVED ONES ALONE!
-- ANGRY VILLAGERS!
I'VE SEEN THIS MOVIE BEFORE --
-- LET'S SKEEDATTLE!
A DOCTOR NEVER SKEEDATTLES.
FRIENDS... NEIGHBORS... COMMUNITY LEADERS...
... IN SITUATIONS LIKE THIS, VIOLENCE IS NOT THE ANSWER.
I CAN ASSURE YOU ALL...
... THIS IS STRICTLY A MEDICAL MATTER --
LEMME SKEWER HIM ON MY PITCHFORK!
BURN HIM AT THE STAKE!
HE'S GOT A PURDY MOUTH, DON'T HE--?!
ON SECOND THOUGHT --
-- EPOCH! WAIT FOR ME!

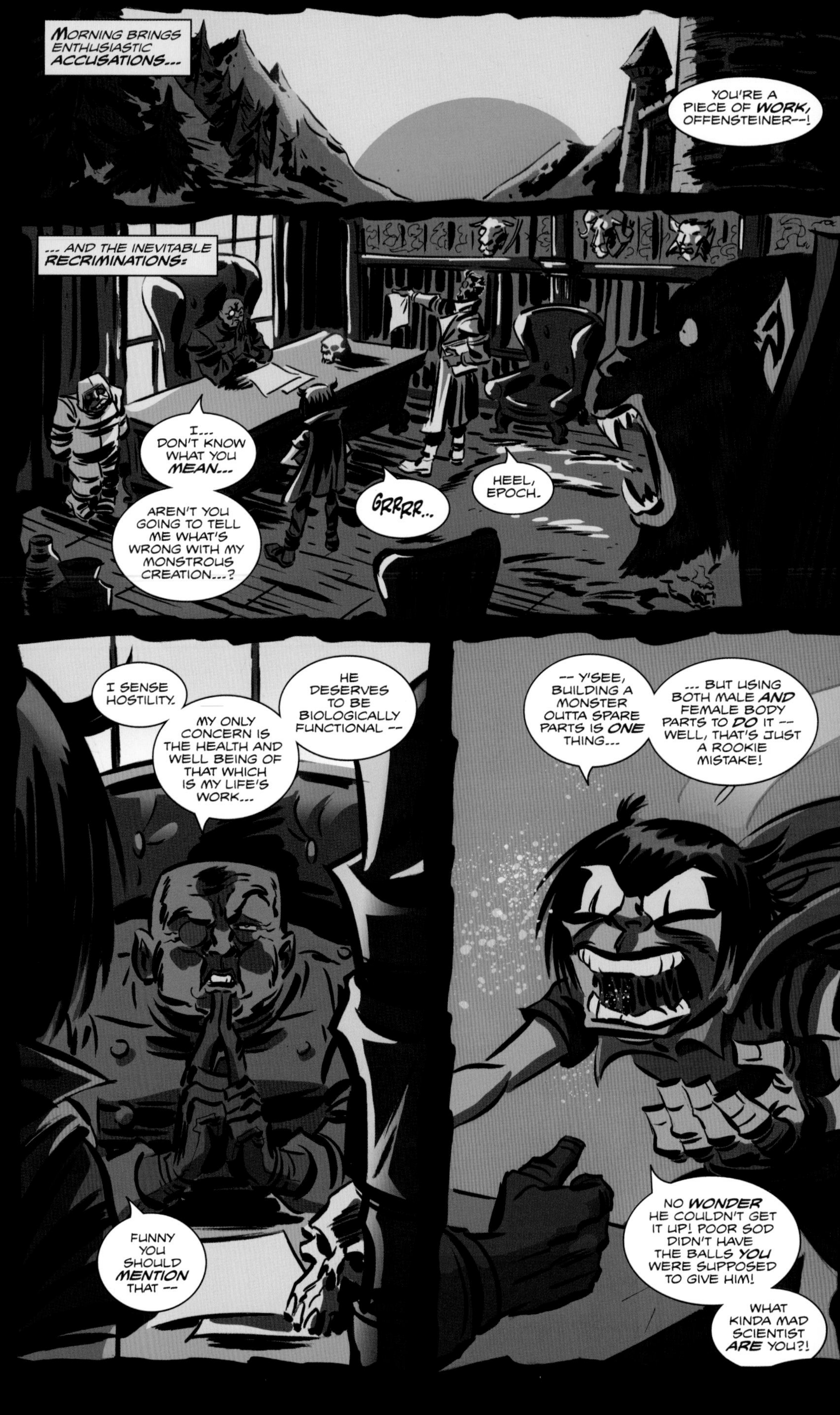
MORNING BRINGS ENTHUSIASTIC ACCUSATIONS...
YOU'RE A PIECE OF WORK, OFFENSTEINER--!
... AND THE INEVITABLE RECRIMINATIONS:
I... DON'T KNOW WHAT YOU MEAN...
ARE'NT YOU GOING TO TELL ME WHAT'S WRONG WITH MY MONSTROUS CREATION...?
GRRRR...
HEEL, EPOCH.
I SENSE HOSTILITY.
MY ONLY CONCERN IS THE HEALTH AND WELL BEING OF THAT WHICH IS MY LIFE'S WORK...
HE DESERVES TO BE BIOLOGICALLY FUNCTIONAL --
FUNNY YOU SHOULD MENTION THAT --
-- Y'SEE, BUILDING A MONSTER OUTTA SPARE PARTS IS ONE THING...
... BUT USING BOTH MALE AND FEMALE BODY PARTS TO DO IT -- WELL, THAT'S JUST A ROOKIE MISTAKE!
NO WONDER HE COULDN'T GET IT UP! POOR SOD DIDN'T HAVE THE BALLS YOU WERE SUPPOSED TO GIVE HIM!
WHAT KINDA MAD SCIENTIST ARE YOU?!

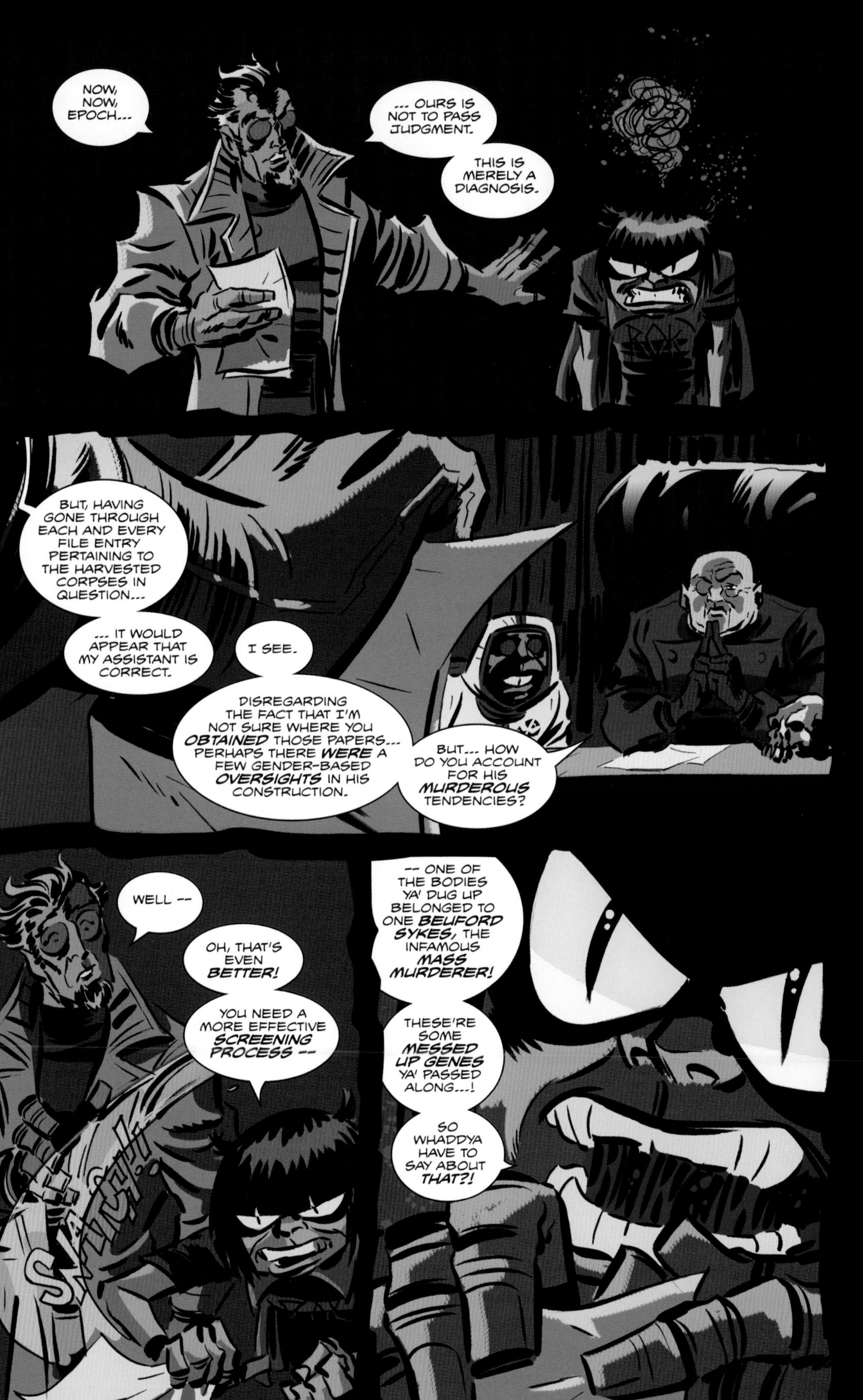
NOW, NOW, EPOCH...
... OURS IS NOT TO PASS JUDGMENT.
THIS IS MERELY A DIAGNOSIS.
BUT, HAVING GONE THROUGH EACH AND EVERY FILE ENTRY PERTAINING TO THE HARVESTED CORPSES IN QUESTION...
... IT WOULD APPEAR THAT MY ASSISTANT IS CORRECT.
I SEE.
DISREGARDING THE FACT THAT I'M NOT SURE WHERE YOU *OBTAINED* THOSE PAPERS... PERHAPS THERE *WERE* A FEW GENDER-BASED *OVERSIGHTS* IN HIS CONSTRUCTION.
BUT... HOW DO YOU ACCOUNT FOR HIS *MURDEROUS* TENDENCIES?
WELL --
OH, THAT'S EVEN *BETTER!*
YOU NEED A MORE EFFECTIVE *SCREENING PROCESS --*
-- ONE OF THE BODIES YA' DUG UP BELONGED TO ONE *BEUFORD SYKES,* THE INFAMOUS *MASS MURDERER!*
THESE'RE SOME *MESSED UP GENES* YA' PASSED ALONG...!
SO WHADDYA HAVE TO SAY ABOUT *THAT?!*

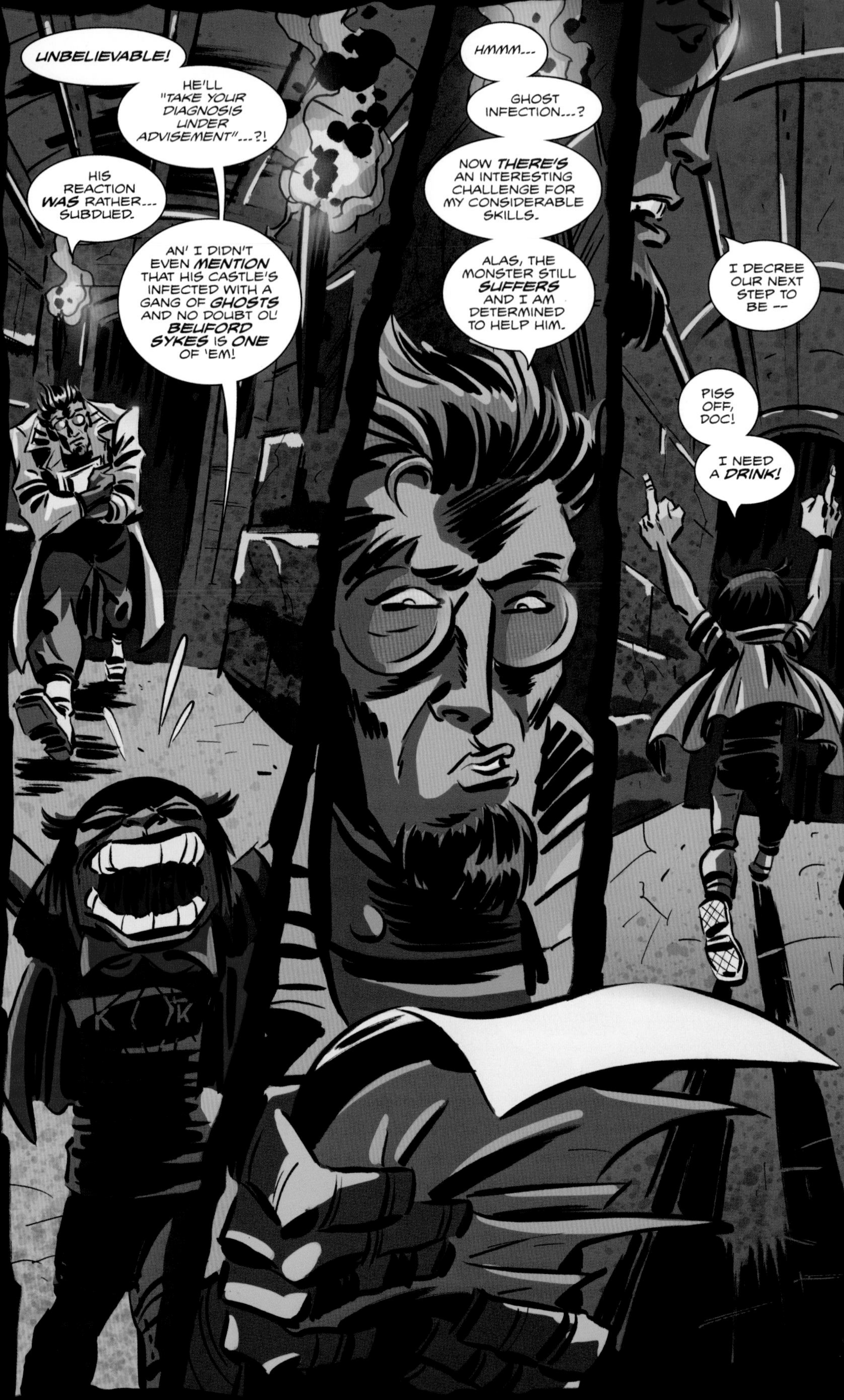
UNBELIEVABLE!
HE'LL "TAKE YOUR DIAGNOSIS UNDER ADVISEMENT"...?!
HIS REACTION WAS RATHER... SUBDUED.
AN' I DIDN'T EVEN MENTION THAT HIS CASTLE'S INFECTED WITH A GANG OF GHOSTS AND NO DOUBT OL' BEUFORD SYKES IS ONE OF 'EM!
HMMM...
GHOST INFECTION...?
NOW THERE'S AN INTERESTING CHALLENGE FOR MY CONSIDERABLE SKILLS.
ALAS, THE MONSTER STILL SUFFERS AND I AM DETERMINED TO HELP HIM.
I DECREE OUR NEXT STEP TO BE --
PISS OFF, DOC!
I NEED A DRINK!

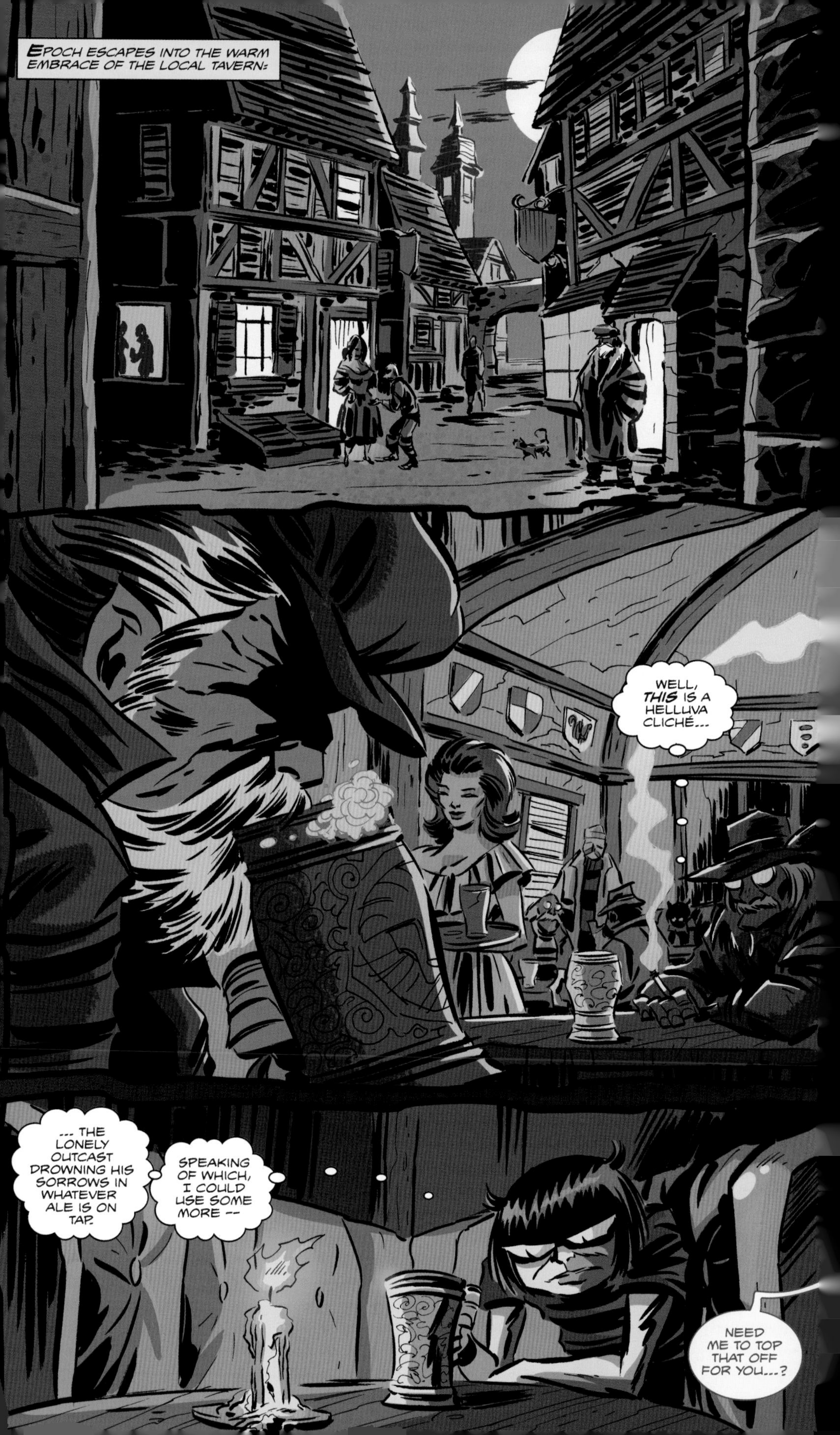
EPOCH ESCAPES INTO THE WARM EMBRACE OF THE LOCAL TAVERN:
WELL, THIS IS A HELLUVA CLICHÉ...
... THE LONELY OUTCAST DROWNING HIS SORROWS IN WHATEVER ALE IS ON TAP.
SPEAKING OF WHICH, I COULD USE SOME MORE --
NEED ME TO TOP THAT OFF FOR YOU...?

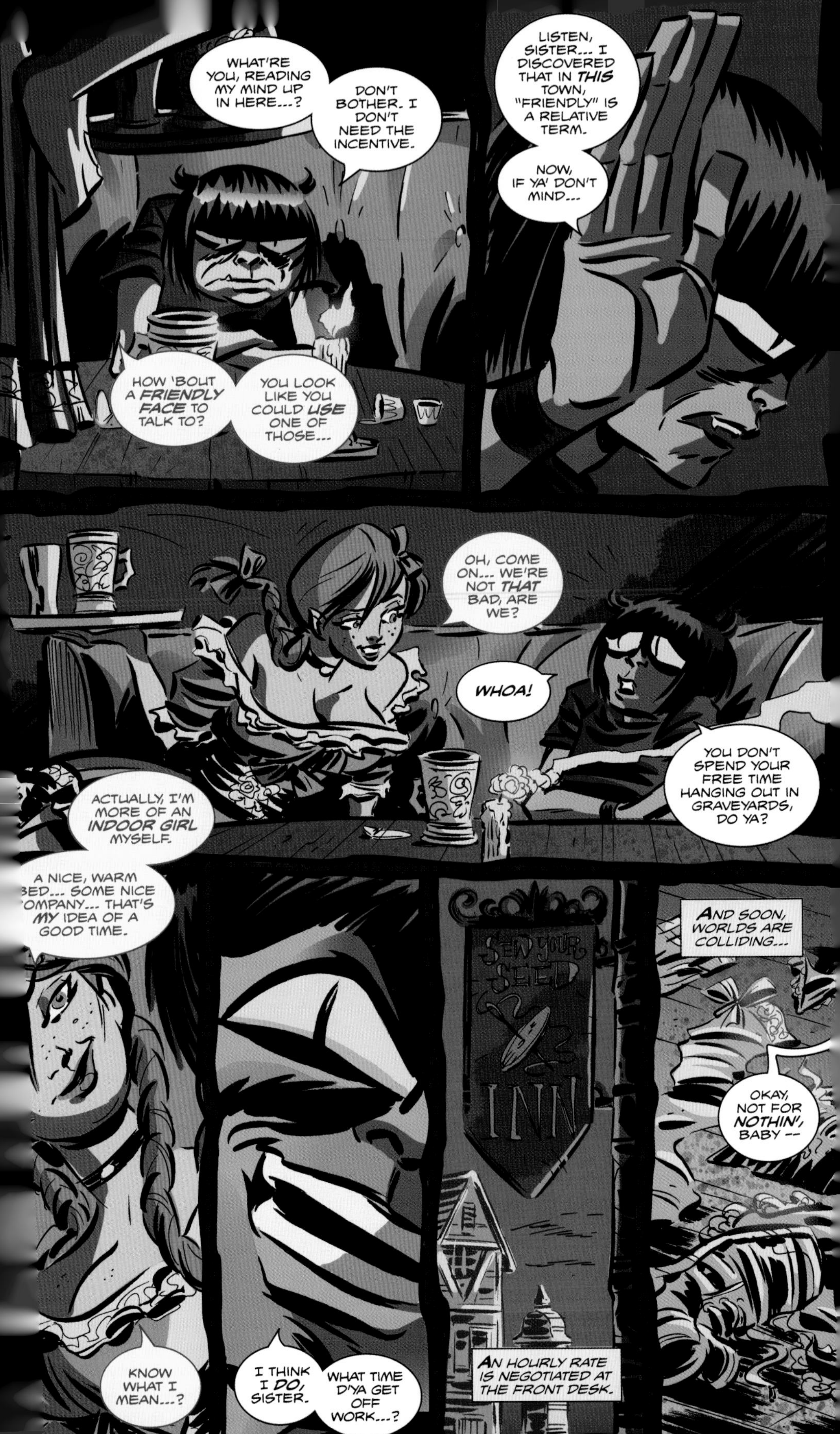

WHAT'RE YOU, READING MY MIND UP IN HERE...?
DON'T BOTHER. I DON'T NEED THE INCENTIVE.
HOW 'BOUT A FRIENDLY FACE TO TALK TO?
YOU LOOK LIKE YOU COULD USE ONE OF THOSE...
LISTEN, SISTER... I DISCOVERED THAT IN THIS TOWN, "FRIENDLY" IS A RELATIVE TERM.
NOW, IF YA' DON'T MIND...
OH, COME ON... WE'RE NOT THAT BAD, ARE WE?
WHOA!
YOU DON'T SPEND YOUR FREE TIME HANGING OUT IN GRAVEYARDS, DO YA?
ACTUALLY, I'M MORE OF AN INDOOR GIRL MYSELF.
A NICE, WARM BED... SOME NICE COMPANY... THAT'S MY IDEA OF A GOOD TIME.
KNOW WHAT I MEAN...?
I THINK I DO, SISTER.
WHAT TIME D'YA GET OFF WORK...?
SEW YOUR SEED
INN
AN HOURLY RATE IS NEGOTIATED AT THE FRONT DESK.
AND SOON, WORLDS ARE COLLIDING...
OKAY, NOT FOR NOTHIN', BABY --

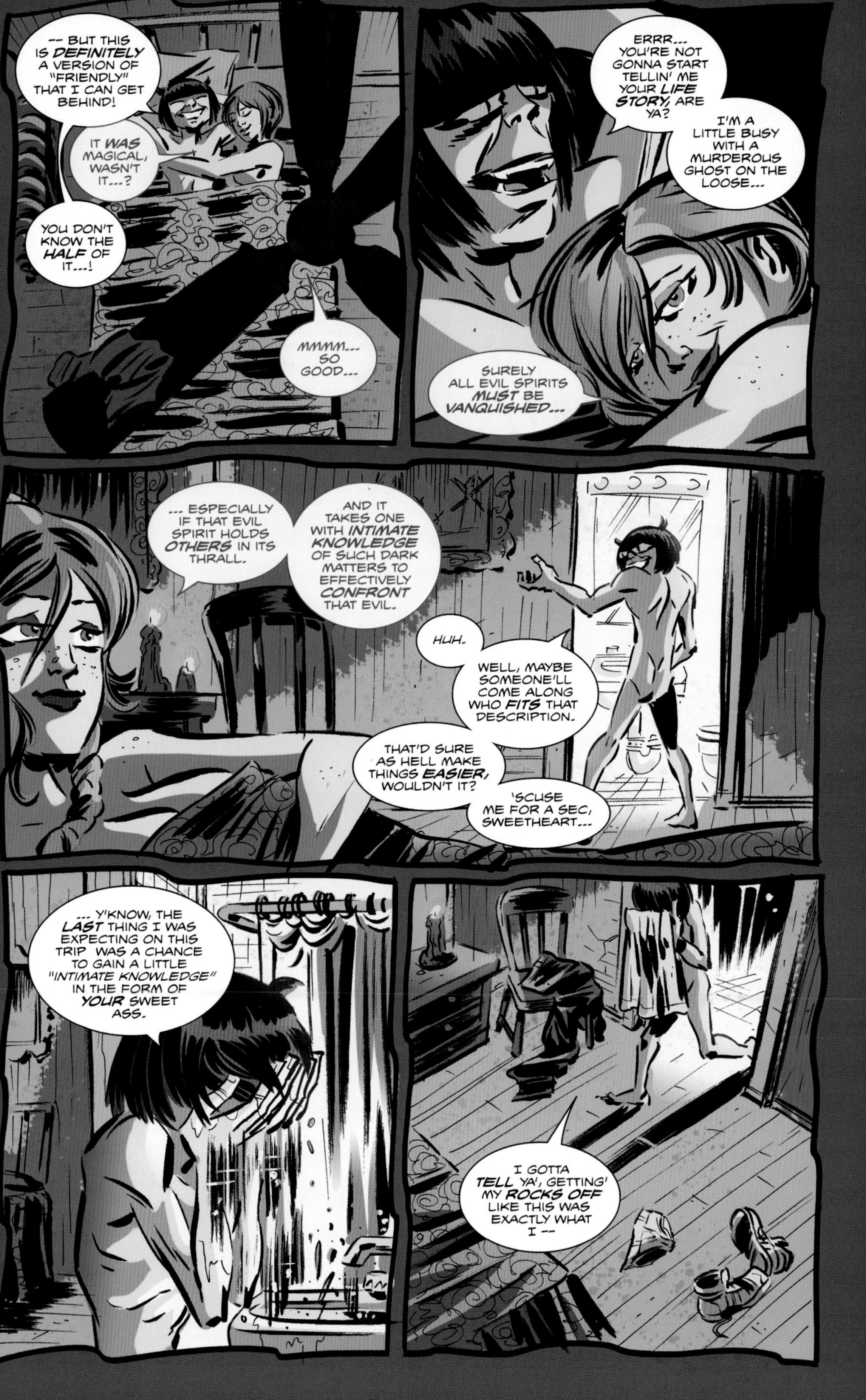
-- BUT THIS IS DEFINITELY A VERSION OF "FRIENDLY" THAT I CAN GET BEHIND!
IT WAS MAGICAL, WASN'T IT...?
YOU DON'T KNOW THE HALF OF IT...!
MMMM... SO GOOD...
ERRR... YOU'RE NOT GONNA START TELLIN' ME YOUR LIFE STORY, ARE YA?
I'M A LITTLE BUSY WITH A MURDEROUS GHOST ON THE LOOSE...
SURELY ALL EVIL SPIRITS MUST BE VANQUISHED...
... ESPECIALLY IF THAT EVIL SPIRIT HOLDS OTHERS IN ITS THRALL.
AND IT TAKES ONE WITH INTIMATE KNOWLEDGE OF SUCH DARK MATTERS TO EFFECTIVELY CONFRONT THAT EVIL.
HUH.
WELL, MAYBE SOMEONE'LL COME ALONG WHO FITS THAT DESCRIPTION.
THAT'D SURE AS HELL MAKE THINGS EASIER, WOULDN'T IT?
'SCUSE ME FOR A SEC, SWEETHEART...
... Y'KNOW, THE LAST THING I WAS EXPECTING ON THIS TRIP WAS A CHANCE TO GAIN A LITTLE "INTIMATE KNOWLEDGE" IN THE FORM OF YOUR SWEET ASS.
I GOTTA TELL YA', GETTING' MY ROCKS OFF LIKE THIS WAS EXACTLY WHAT I --

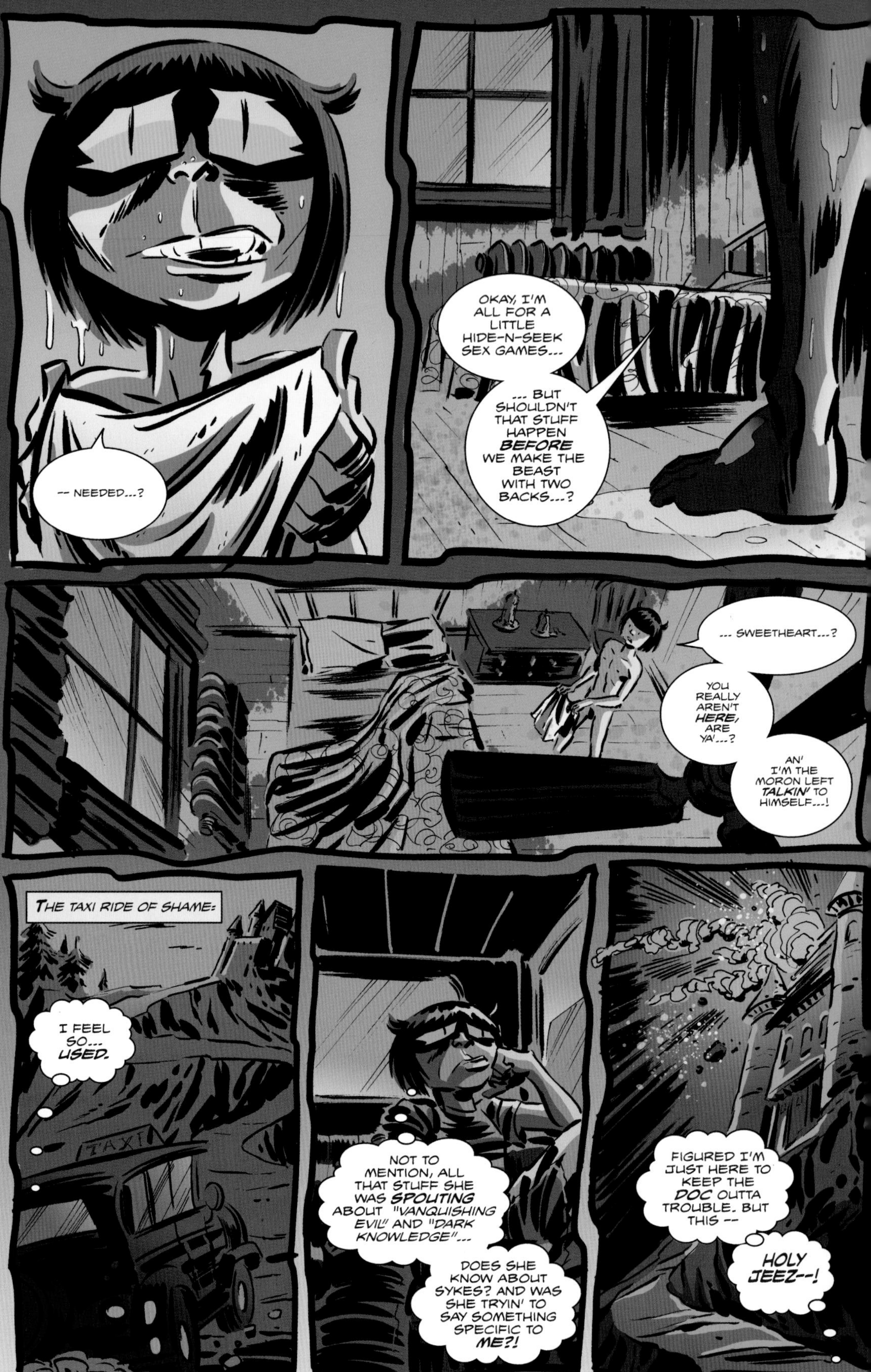
-- NEEDED...?
OKAY, I'M ALL FOR A LITTLE HIDE-N-SEEK SEX GAMES...
... BUT SHOULDN'T THAT STUFF HAPPEN BEFORE WE MAKE THE BEAST WITH TWO BACKS...?
... SWEETHEART...?
YOU REALLY AREN'T HERE, ARE YA'...?
AN' I'M THE MORON LEFT TALKIN' TO HIMSELF...!
THE TAXI RIDE OF SHAME:
I FEEL SO... USED.
TAXI
NOT TO MENTION, ALL THAT STUFF SHE WAS SPOUTING ABOUT "VANQUISHING EVIL" AND "DARK KNOWLEDGE"...
DOES SHE KNOW ABOUT SYKES? AND WAS SHE TRYIN' TO SAY SOMETHING SPECIFIC TO ME?!
FIGURED I'M JUST HERE TO KEEP THE DOC OUTTA TROUBLE. BUT THIS --
HOLY JEEZ--!

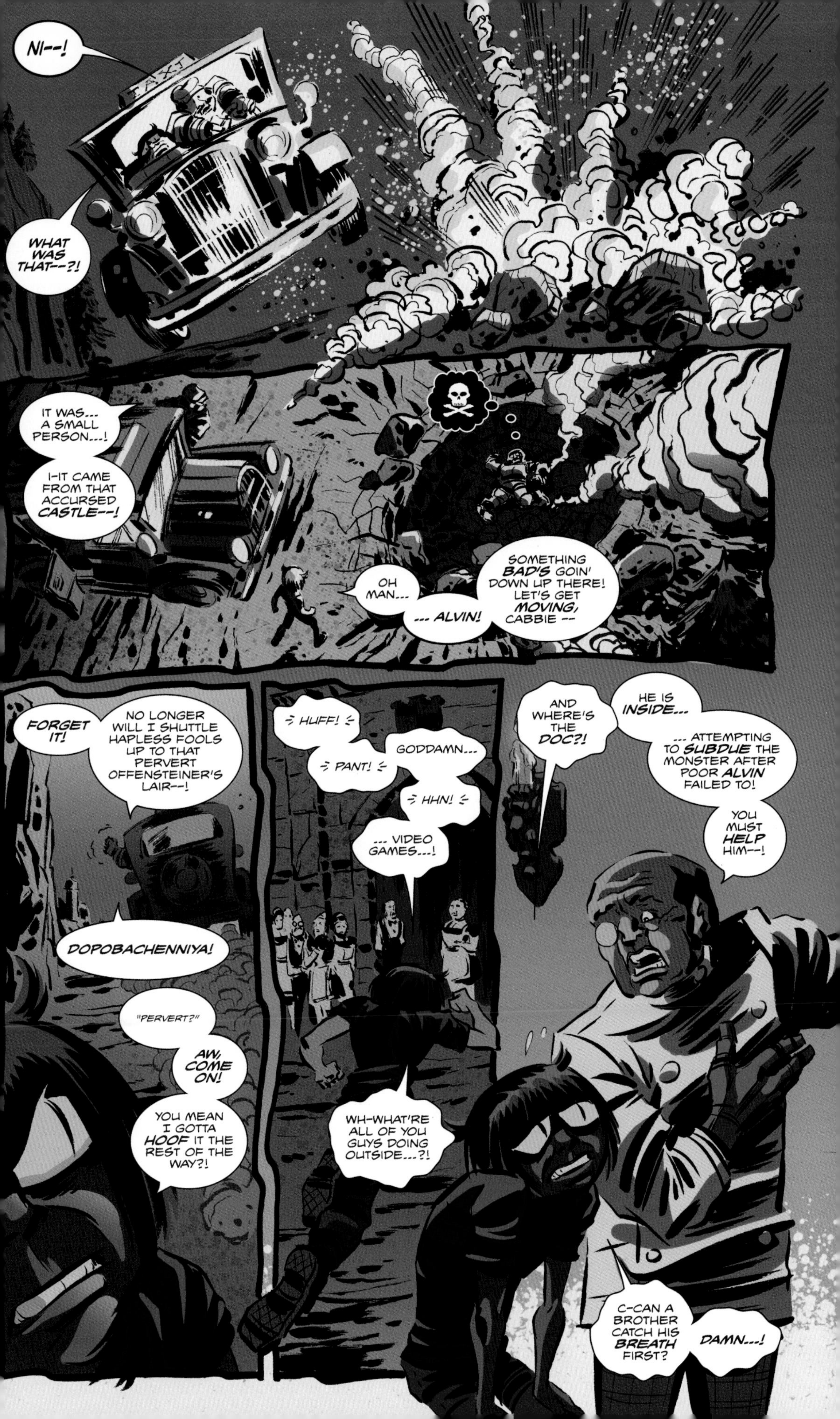
NI--!
WHAT WAS THAT--?!
IT WAS... A SMALL PERSON...!
I-IT CAME FROM THAT ACCURSED CASTLE--!
OH MAN...
--- ALVIN!
SOMETHING BAD'S GOIN' DOWN UP THERE! LET'S GET MOVING, CABBIE --
FORGET IT!
NO LONGER WILL I SHUTTLE HAPLESS FOOLS UP TO THAT PERVERT OFFENSTEINER'S LAIR--!
DOPOBACHENNIYA!
"PERVERT?"
AW, COME ON!
YOU MEAN I GOTTA HOOF IT THE REST OF THE WAY?!
HUFF!
GODDAMN...
PANT!
HHN!
... VIDEO GAMES...!
WH-WHAT'RE ALL OF YOU GUYS DOING OUTSIDE...?!
AND WHERE'S THE DOC?!
HE IS INSIDE...
... ATTEMPTING TO SUBDUE THE MONSTER AFTER POOR ALVIN FAILED TO!
YOU MUST HELP HIM--!
C-CAN A BROTHER CATCH HIS BREATH FIRST?
DAMN...!

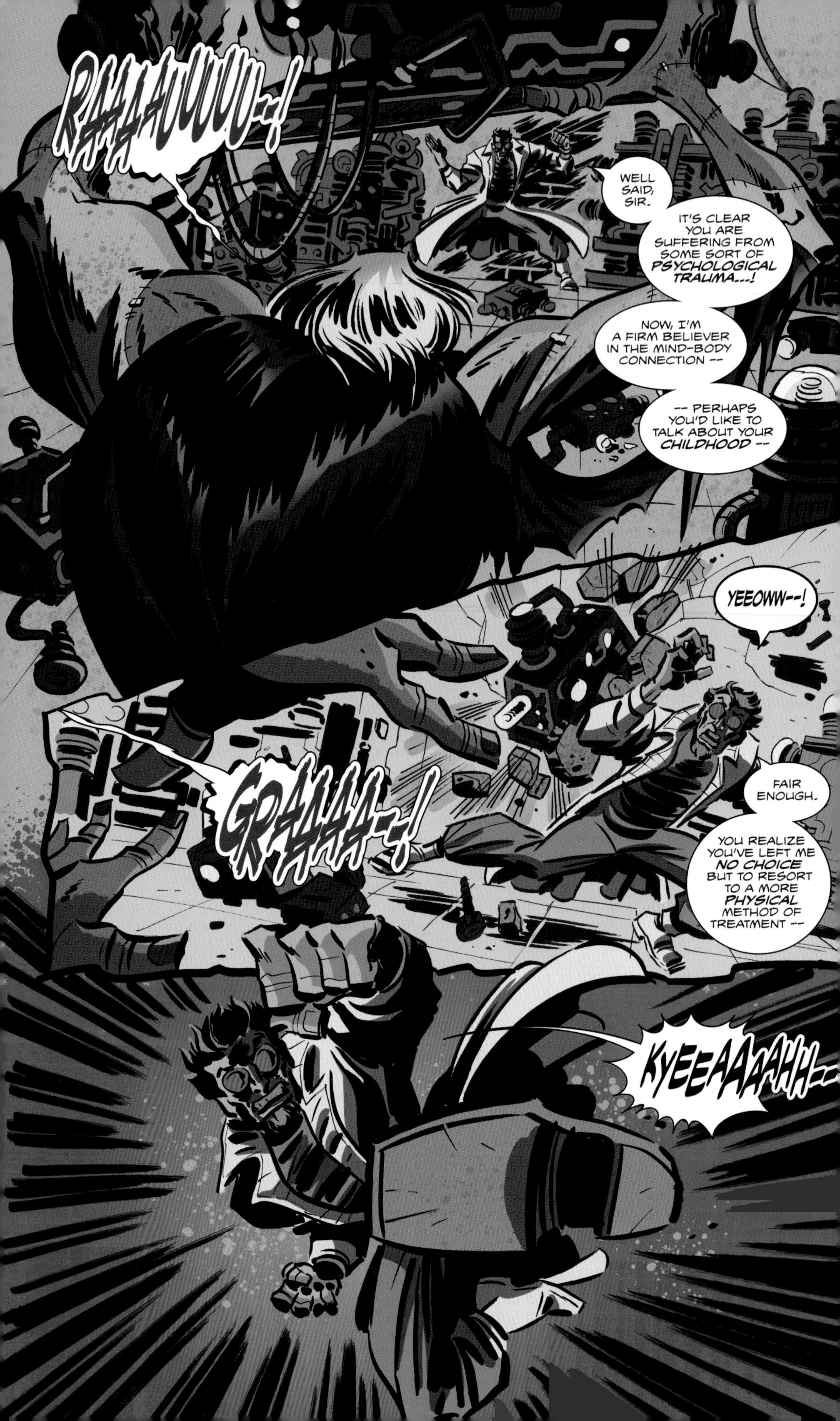
RAAAOUUUU--!
WELL SAID, SIR.
IT'S CLEAR YOU ARE SUFFERING FROM SOME SORT OF *PSYCHOLOGICAL TRAUMA*...!
NOW, I'M A FIRM BELIEVER IN THE MIND-BODY CONNECTION --
-- PERHAPS YOU'D LIKE TO TALK ABOUT YOUR *CHILDHOOD* --
YEEOWW--!
GRAAAA--!
FAIR ENOUGH.
YOU REALIZE YOU'VE LEFT ME *NO CHOICE* BUT TO RESORT TO A MORE *PHYSICAL* METHOD OF TREATMENT --
KYEEAAAAHH--

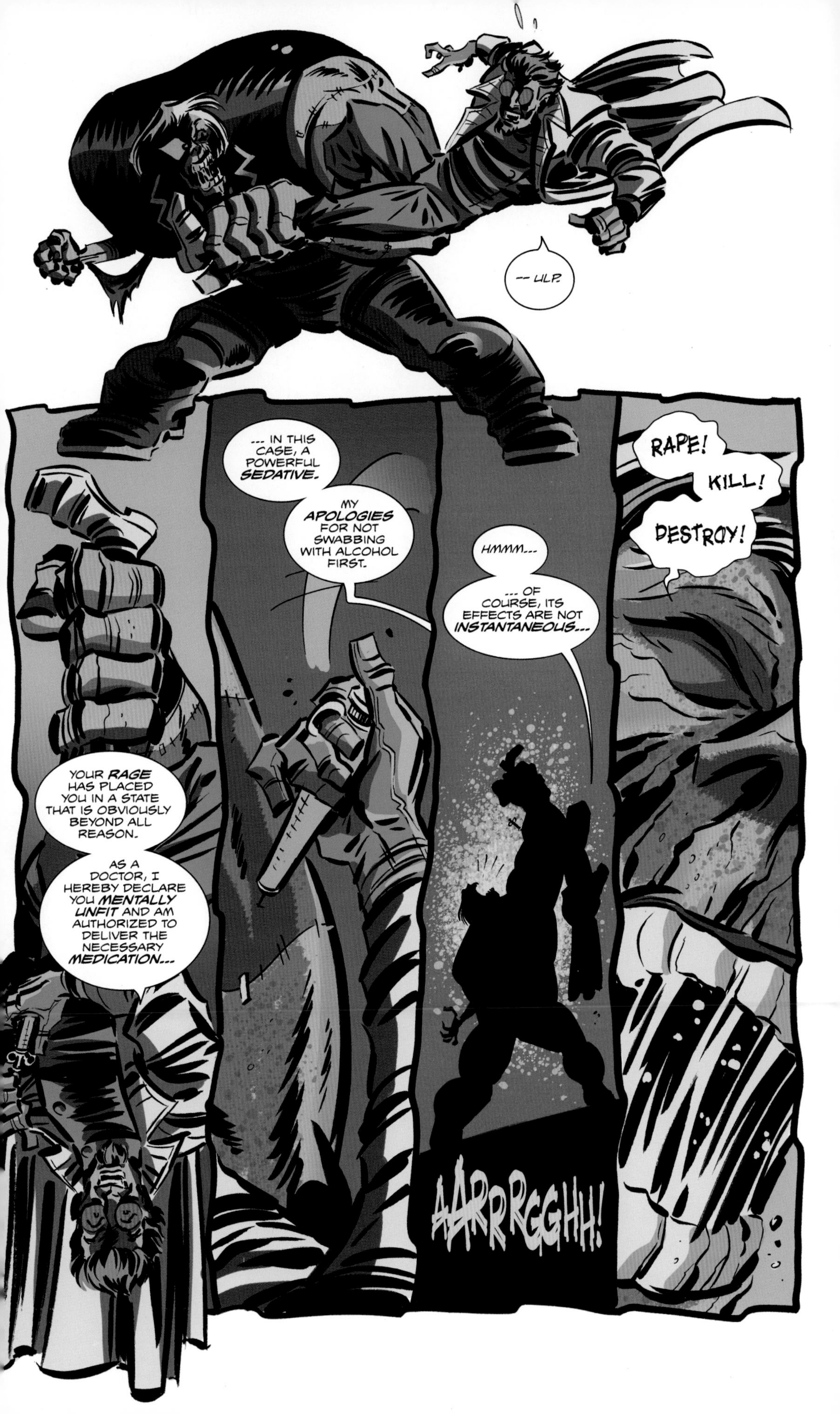
-- ULP.
... IN THIS CASE, A POWERFUL SEDATIVE.
MY APOLOGIES FOR NOT SWABBING WITH ALCOHOL FIRST.
YOUR RAGE HAS PLACED YOU IN A STATE THAT IS OBVIOUSLY BEYOND ALL REASON.
AS A DOCTOR, I HEREBY DECLARE YOU MENTALLY UNFIT AND AM AUTHORIZED TO DELIVER THE NECESSARY MEDICATION...
HMMM...
... OF COURSE, ITS EFFECTS ARE NOT INSTANTANEOUS...
AARRRGGHH!
RAPE!
KILL!
DESTROY!

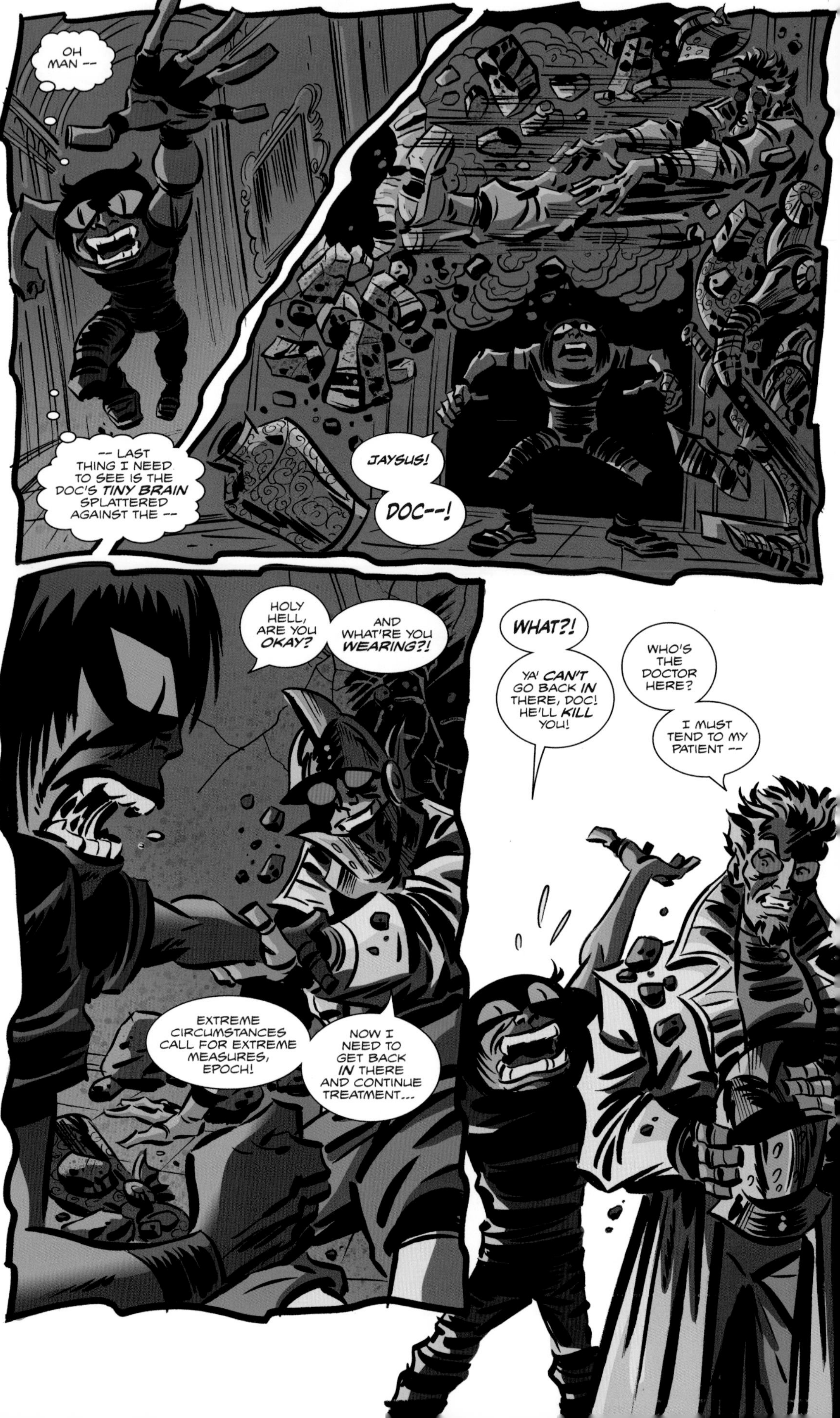
OH MAN --
-- LAST THING I NEED TO SEE IS THE DOC'S TINY BRAIN SPLATTERED AGAINST THE --
JAYSUS!
DOC--!
HOLY HELL, ARE YOU OKAY?
AND WHAT'RE YOU WEARING?!
EXTREME CIRCUMSTANCES CALL FOR EXTREME MEASURES, EPOCH!
NOW I NEED TO GET BACK IN THERE AND CONTINUE TREATMENT...
WHAT?!
YA' CAN'T GO BACK IN THERE, DOC! HE'LL KILL YOU!
WHO'S THE DOCTOR HERE?
I MUST TEND TO MY PATIENT --

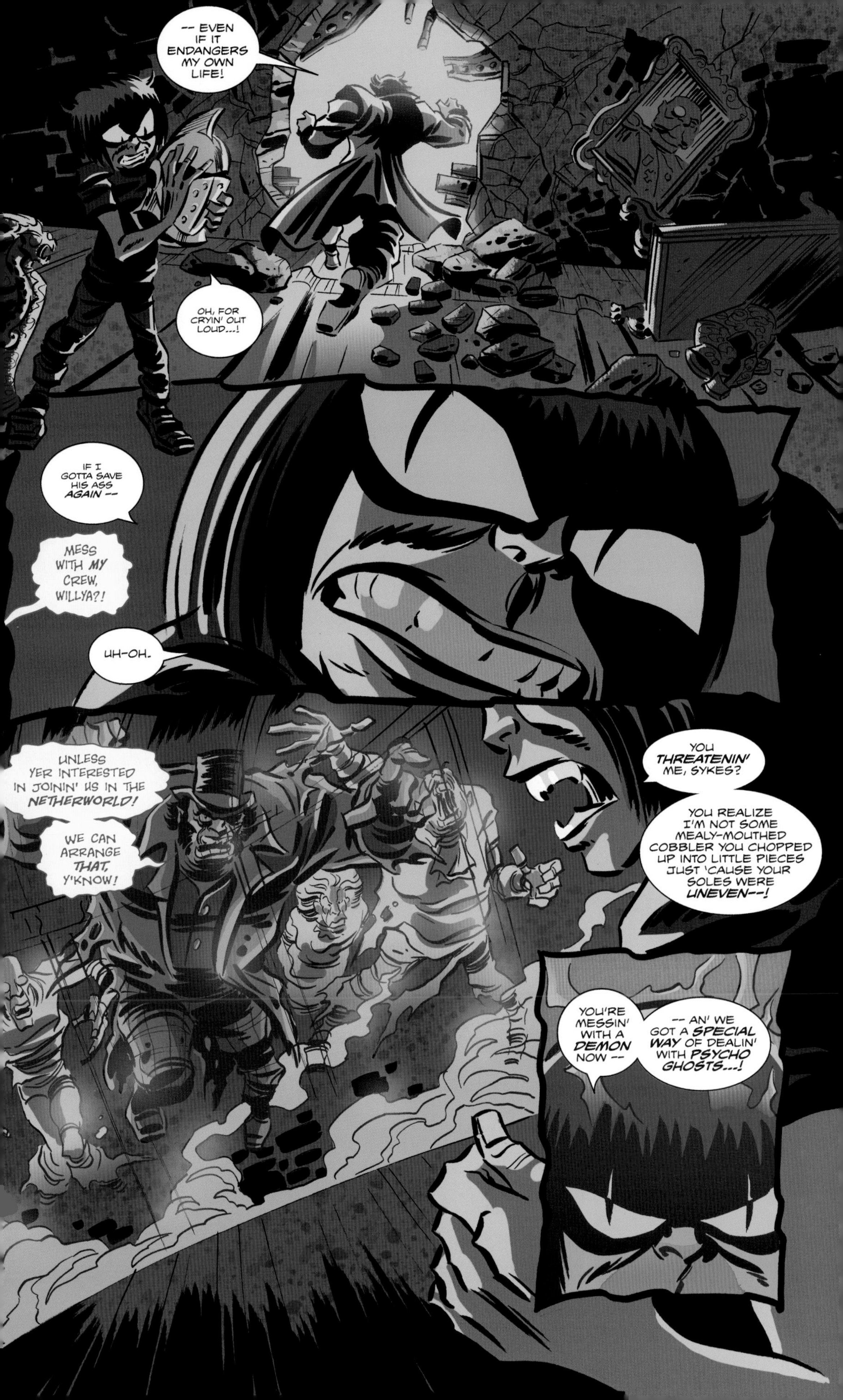
-- EVEN IF IT ENDANGERS MY OWN LIFE!
OH, FOR CRYIN' OUT LOUD...!
IF I GOTTA SAVE HIS ASS AGAIN --
MESS WITH MY CREW, WILLYA?!
UH-OH.
UNLESS YER INTERESTED IN JOININ' US IN THE NETHERWORLD!
WE CAN ARRANGE THAT, Y'KNOW!
YOU THREATENIN' ME, SYKES?
YOU REALIZE I'M NOT SOME MEALY-MOUTHED COBBLER YOU CHOPPED UP INTO LITTLE PIECES JUST 'CAUSE YOUR SOLES WERE UNEVEN--!
YOU'RE MESSIN' WITH A DEMON NOW --
-- AN' WE GOT A SPECIAL WAY OF DEALIN' WITH PSYCHO GHOSTS...!

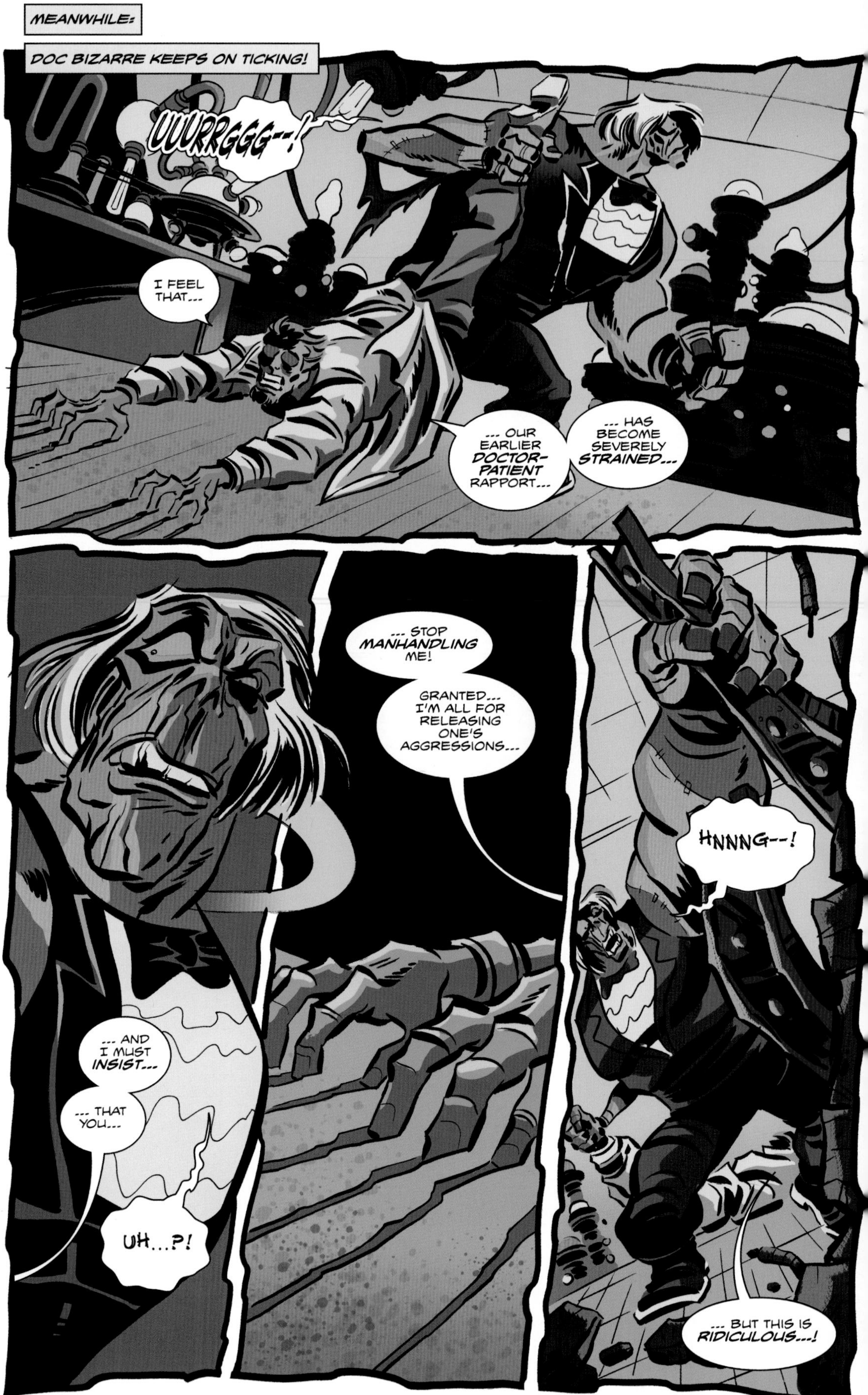
MEANWHILE:
DOC BIZARRE KEEPS ON TICKING!
UUURRGGG--!
I FEEL THAT...
... OUR EARLIER DOCTOR-PATIENT RAPPORT...
... HAS BECOME SEVERELY STRAINED...
... STOP MANHANDLING ME!
GRANTED... I'M ALL FOR RELEASING ONE'S AGGRESSIONS...
... AND I MUST INSIST...
... THAT YOU...
UH...?!
HNNNG--!
... BUT THIS IS RIDICULOUS...!

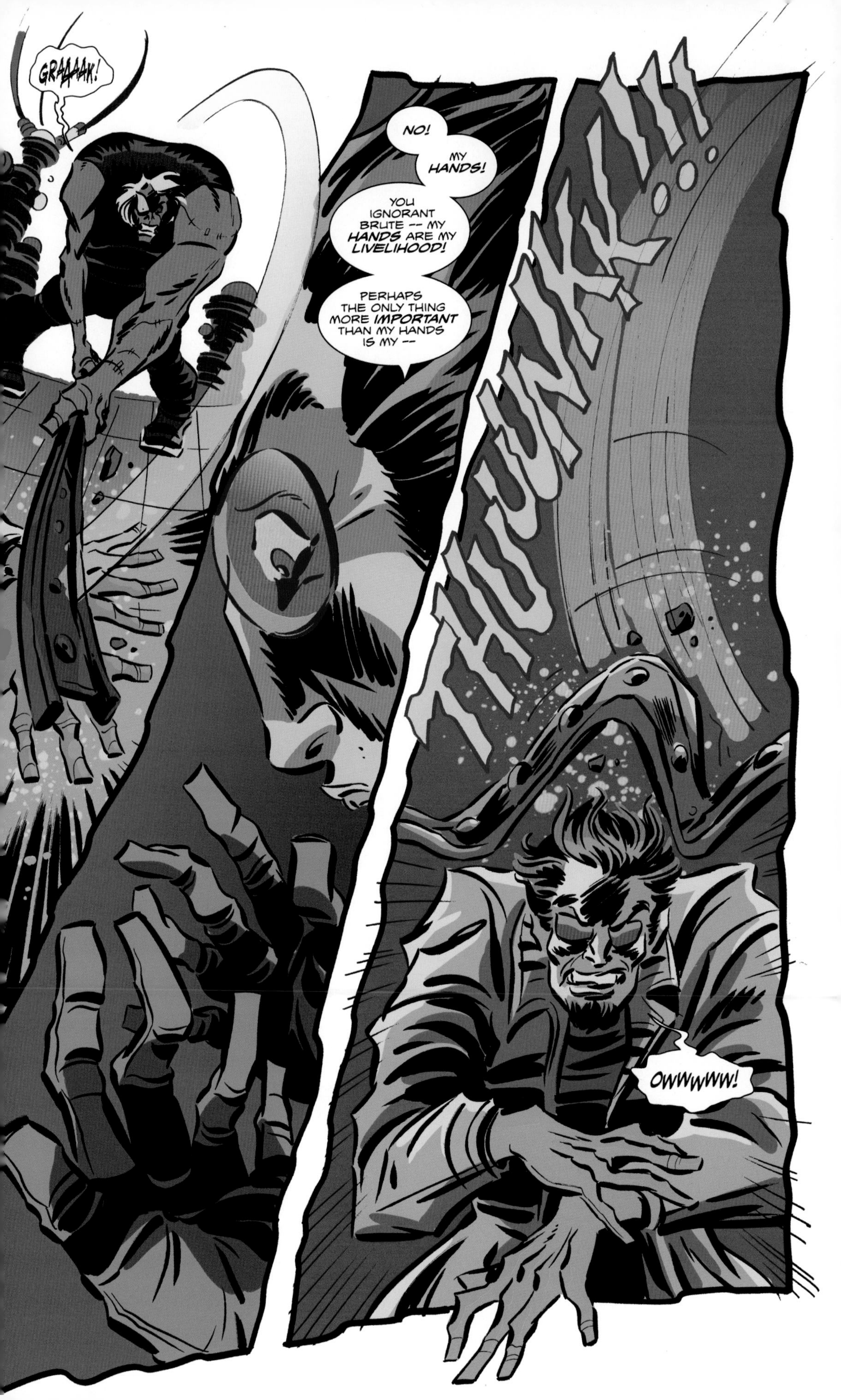
GRAAAAK!
NO!
MY HANDS!
YOU IGNORANT BRUTE -- MY HANDS ARE MY LIVELIHOOD!
PERHAPS THE ONLY THING MORE IMPORTANT THAN MY HANDS IS MY --
THUNK!!!
OWWWWW!

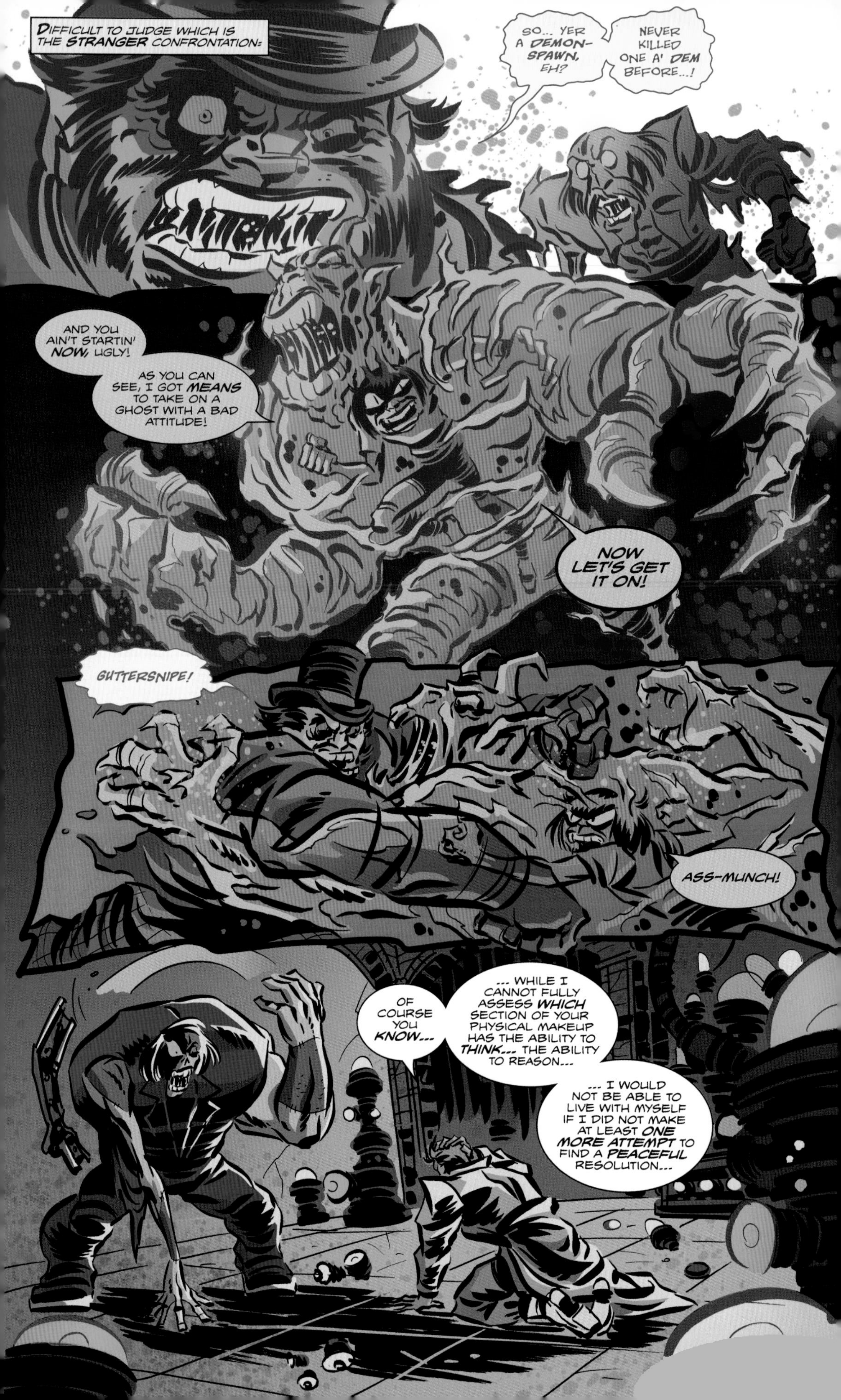
DIFFICULT TO JUDGE WHICH IS THE STRANGER CONFRONTATION:
SO... YER A DEMON-SPAWN, EH?
NEVER KILLED ONE A' DEM BEFORE...!
AND YOU AIN'T STARTIN' NOW, UGLY!
AS YOU CAN SEE, I GOT MEANS TO TAKE ON A GHOST WITH A BAD ATTITUDE!
NOW LET'S GET IT ON!
GUTTERSNIPE!
ASS-MUNCH!
OF COURSE YOU KNOW...
... WHILE I CANNOT FULLY ASSESS WHICH SECTION OF YOUR PHYSICAL MAKEUP HAS THE ABILITY TO THINK... THE ABILITY TO REASON...
... I WOULD NOT BE ABLE TO LIVE WITH MYSELF IF I DID NOT MAKE AT LEAST ONE MORE ATTEMPT TO FIND A PEACEFUL RESOLUTION...

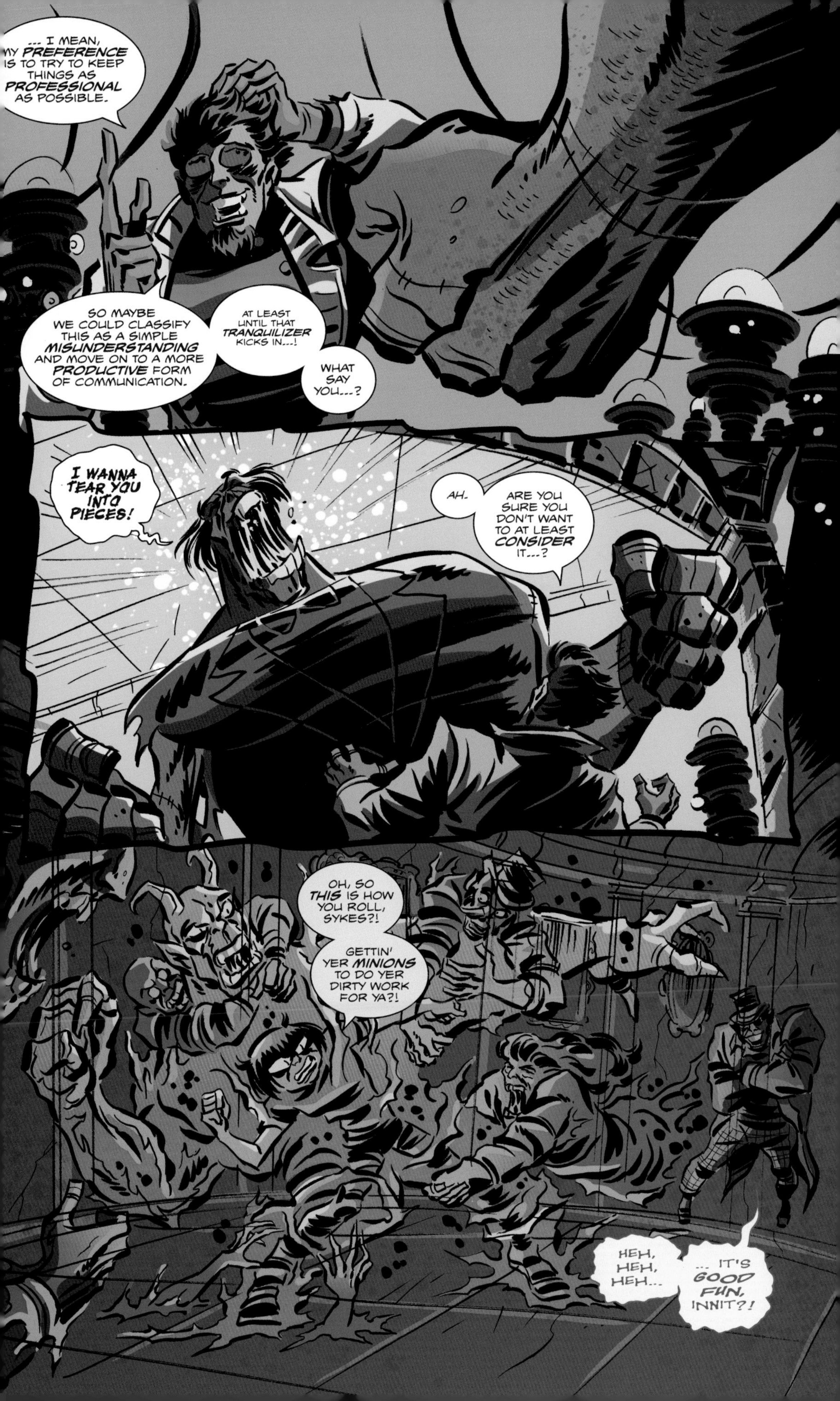
... I MEAN, MY PREFERENCE IS TO TRY TO KEEP THINGS AS PROFESSIONAL AS POSSIBLE.
SO MAYBE WE COULD CLASSIFY THIS AS A SIMPLE MISUNDERSTANDING AND MOVE ON TO A MORE PRODUCTIVE FORM OF COMMUNICATION.
AT LEAST UNTIL THAT TRANQUILIZER KICKS IN...!
WHAT SAY YOU...?
I WANNA TEAR YOU INTO PIECES!
AH.
ARE YOU SURE YOU DON'T WANT TO AT LEAST CONSIDER IT...?
OH, SO THIS IS HOW YOU ROLL, SYKES?!
GETTIN' YER MINIONS TO DO YER DIRTY WORK FOR YA?!
HEH, HEH, HEH...
... IT'S GOOD FUN, INNIT?!

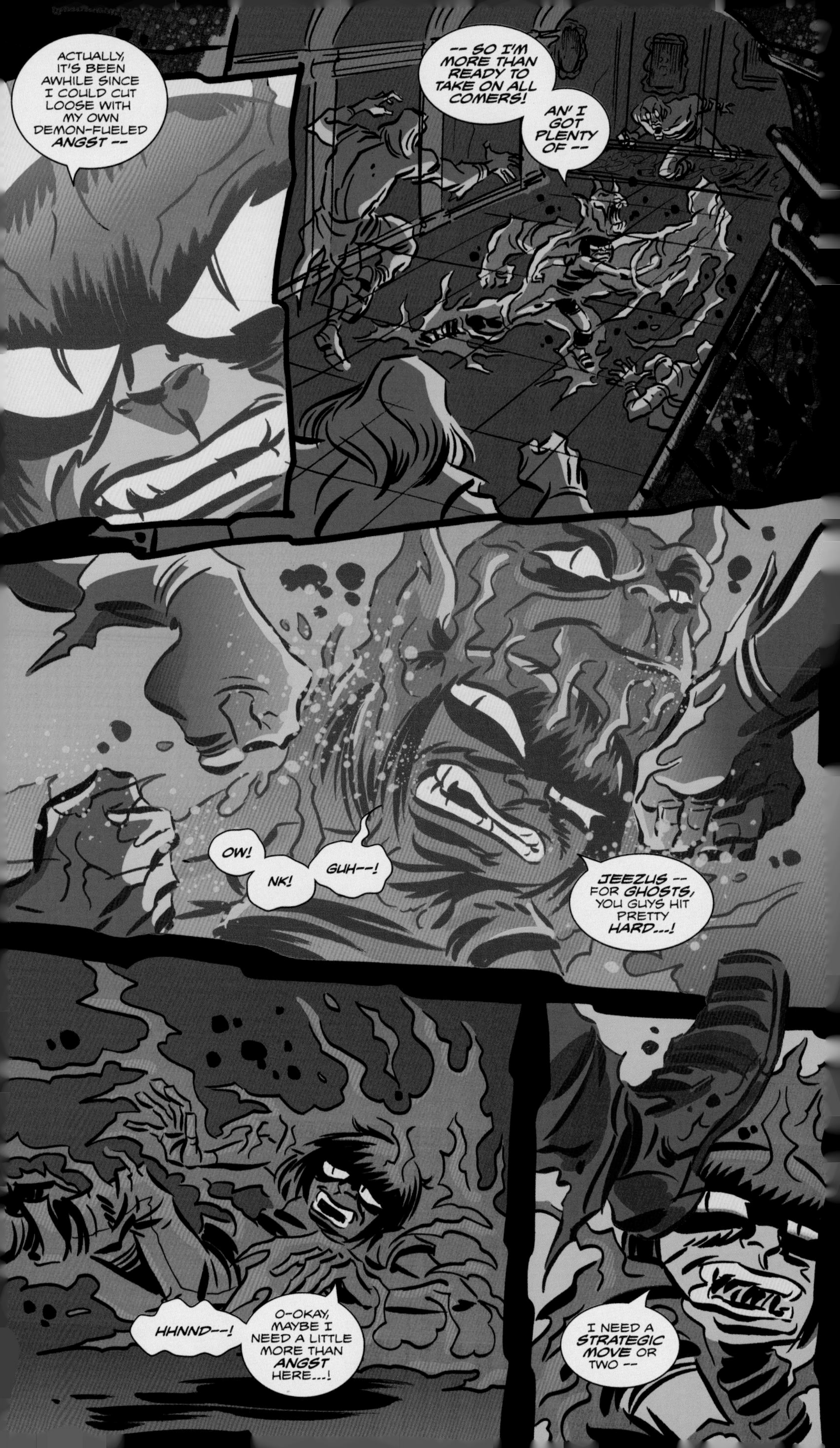
ACTUALLY, IT'S BEEN AWHILE SINCE I COULD CUT LOOSE WITH MY OWN DEMON-FUELED ANGST --
-- SO I'M MORE THAN READY TO TAKE ON ALL COMERS!
AN' I GOT PLENTY OF --
OW!
NK!
GUH--!
JEEZUS -- FOR GHOSTS, YOU GUYS HIT PRETTY HARD...!
HHNND--!
O-OKAY, MAYBE I NEED A LITTLE MORE THAN ANGST HERE...!
I NEED A STRATEGIC MOVE OR TWO --

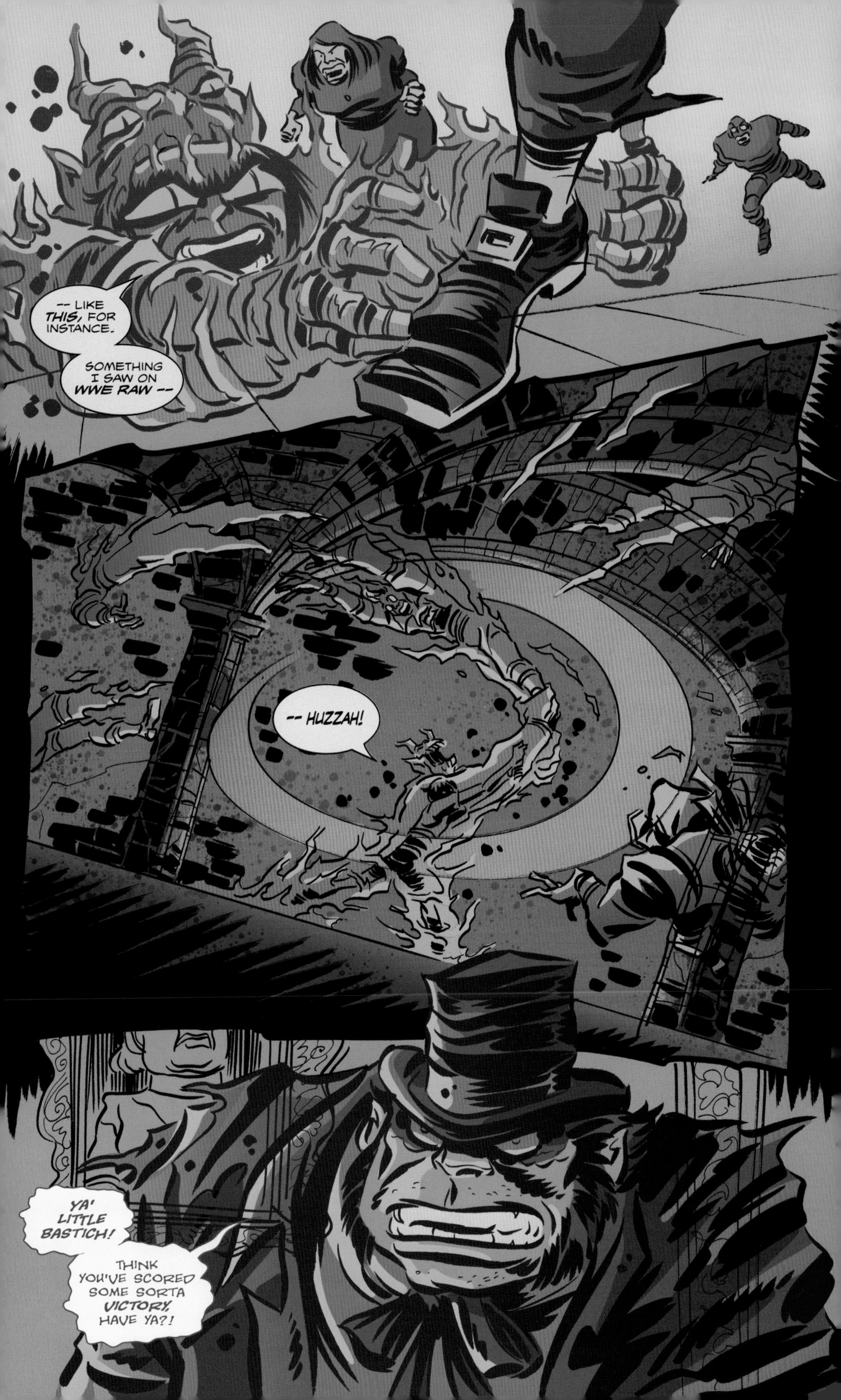
-- LIKE THIS, FOR INSTANCE.
SOMETHING I SAW ON WWE RAW --
-- HUZZAH!
YA' LITTLE BASTICH!
THINK YOU'VE SCORED SOME SORTA VICTORY, HAVE YA?!

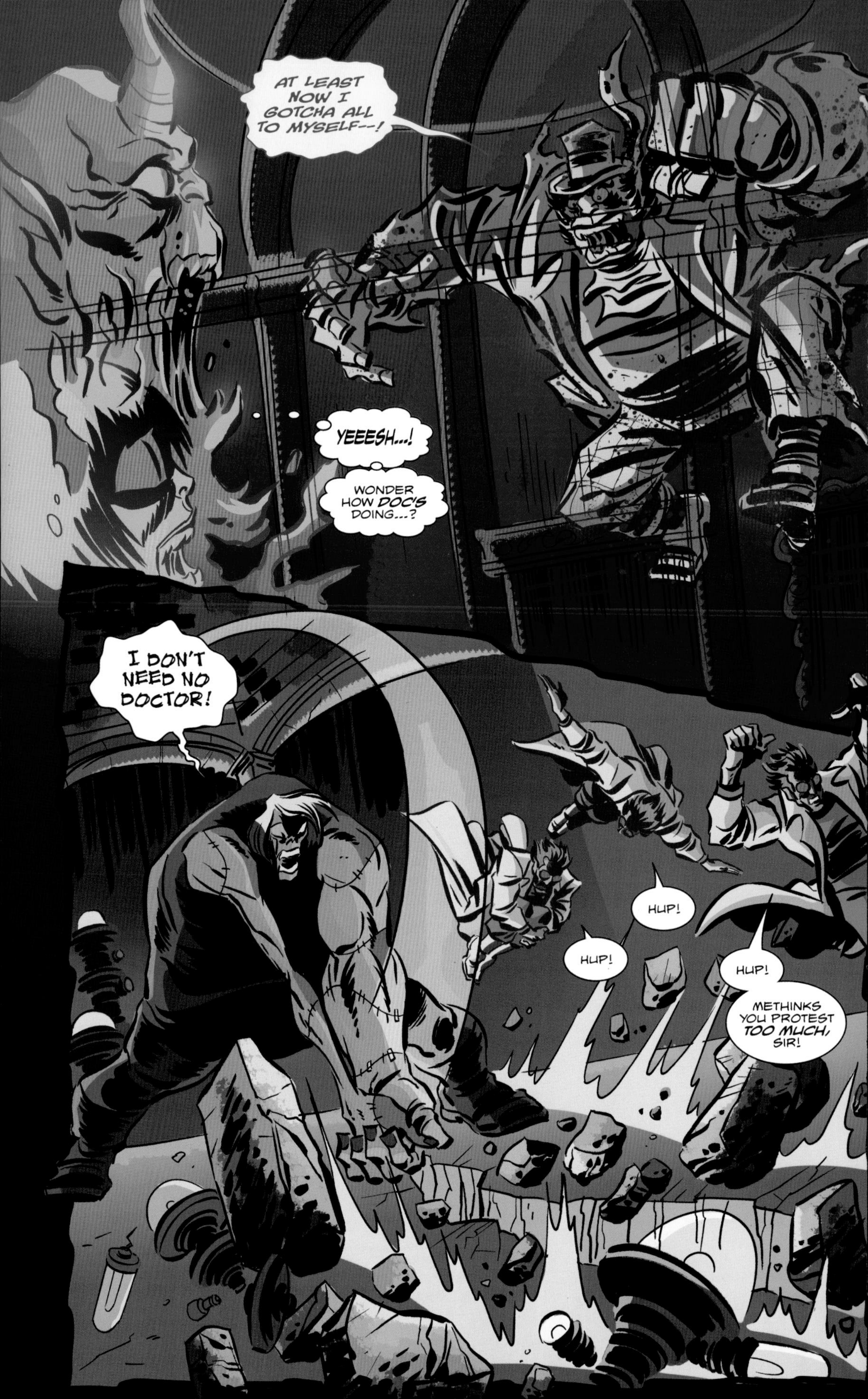
AT LEAST NOW I GOTCHA ALL TO MYSELF--!
YEEESH...!
WONDER HOW DOC'S DOING...?
I DON'T NEED NO DOCTOR!
HUP!
HUP!
HUP!
METHINKS YOU PROTEST TOO MUCH, SIR!

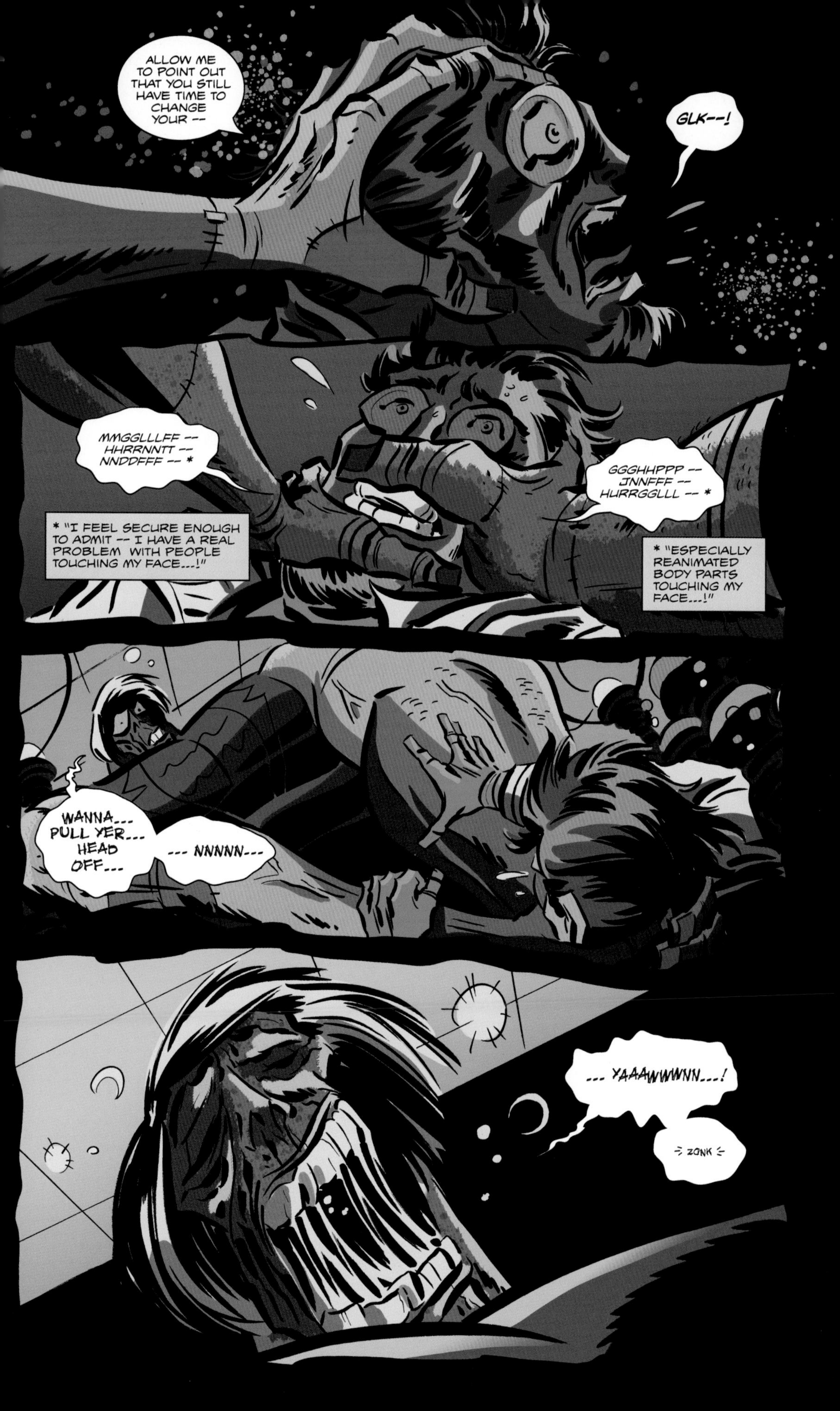
ALLOW ME TO POINT OUT THAT YOU STILL HAVE TIME TO CHANGE YOUR --
GLK--!
MMGGLLLFF -- HHRRNNTT -- NNDDFFF -- *
GGGHHPPP -- JNNFFF -- HURRGGLLL -- *
* "I FEEL SECURE ENOUGH TO ADMIT -- I HAVE A REAL PROBLEM WITH PEOPLE TOUCHING MY FACE...!"
* "ESPECIALLY REANIMATED BODY PARTS TOUCHING MY FACE...!"
WANNA... PULL YER... HEAD OFF...
--- NNNNN---
--- YAAAWWWNN...!
ZONK

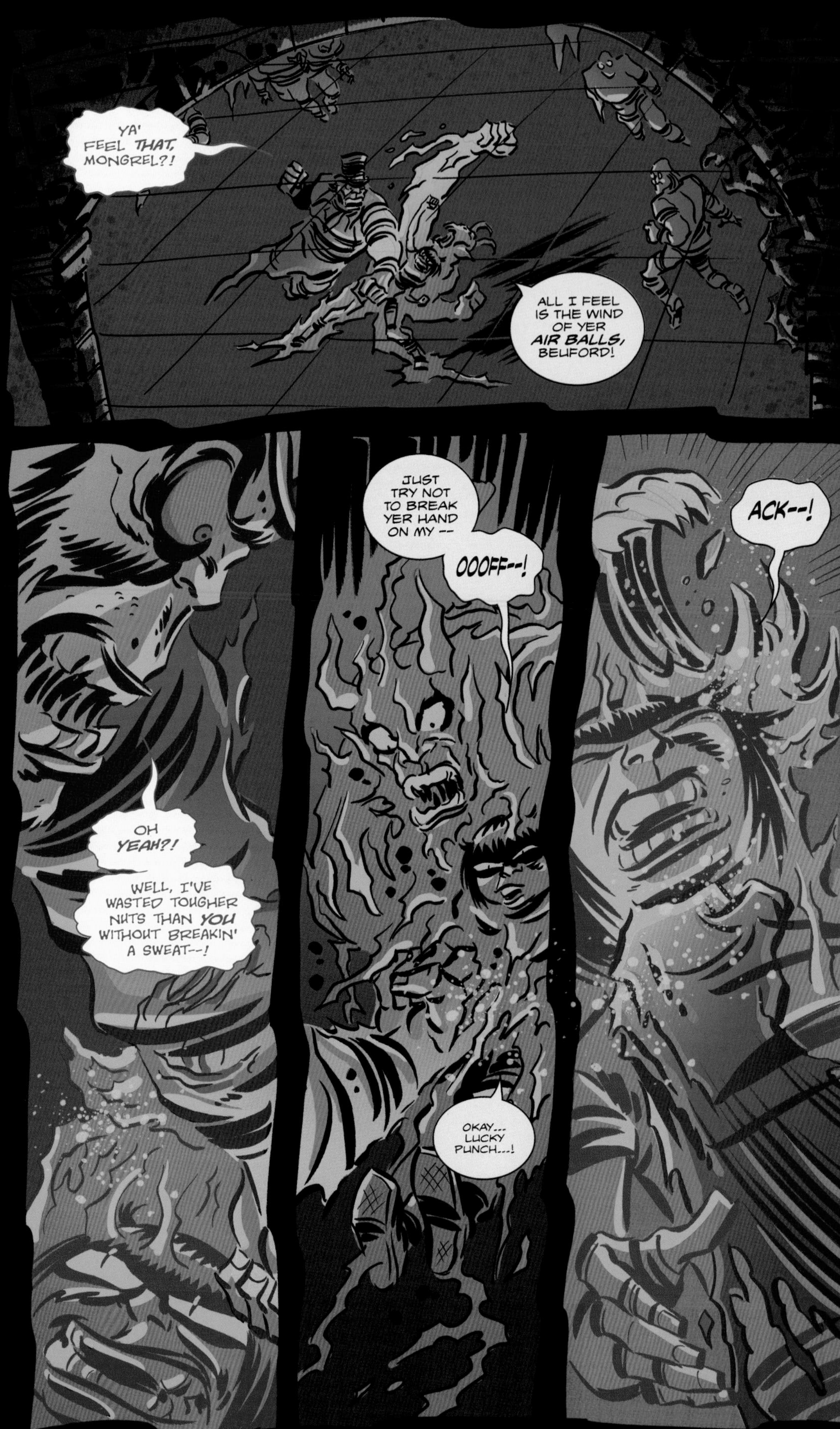
YA' FEEL THAT, MONGREL?!
ALL I FEEL IS THE WIND OF YER AIR BALLS, BEUFORD!
OH YEAH?!
WELL, I'VE WASTED TOUGHER NUTS THAN YOU WITHOUT BREAKIN' A SWEAT--!
JUST TRY NOT TO BREAK YER HAND ON MY --
OOOFF--!
OKAY... LUCKY PUNCH...!
ACK--!

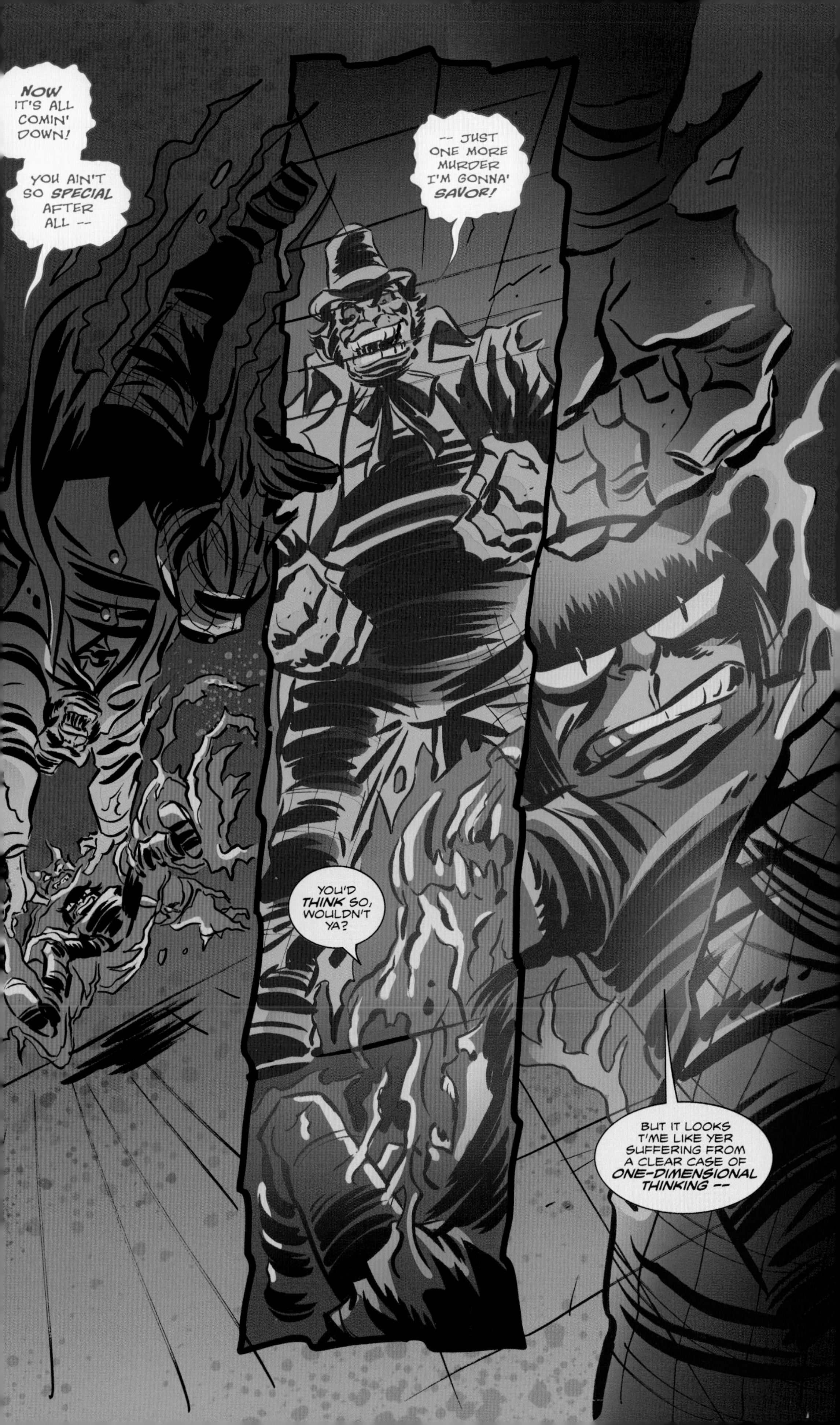
NOW IT'S ALL COMIN' DOWN!
YOU AIN'T SO SPECIAL AFTER ALL --
-- JUST ONE MORE MURDER I'M GONNA' SAVOR!
YOU'D THINK SO, WOULDN'T YA?
BUT IT LOOKS T'ME LIKE YER SUFFERING FROM A CLEAR CASE OF ONE-DIMENSIONAL THINKING --

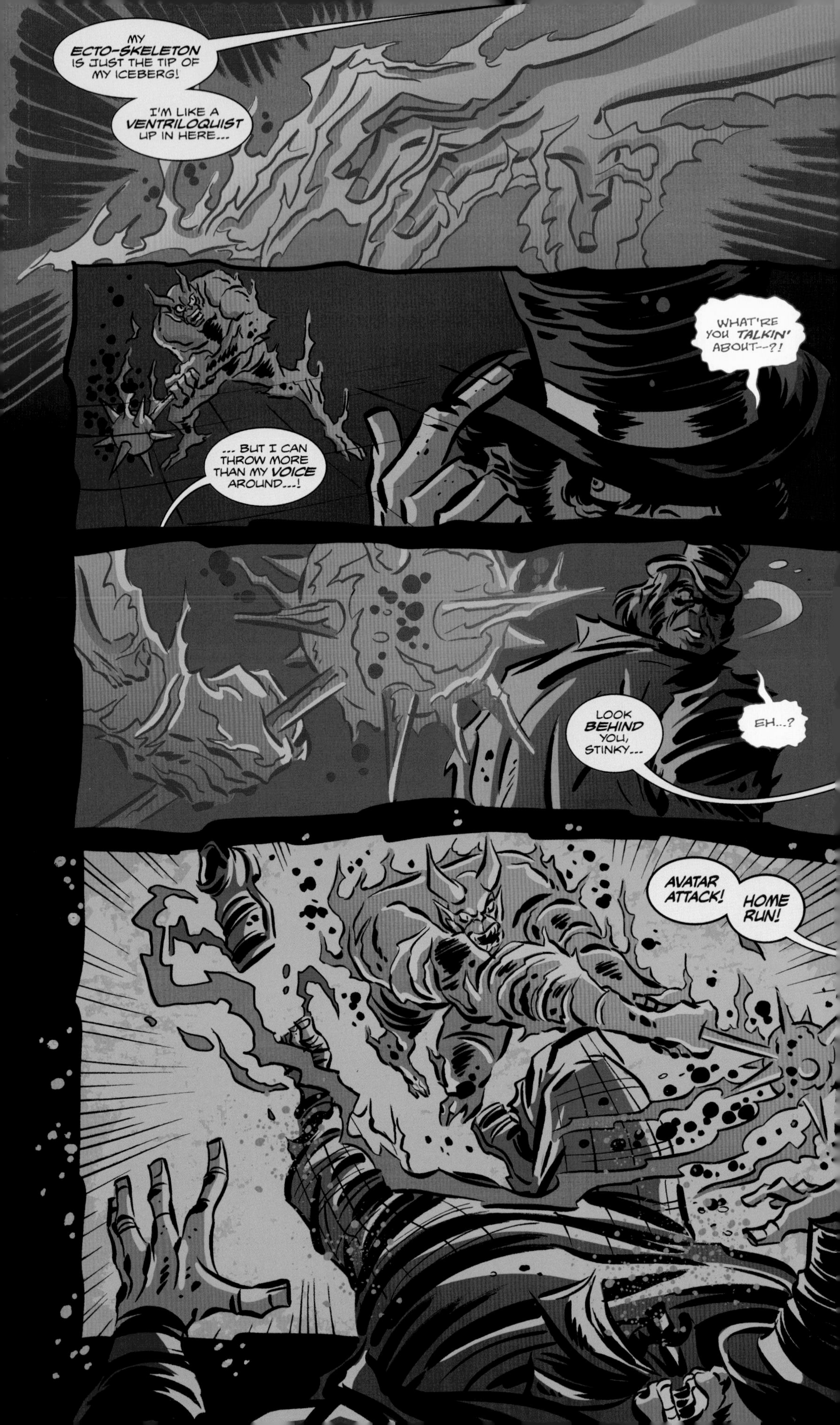
MY ECTO-SKELETON IS JUST THE TIP OF MY ICEBERG!
I'M LIKE A VENTRILOQUIST UP IN HERE...
WHAT'RE YOU TALKIN' ABOUT--?!
... BUT I CAN THROW MORE THAN MY VOICE AROUND...!
LOOK BEHIND YOU, STINKY...
EH...?
AVATAR ATTACK!
HOME RUN!

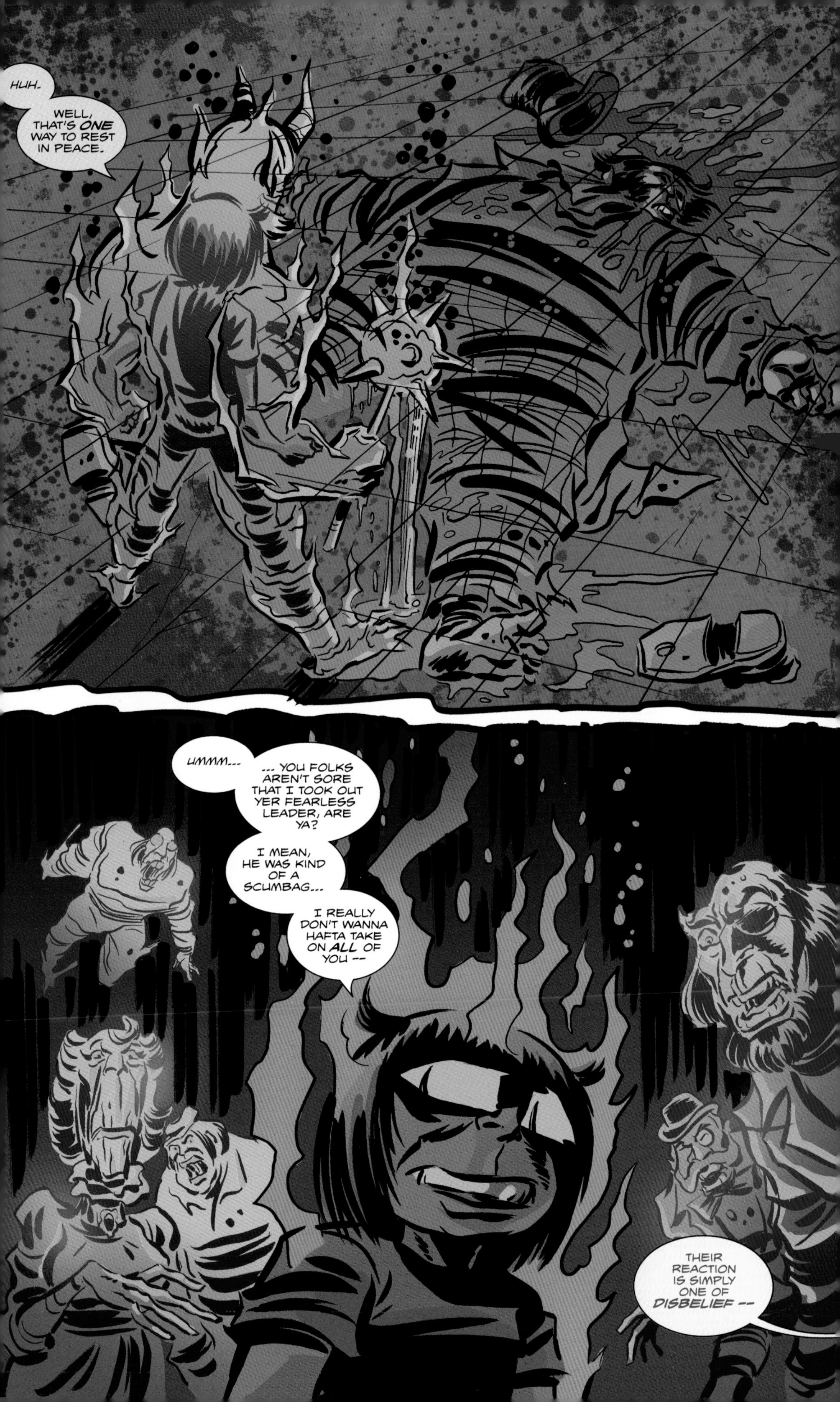
HUH.
WELL, THAT'S ONE WAY TO REST IN PEACE.
UMMM...
... YOU FOLKS AREN'T SORE THAT I TOOK OUT YER FEARLESS LEADER, ARE YA?
I MEAN, HE WAS KIND OF A SCUMBAG...
I REALLY DON'T WANNA HAFTA TAKE ON ALL OF YOU --
THEIR REACTION IS SIMPLY ONE OF DISBELIEF --

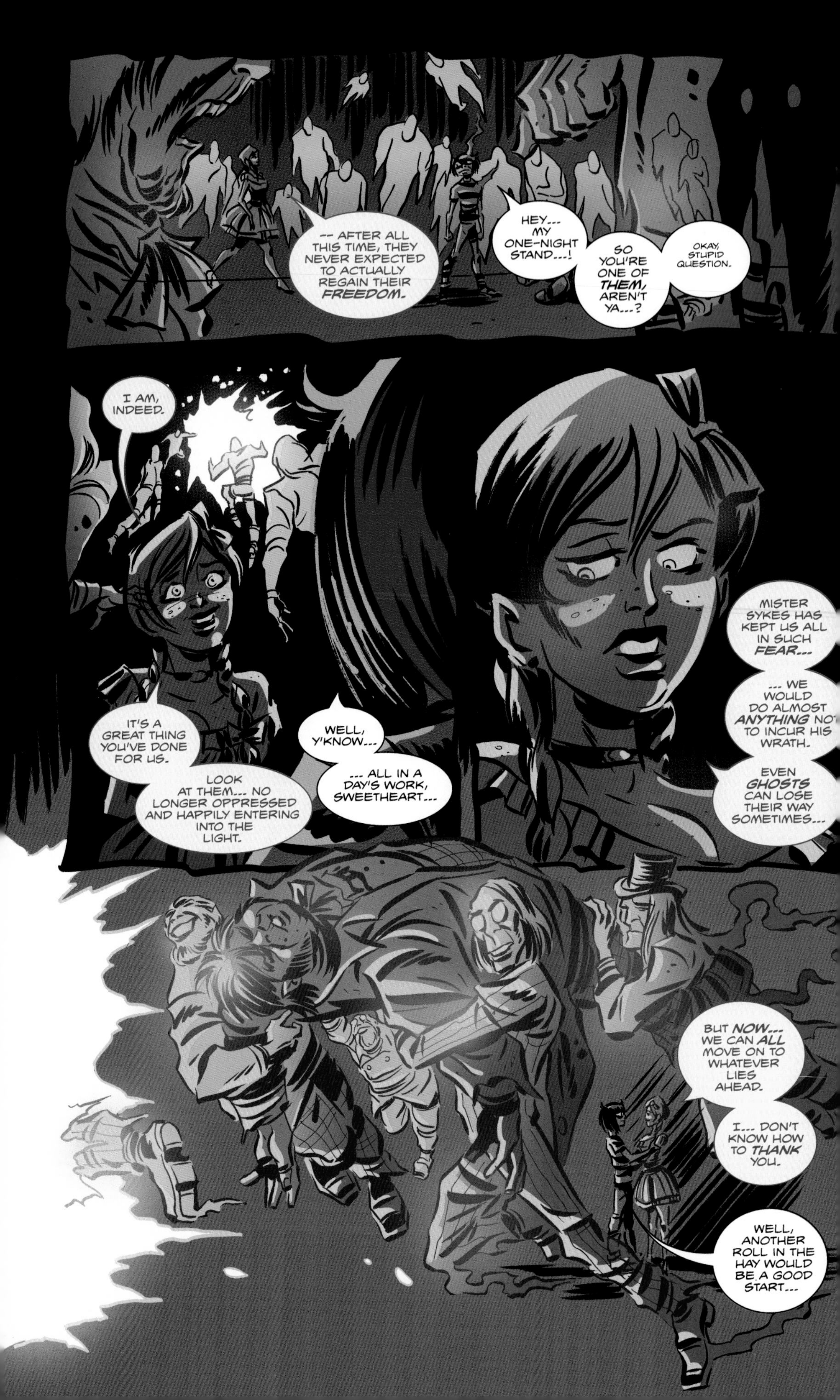
-- AFTER ALL THIS TIME, THEY NEVER EXPECTED TO ACTUALLY REGAIN THEIR FREEDOM.
HEY... MY ONE-NIGHT STAND...!
SO YOU'RE ONE OF THEM, AREN'T YA...?
OKAY, STUPID QUESTION.
I AM, INDEED.
MISTER SYKES HAS KEPT US ALL IN SUCH FEAR...
... WE WOULD DO ALMOST ANYTHING NOT TO INCUR HIS WRATH.
EVEN GHOSTS CAN LOSE THEIR WAY SOMETIMES...
IT'S A GREAT THING YOU'VE DONE FOR US.
LOOK AT THEM... NO LONGER OPPRESSED AND HAPPILY ENTERING INTO THE LIGHT.
WELL, Y'KNOW...
... ALL IN A DAY'S WORK, SWEETHEART...
BUT NOW... WE CAN ALL MOVE ON TO WHATEVER LIES AHEAD.
I... DON'T KNOW HOW TO THANK YOU.
WELL, ANOTHER ROLL IN THE HAY WOULD BE A GOOD START...

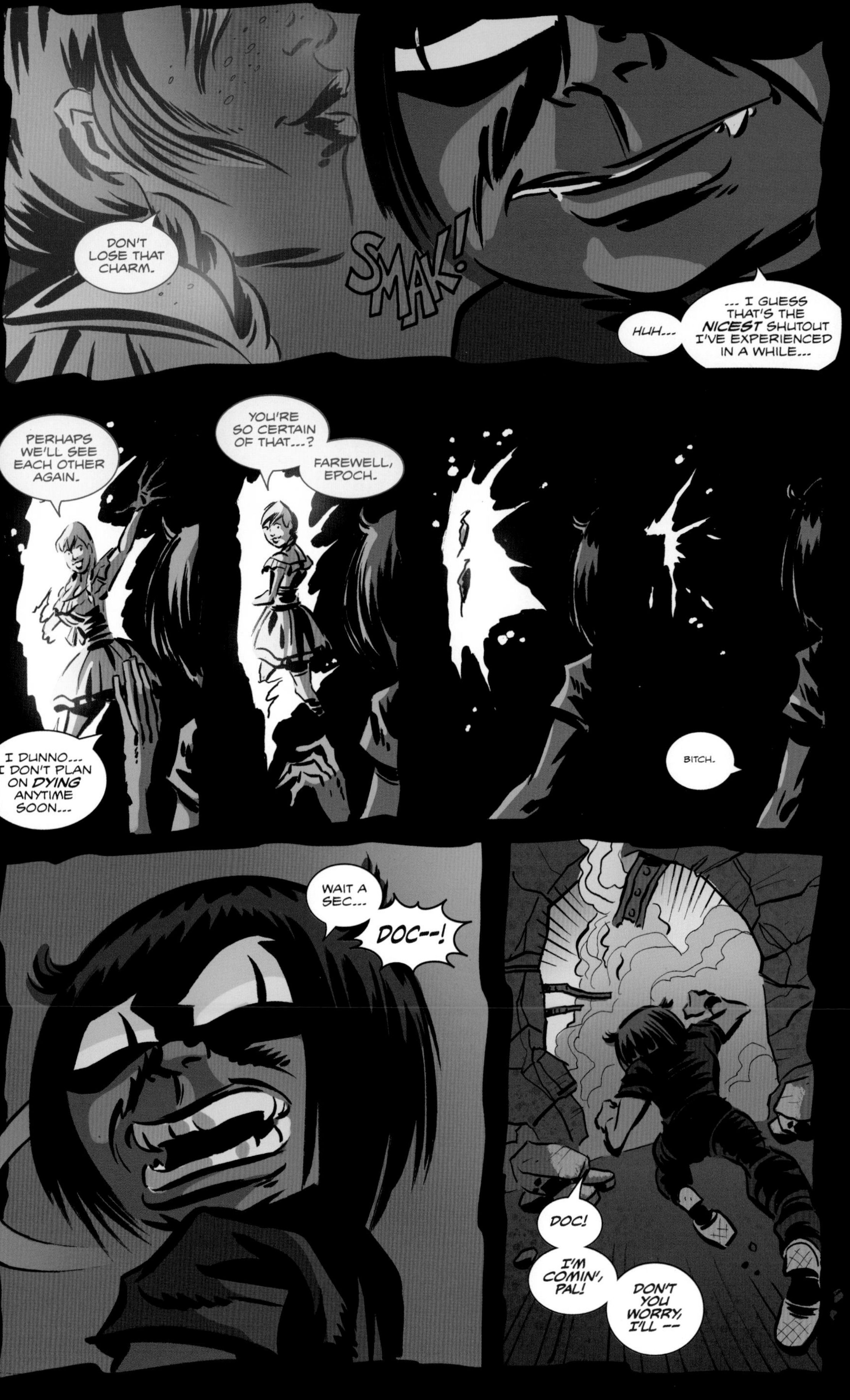
DON'T LOSE THAT CHARM.
SMAK!
HUH...
... I GUESS THAT'S THE NICEST SHUTOUT I'VE EXPERIENCED IN A WHILE...
PERHAPS WE'LL SEE EACH OTHER AGAIN.
I DUNNO... I DON'T PLAN ON DYING ANYTIME SOON...
YOU'RE SO CERTAIN OF THAT...?
FAREWELL, EPOCH.
BITCH.
WAIT A SEC...
DOC--!
DOC!
I'M COMIN', PAL!
DON'T YOU WORRY, I'LL --

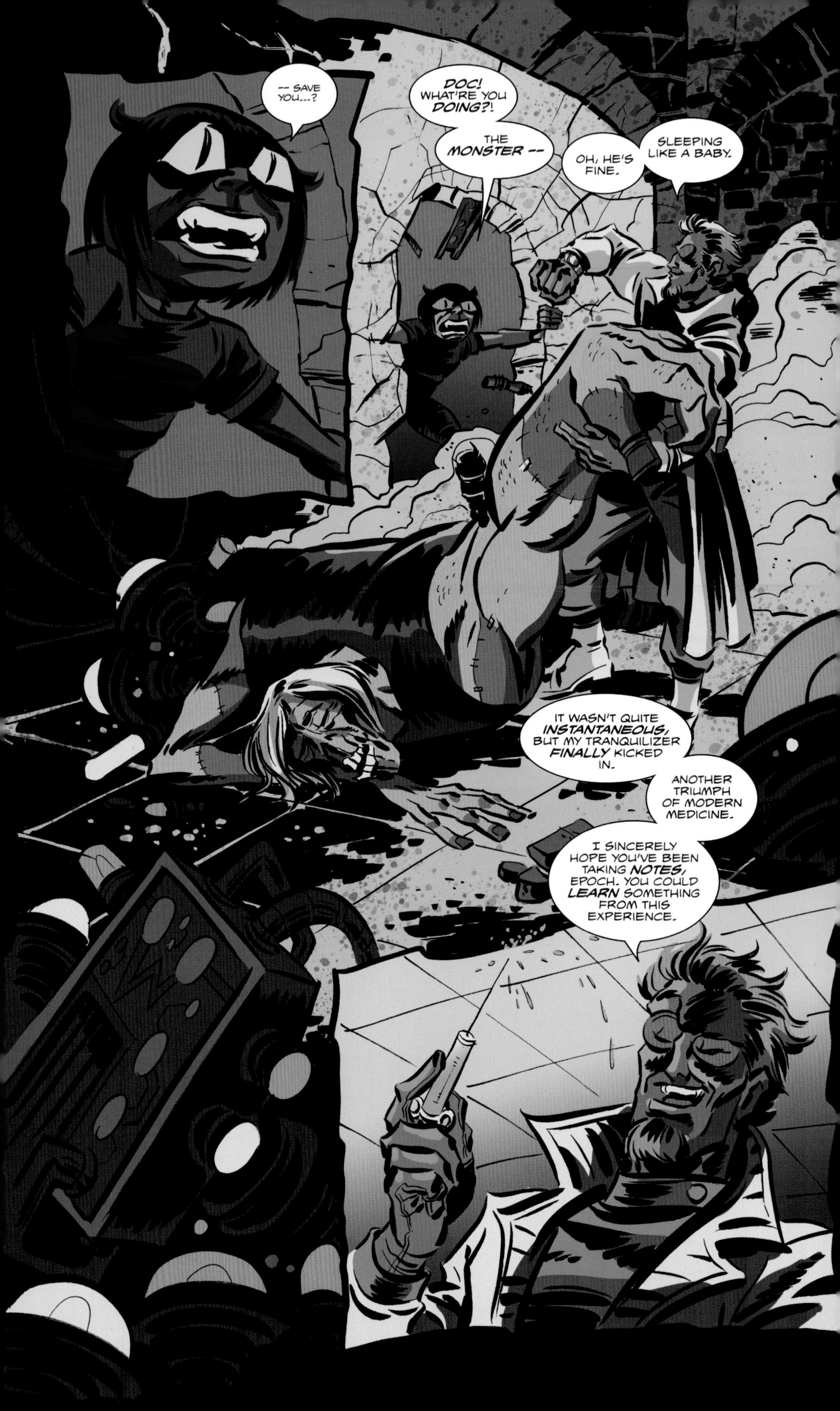
-- SAVE YOU...?
DOC! WHAT'RE YOU DOING?!
THE MONSTER --
OH, HE'S FINE.
SLEEPING LIKE A BABY.
IT WASN'T QUITE INSTANTANEOUS, BUT MY TRANQUILIZER FINALLY KICKED IN.
ANOTHER TRIUMPH OF MODERN MEDICINE.
I SINCERELY HOPE YOU'VE BEEN TAKING NOTES, EPOCH. YOU COULD LEARN SOMETHING FROM THIS EXPERIENCE.

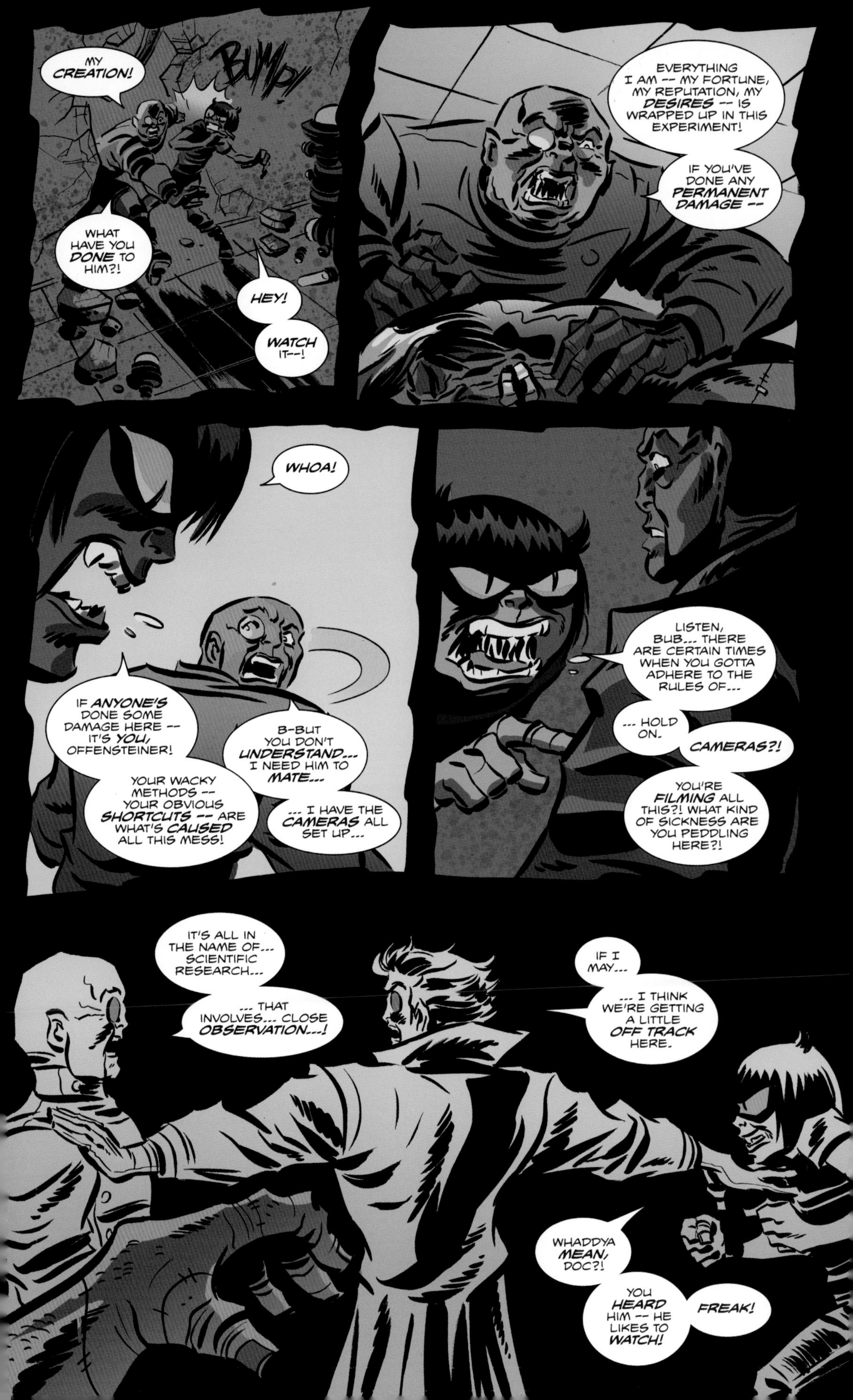
MY CREATION!
BUMP!
WHAT HAVE YOU DONE TO HIM?!
HEY!
WATCH IT--!
EVERYTHING I AM -- MY FORTUNE, MY REPUTATION, MY DESIRES -- IS WRAPPED UP IN THIS EXPERIMENT!
IF YOU'VE DONE ANY PERMANENT DAMAGE --
WHOA!
IF ANYONE'S DONE SOME DAMAGE HERE -- IT'S YOU, OFFENSTEINER!
YOUR WACKY METHODS -- YOUR OBVIOUS SHORTCUTS -- ARE WHAT'S CAUSED ALL THIS MESS!
B-BUT YOU DON'T UNDERSTAND... I NEED HIM TO MATE...
... I HAVE THE CAMERAS ALL SET UP...
LISTEN, BUB... THERE ARE CERTAIN TIMES WHEN YOU GOTTA ADHERE TO THE RULES OF...
... HOLD ON.
CAMERAS?!
YOU'RE FILMING ALL THIS?! WHAT KIND OF SICKNESS ARE YOU PEDDLING HERE?!
IT'S ALL IN THE NAME OF... SCIENTIFIC RESEARCH...
... THAT INVOLVES... CLOSE OBSERVATION...!
IF I MAY...
... I THINK WE'RE GETTING A LITTLE OFF TRACK HERE.
WHADDYA MEAN, DOC?!
YOU HEARD HIM -- HE LIKES TO WATCH!
FREAK!

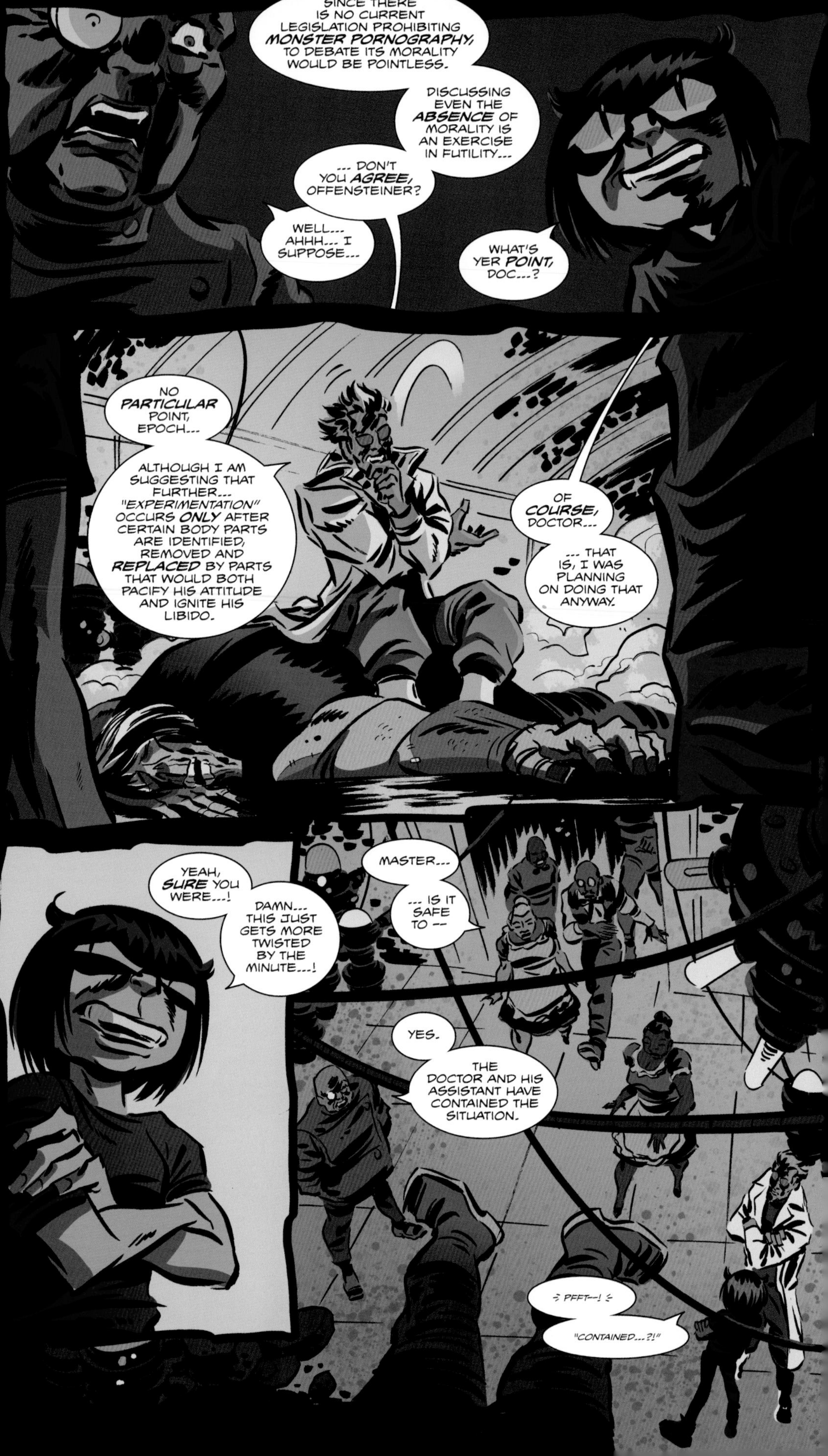
SINCE THERE IS NO CURRENT LEGISLATION PROHIBITING MONSTER PORNOGRAPHY, TO DEBATE ITS MORALITY WOULD BE POINTLESS.
DISCUSSING EVEN THE ABSENCE OF MORALITY IS AN EXERCISE IN FUTILITY...
... DON'T YOU AGREE, OFFENSTEINER?
WELL... AHHH... I SUPPOSE...
WHAT'S YER POINT, DOC...?
NO PARTICULAR POINT, EPOCH...
ALTHOUGH I AM SUGGESTING THAT FURTHER... "EXPERIMENTATION" OCCURS ONLY AFTER CERTAIN BODY PARTS ARE IDENTIFIED, REMOVED AND REPLACED BY PARTS THAT WOULD BOTH PACIFY HIS ATTITUDE AND IGNITE HIS LIBIDO.
OF COURSE, DOCTOR...
... THAT IS, I WAS PLANNING ON DOING THAT ANYWAY.
YEAH, SURE YOU WERE...!
DAMN... THIS JUST GETS MORE TWISTED BY THE MINUTE...!
MASTER...
... IS IT SAFE TO --
YES.
THE DOCTOR AND HIS ASSISTANT HAVE CONTAINED THE SITUATION.
PFFT--!
"CONTAINED...?!"

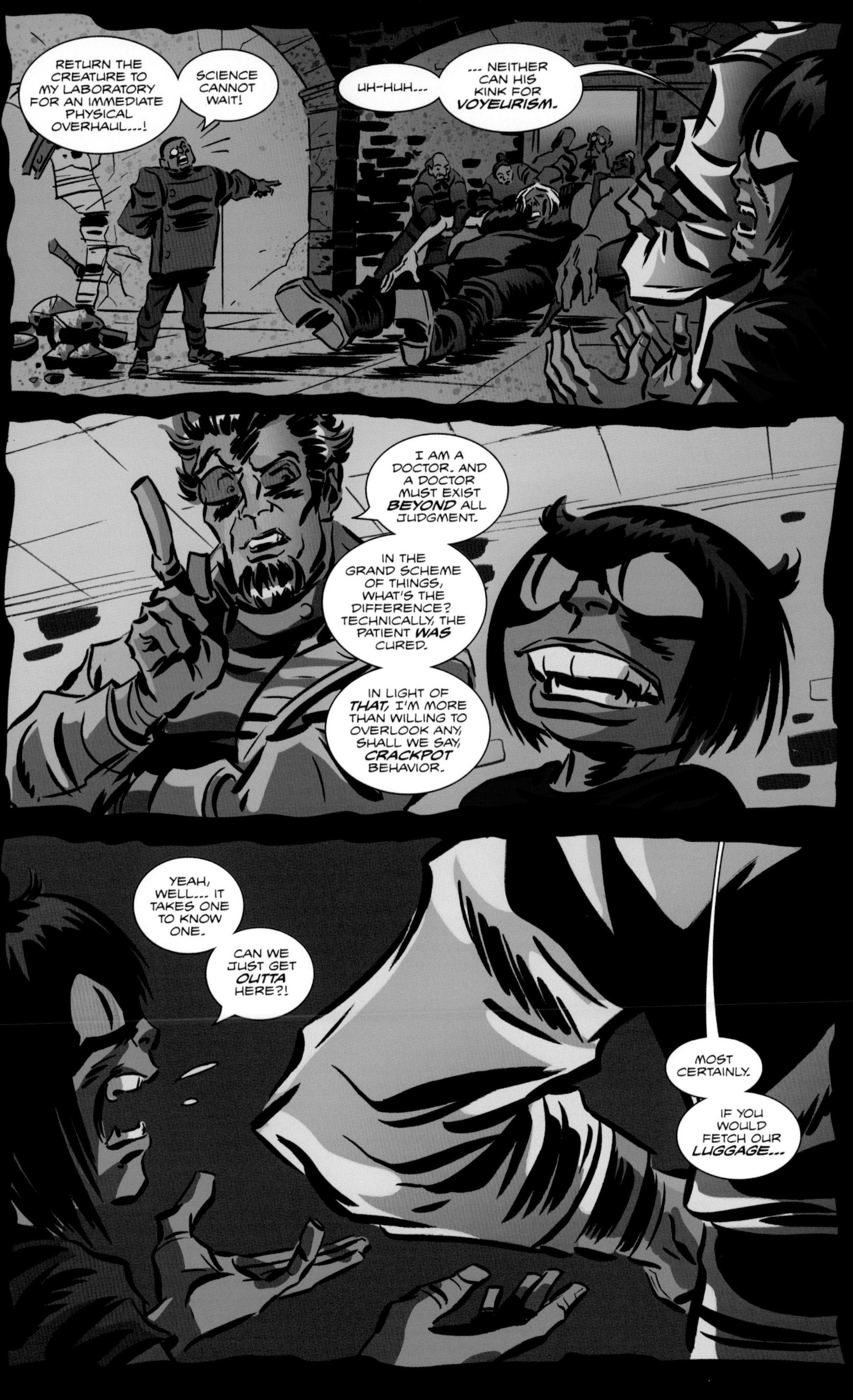
RETURN THE CREATURE TO MY LABORATORY FOR AN IMMEDIATE PHYSICAL OVERHAUL...!
SCIENCE CANNOT WAIT!
UH-HUH...
... NEITHER CAN HIS KINK FOR VOYEURISM.
I AM A DOCTOR. AND A DOCTOR MUST EXIST BEYOND ALL JUDGMENT.
IN THE GRAND SCHEME OF THINGS, WHAT'S THE DIFFERENCE? TECHNICALLY, THE PATIENT WAS CURED.
IN LIGHT OF THAT, I'M MORE THAN WILLING TO OVERLOOK ANY, SHALL WE SAY, CRACKPOT BEHAVIOR.
YEAH, WELL... IT TAKES ONE TO KNOW ONE.
CAN WE JUST GET OUTTA HERE?!
MOST CERTAINLY.
IF YOU WOULD FETCH OUR LUGGAGE...

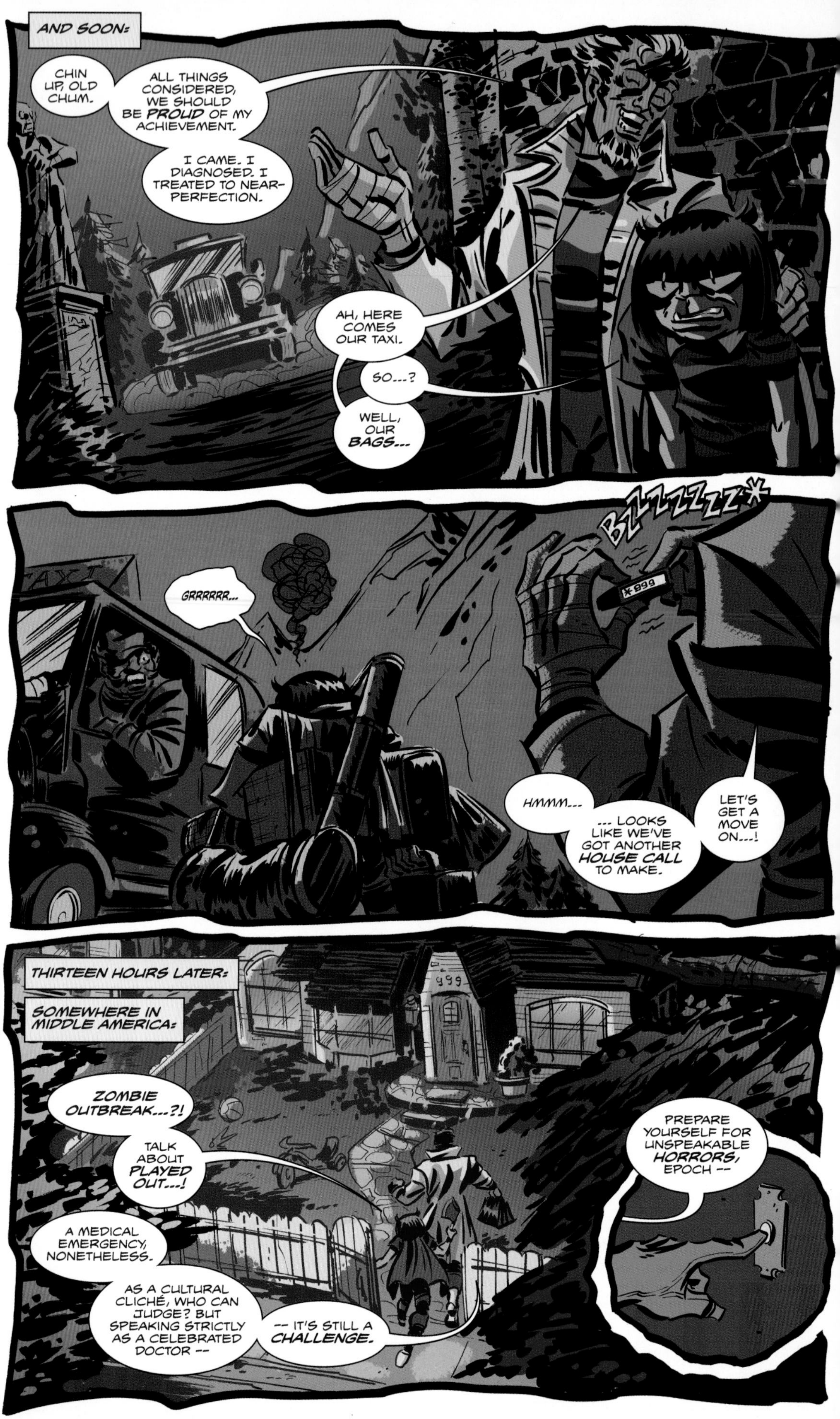
AND SOON:
CHIN UP, OLD CHUM.
ALL THINGS CONSIDERED, WE SHOULD BE PROUD OF MY ACHIEVEMENT.
I CAME. I DIAGNOSED. I TREATED TO NEAR-PERFECTION.
AH, HERE COMES OUR TAXI.
SO...?
WELL, OUR BAGS...
BZZZZZZZ*
GRRRRRR...
*999
HMMM...
... LOOKS LIKE WE'VE GOT ANOTHER HOUSE CALL TO MAKE.
LET'S GET A MOVE ON...!
THIRTEEN HOURS LATER:
SOMEWHERE IN MIDDLE AMERICA:
999
ZOMBIE OUTBREAK...?!
TALK ABOUT PLAYED OUT...!
A MEDICAL EMERGENCY, NONETHELESS.
AS A CULTURAL CLICHÉ, WHO CAN JUDGE? BUT SPEAKING STRICTLY AS A CELEBRATED DOCTOR --
-- IT'S STILL A CHALLENGE.
PREPARE YOURSELF FOR UNSPEAKABLE HORRORS, EPOCH --

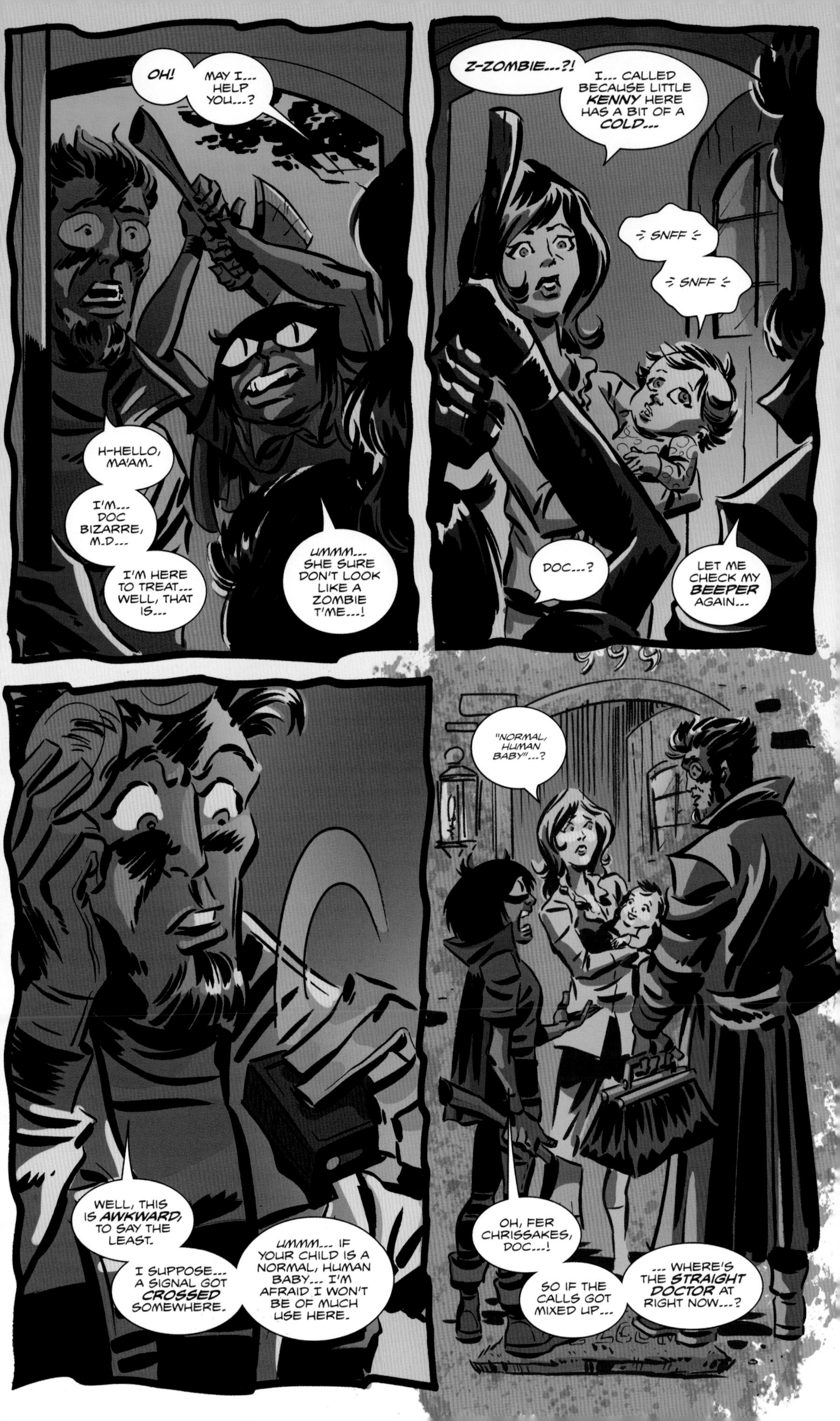
OH!
MAY I... HELP YOU...?
H-HELLO, MA'AM.
I'M... DOC BIZARRE, M.D...
I'M HERE TO TREAT... WELL, THAT IS...
UMMM... SHE SURE DON'T LOOK LIKE A ZOMBIE T'ME...!
Z-ZOMBIE...?!
I... CALLED BECAUSE LITTLE KENNY HERE HAS A BIT OF A COLD...
SNFF
SNFF
DOC...?
LET ME CHECK MY BEEPER AGAIN...
WELL, THIS IS AWKWARD, TO SAY THE LEAST.
I SUPPOSE... A SIGNAL GOT CROSSED SOMEWHERE.
UMMM... IF YOUR CHILD IS A NORMAL, HUMAN BABY... I'M AFRAID I WON'T BE OF MUCH USE HERE.
"NORMAL, HUMAN BABY"...?
OH, FER CHRISSAKES, DOC...!
SO IF THE CALLS GOT MIXED UP...
... WHERE'S THE STRAIGHT DOCTOR AT RIGHT NOW...?

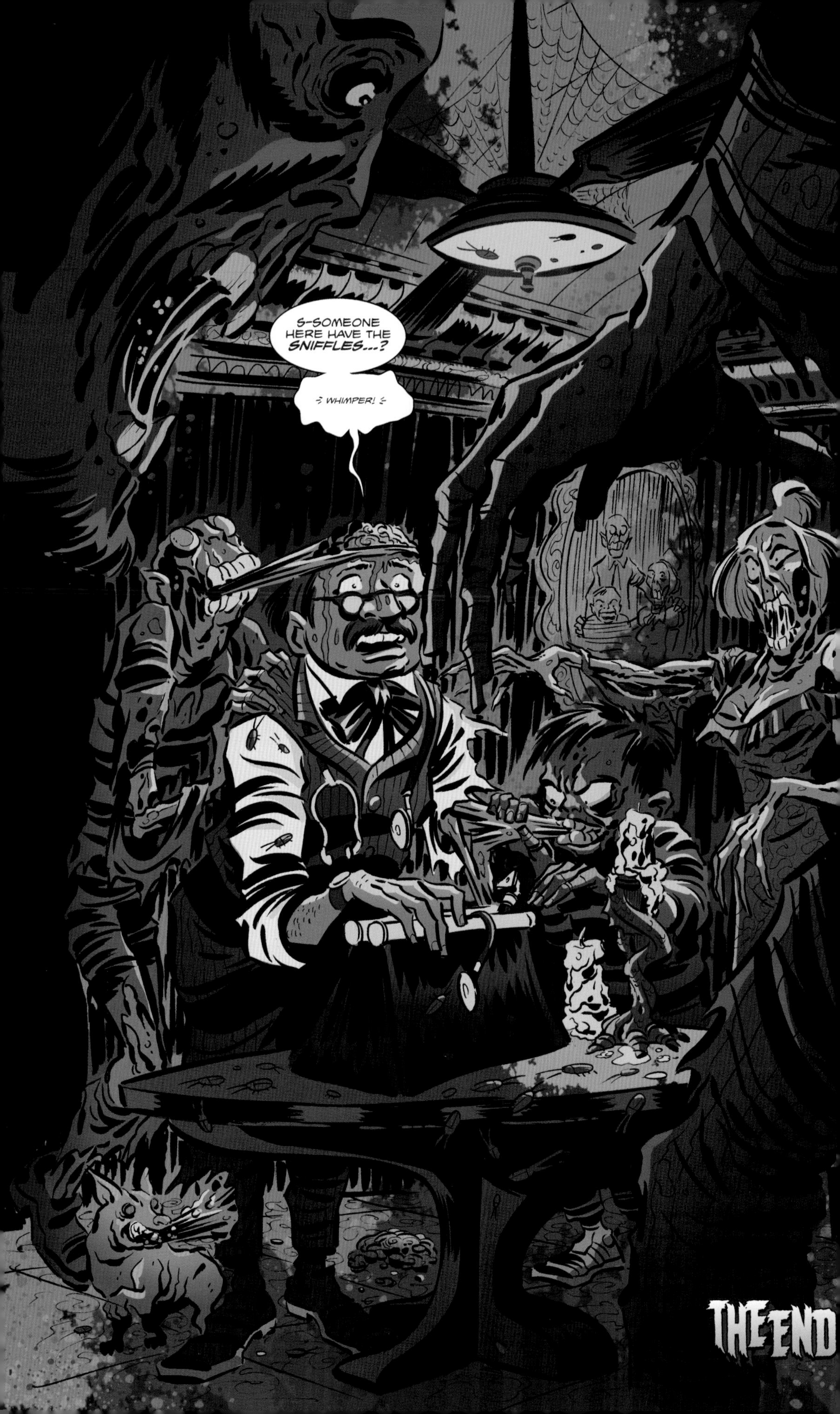
S-SOMEONE HERE HAVE THE SNIFFLES...?
WHIMPER!
THE END

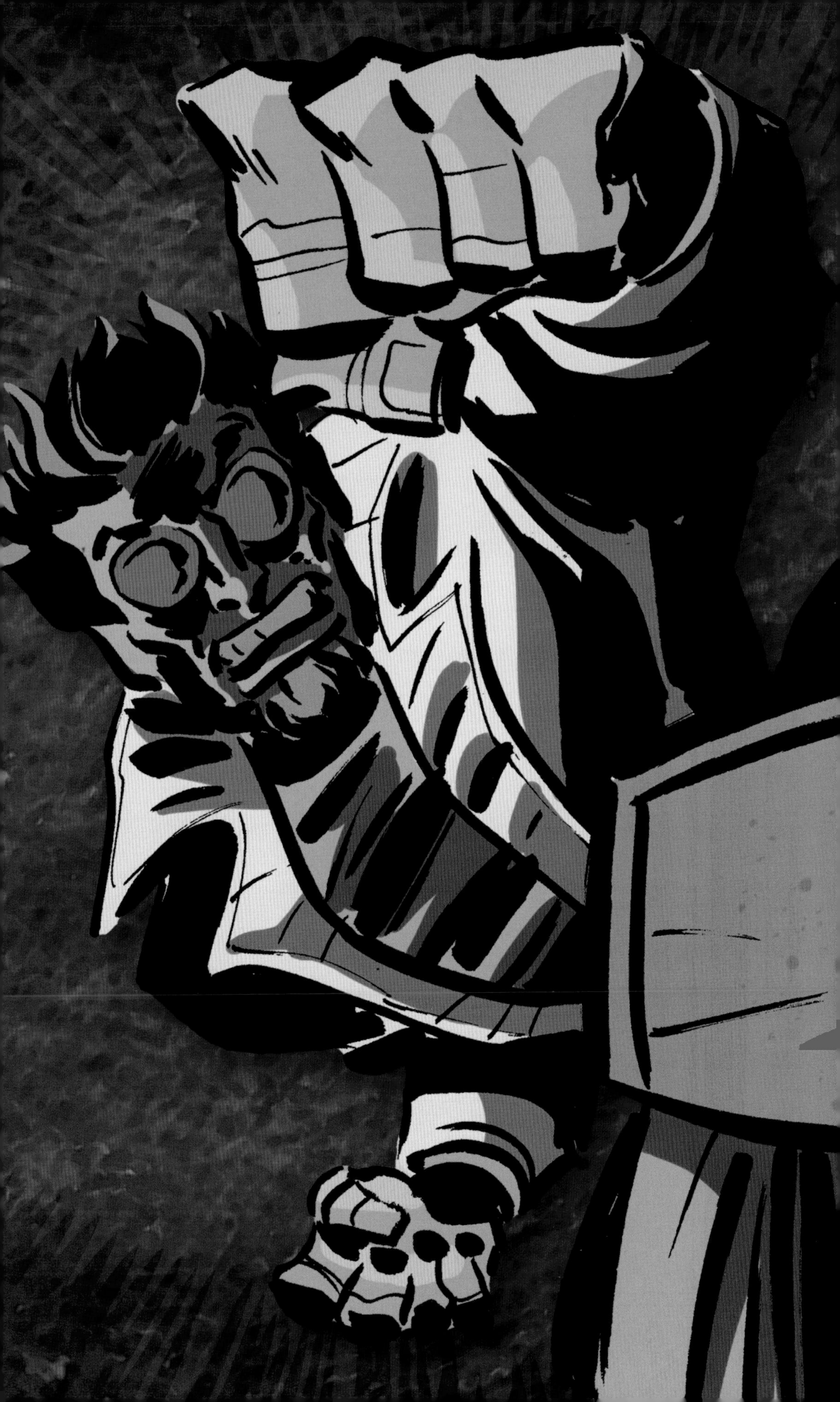

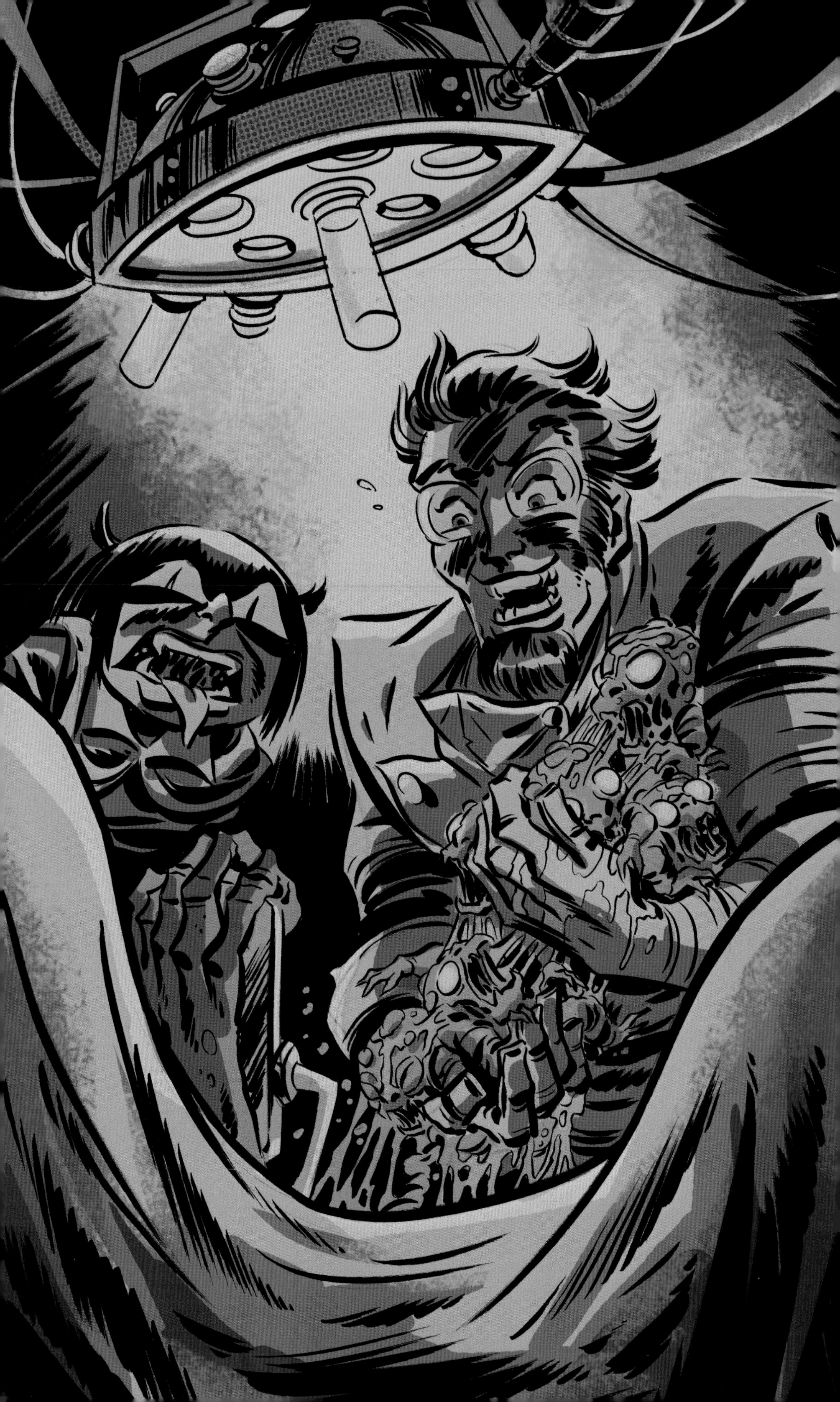

THE BIRTH OF BIZARRE

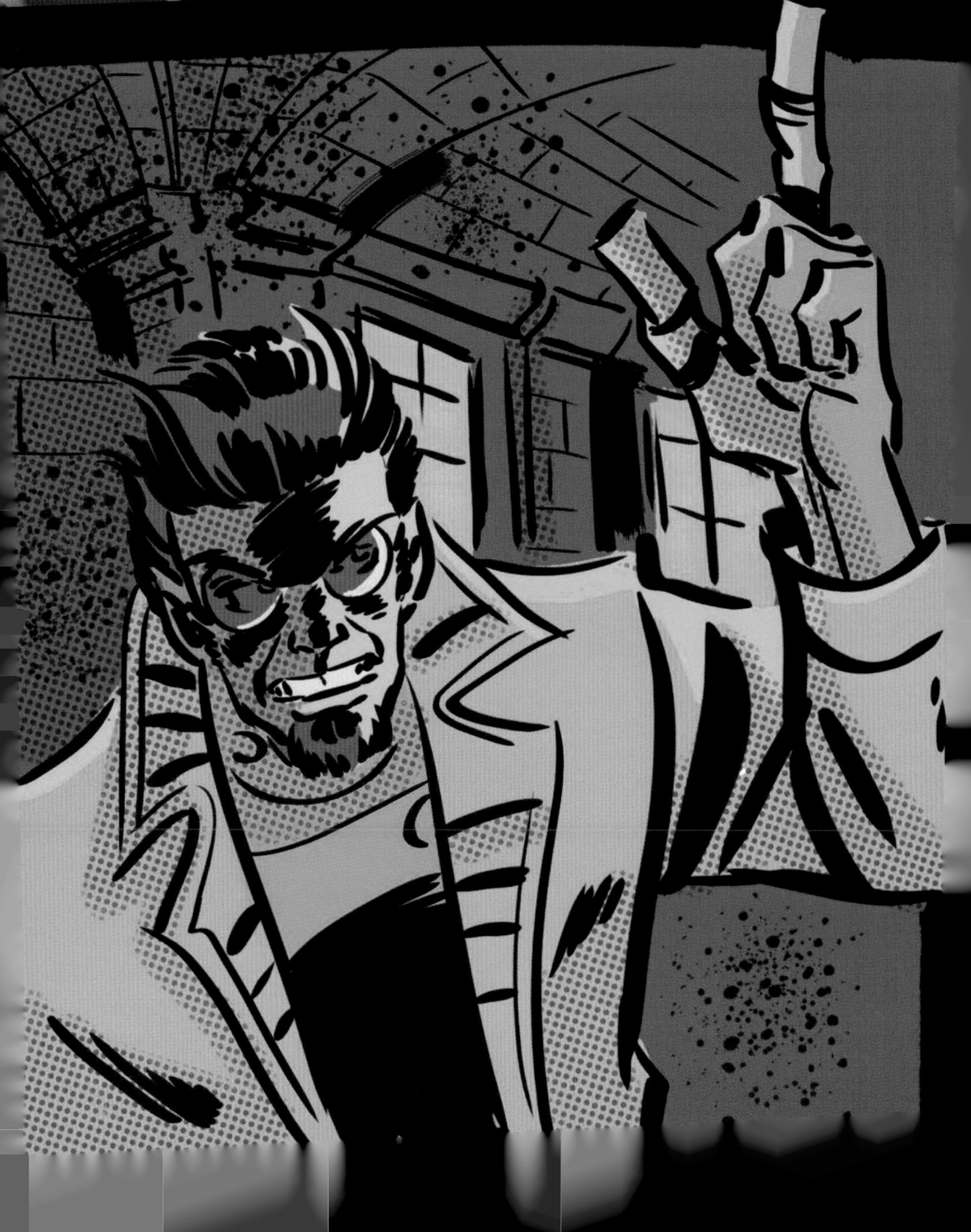

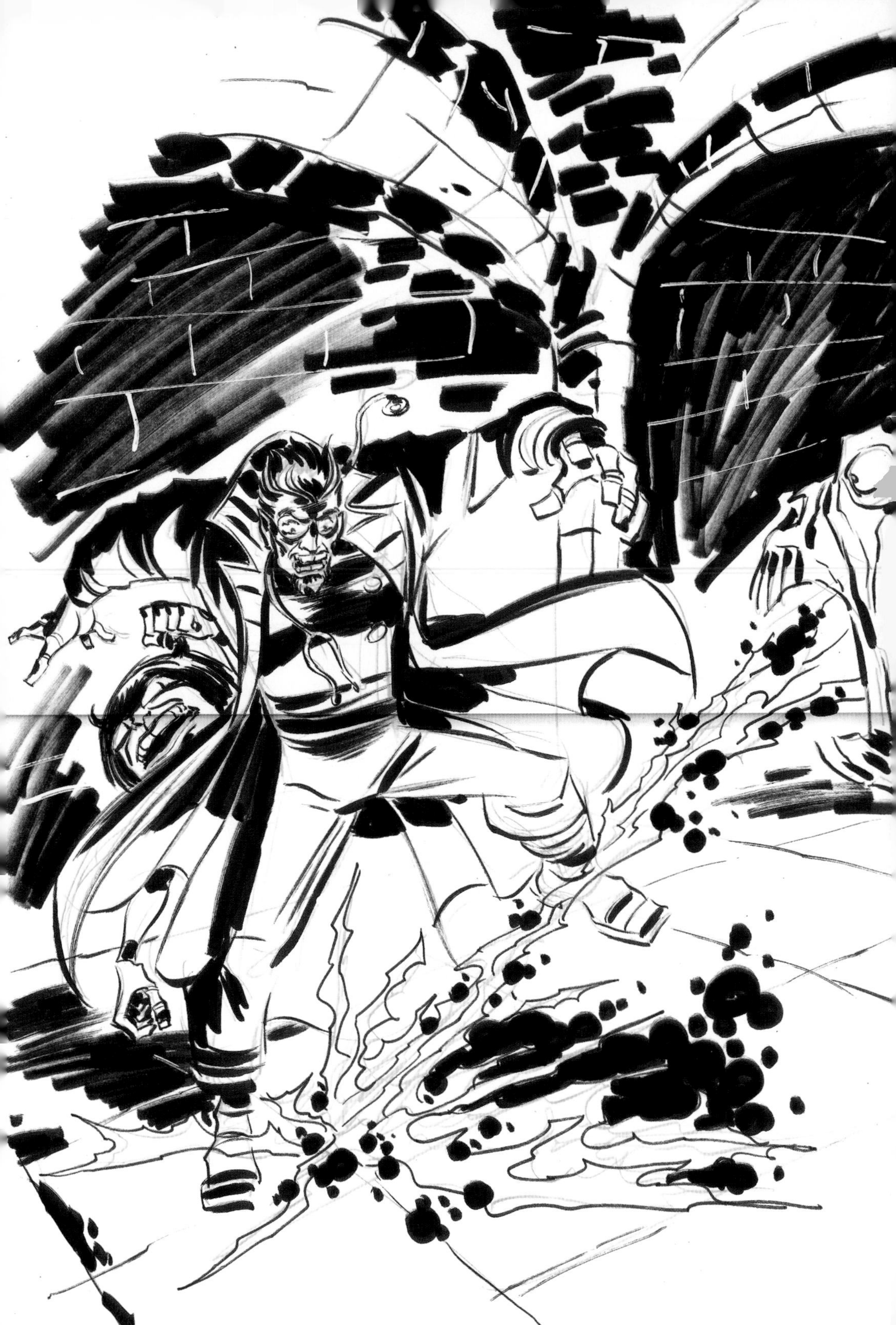

DOC BIZARRE M.D.™

Doc

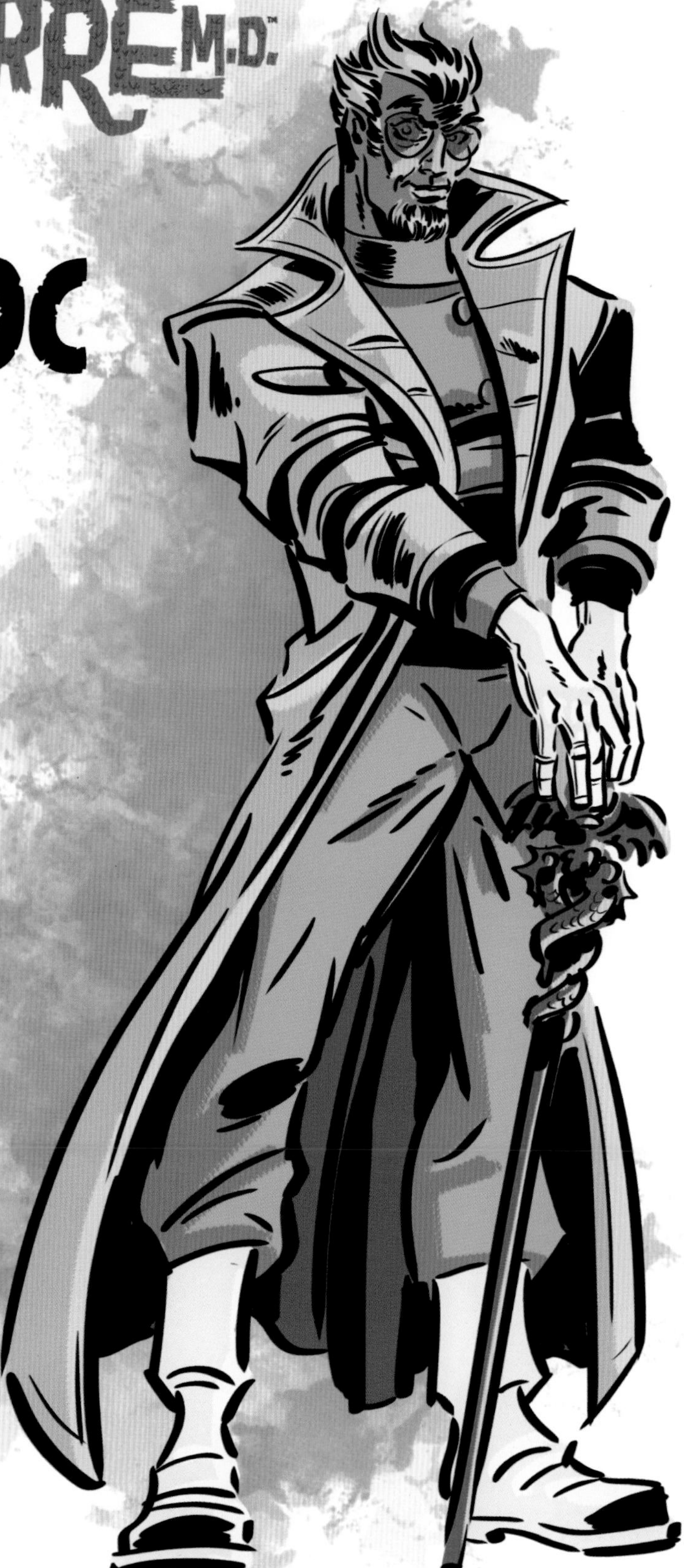

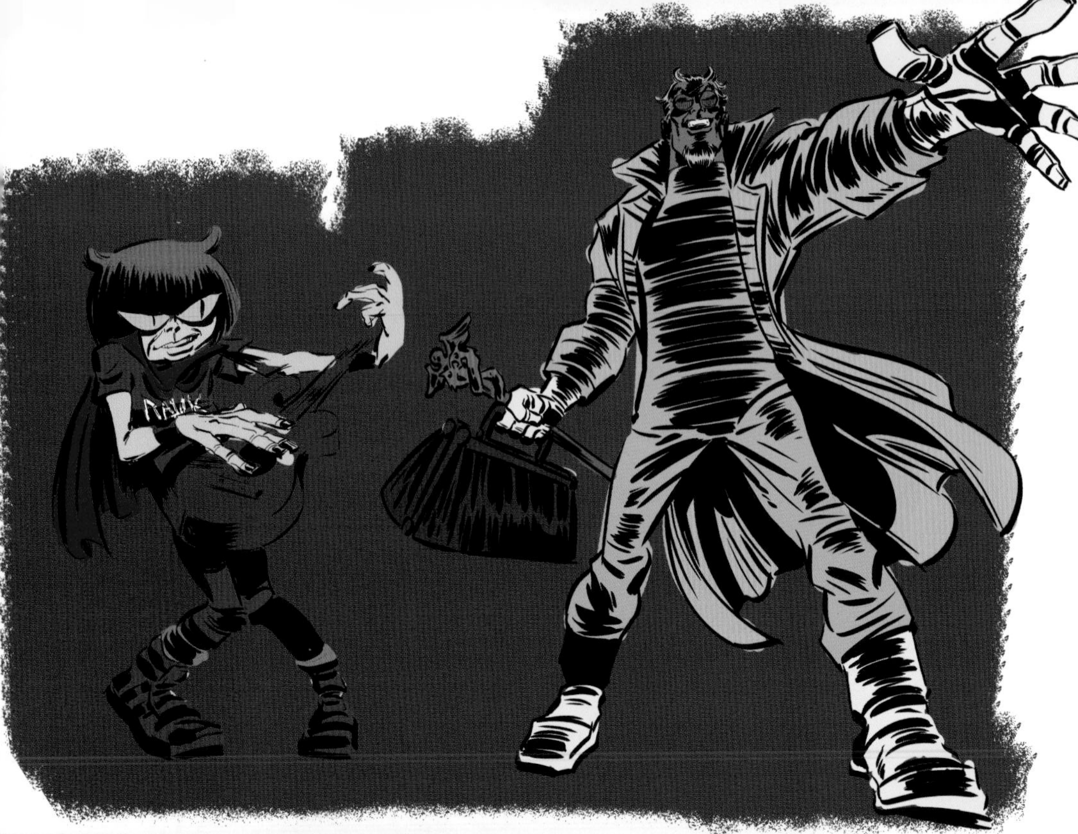

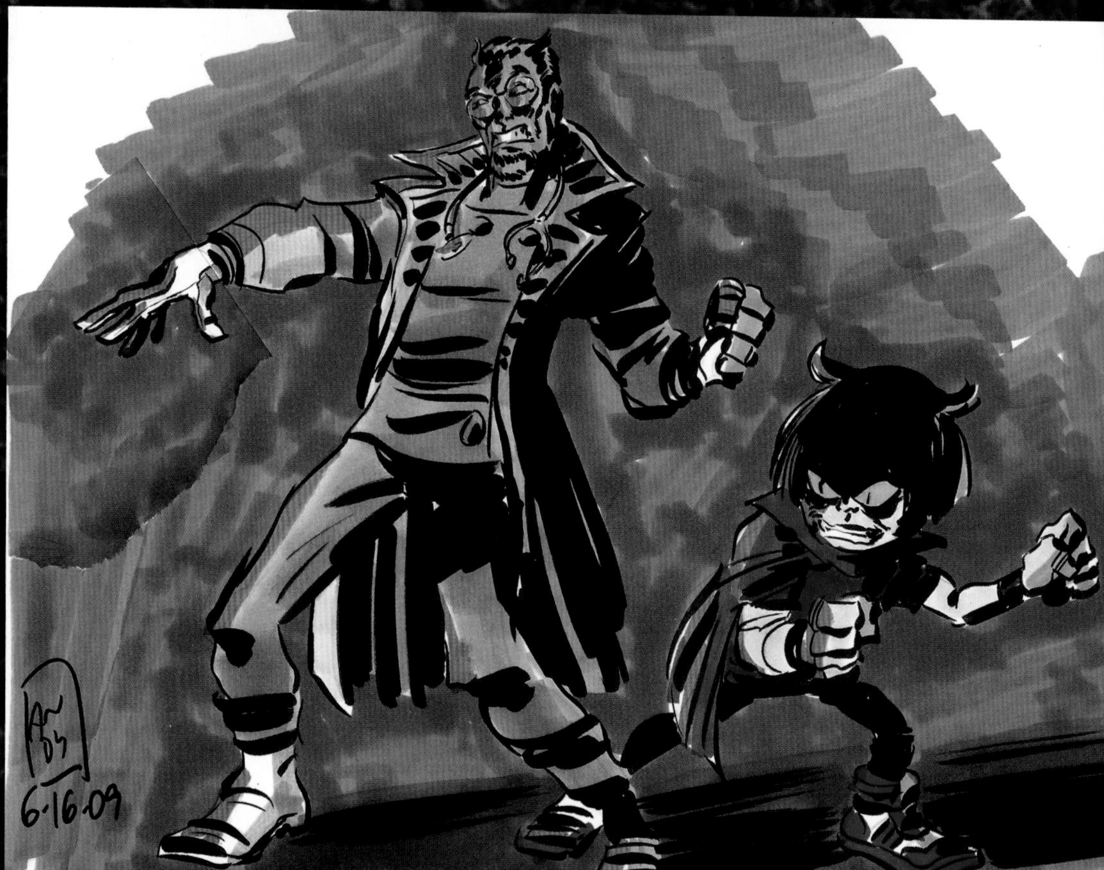
6-16-09

DOC BIZARRE MD

I STILL DON'T UNDERSTAND WHY I HAVE TO WEAR THIS CAPE!?

PART OF THE GIMMIC. IT'S ALL TRUST ME...

A MACABRE MEDICAL TALE

BY

JOE CASEY & ANDY SURIANO

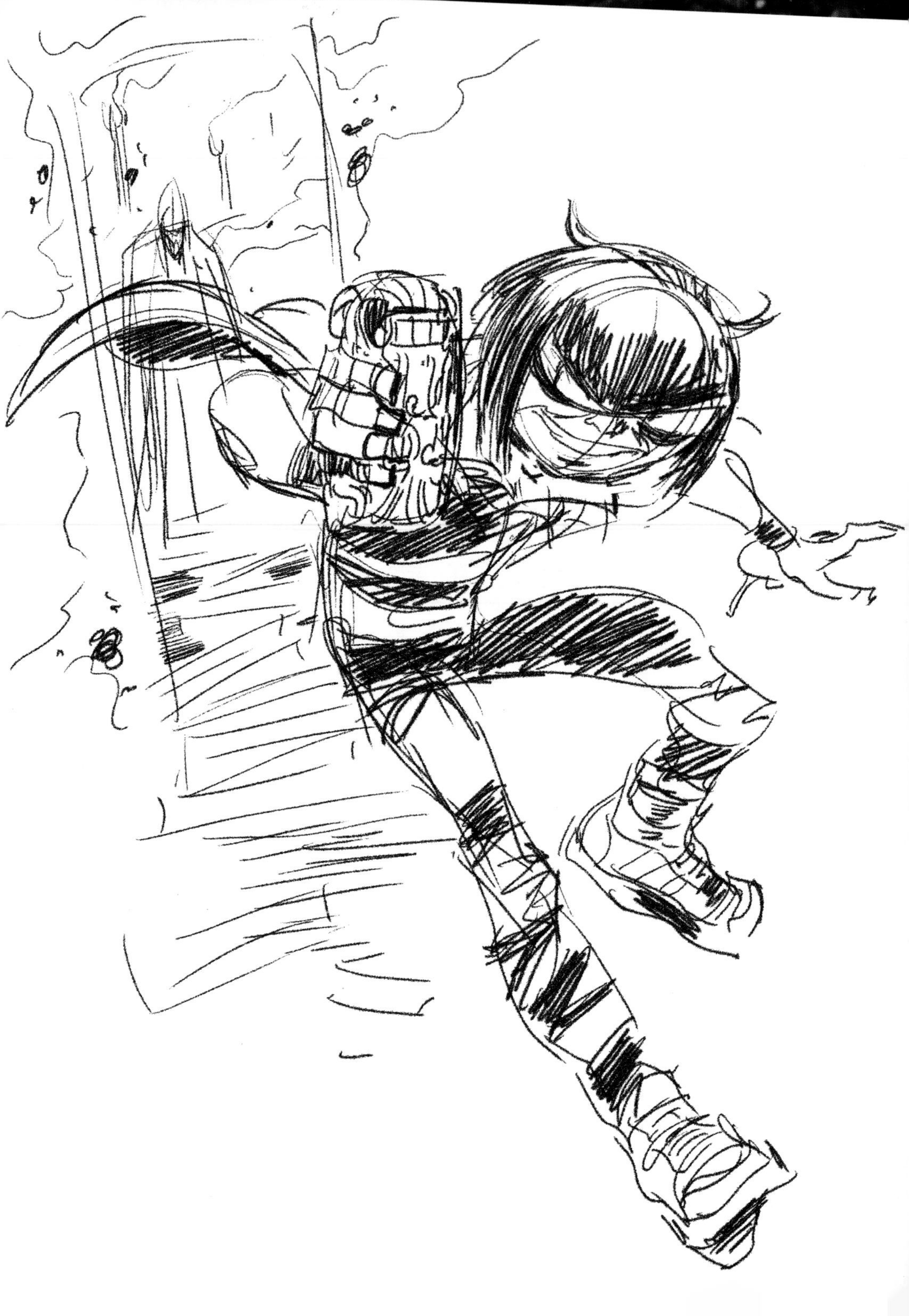

DOC BIZARRE M.D.™

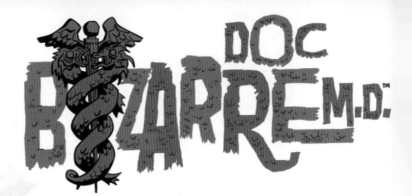

Epoch

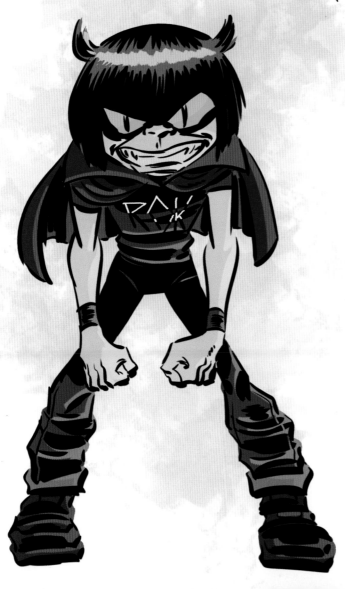

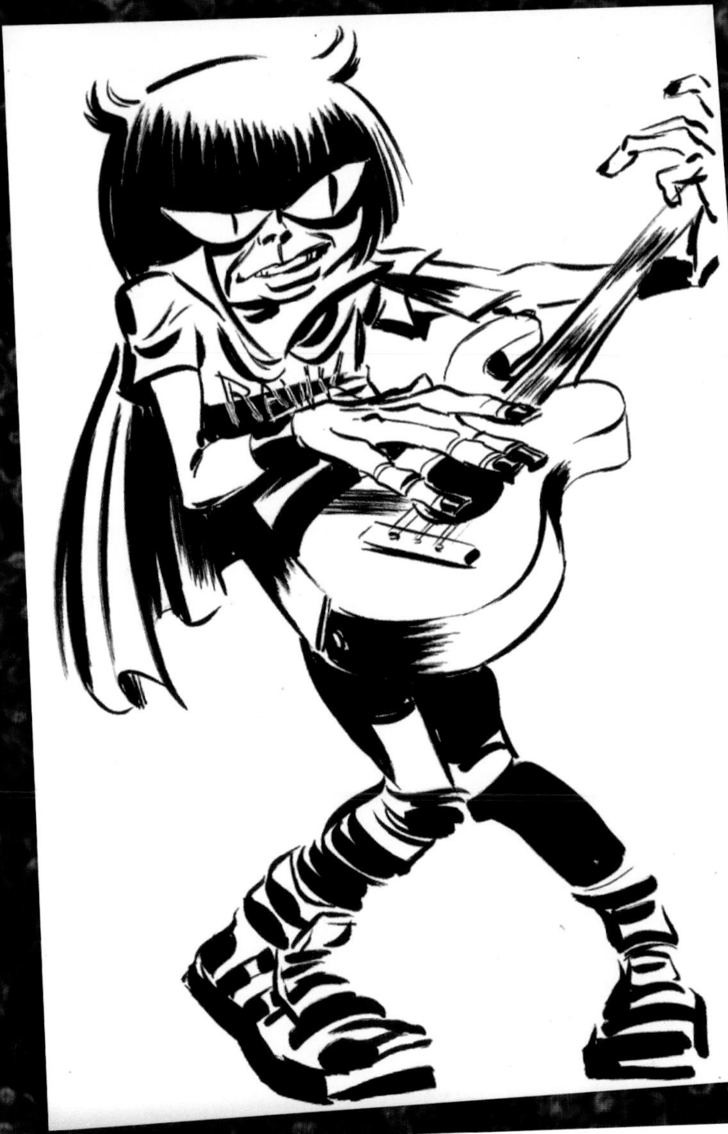

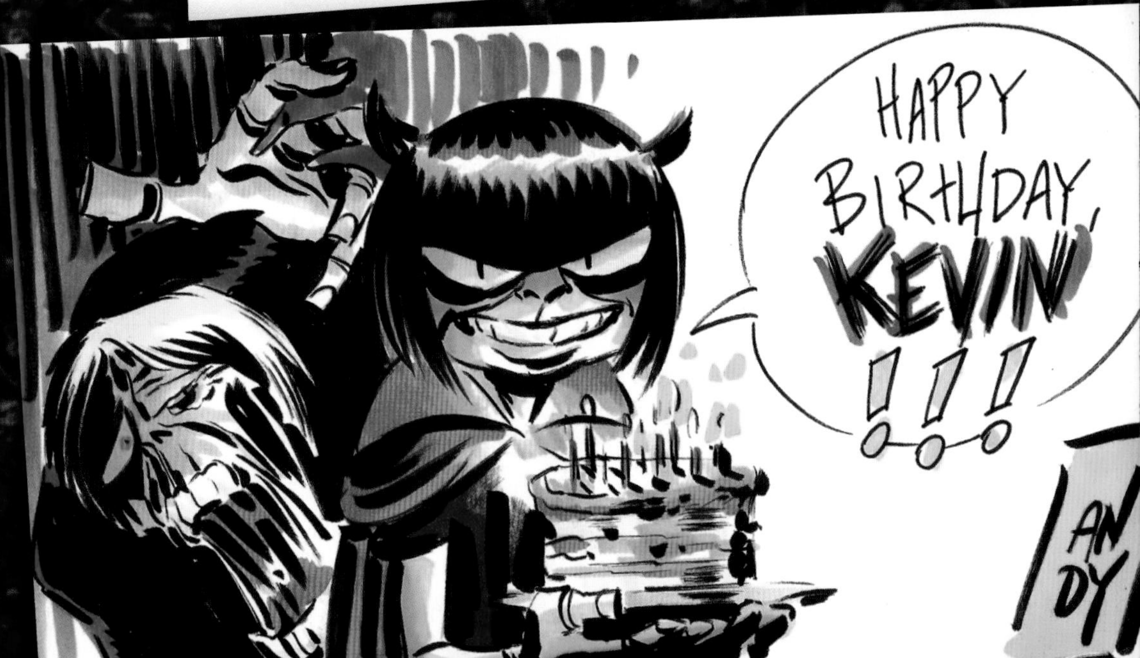
HAPPY BIRTHDAY, KEVIN !!!
ANDY

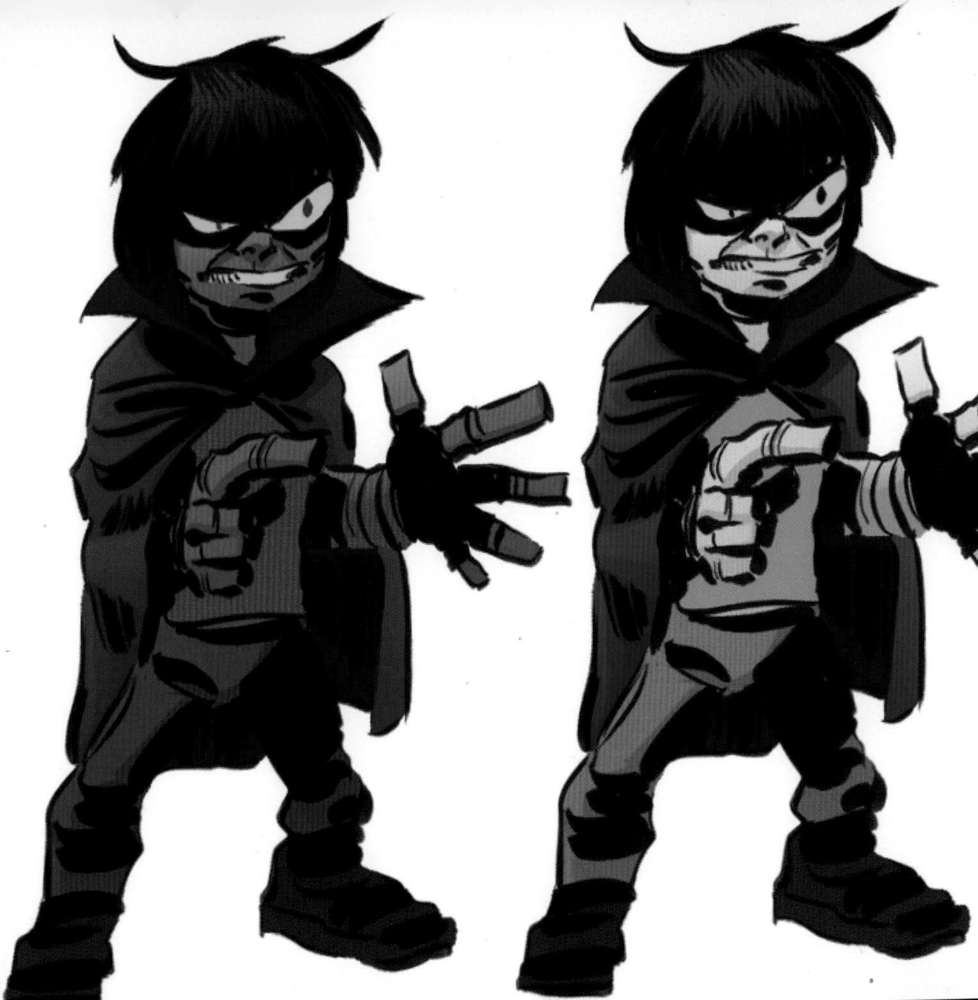

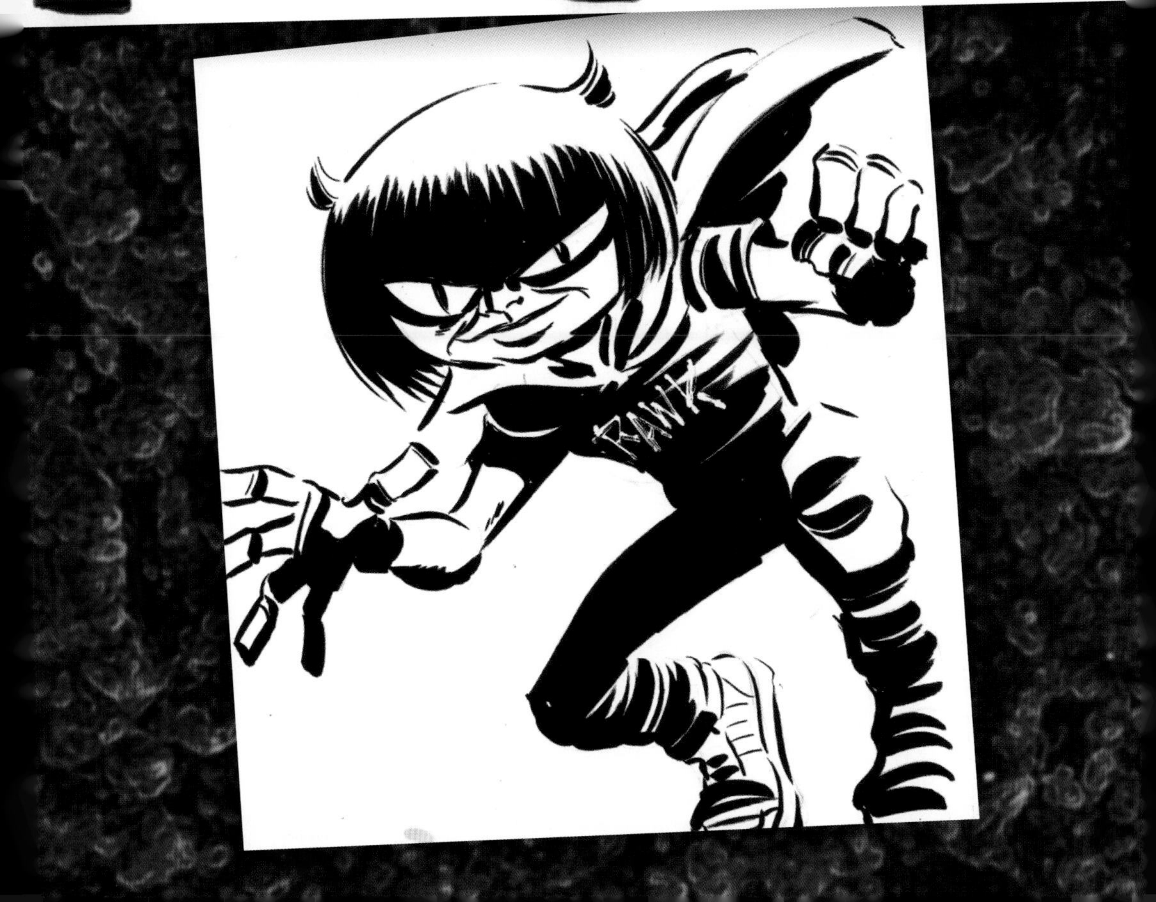
RAWK

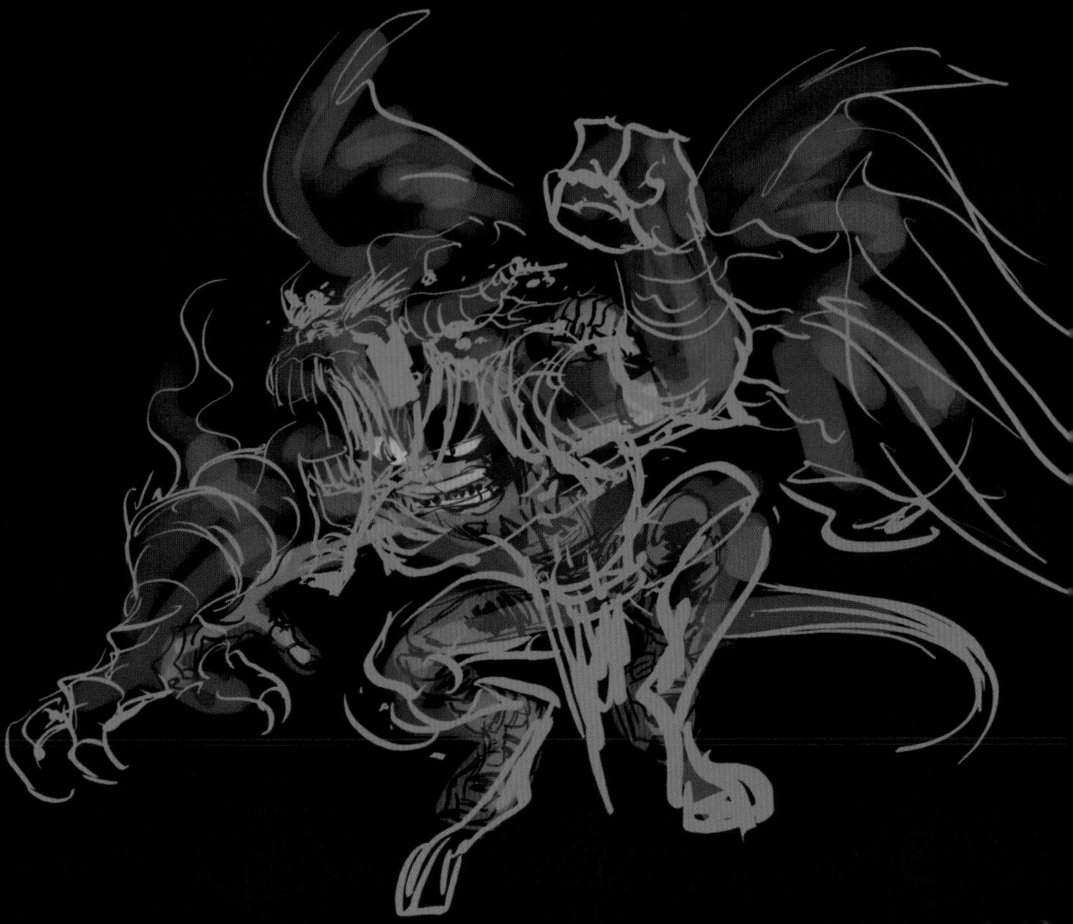

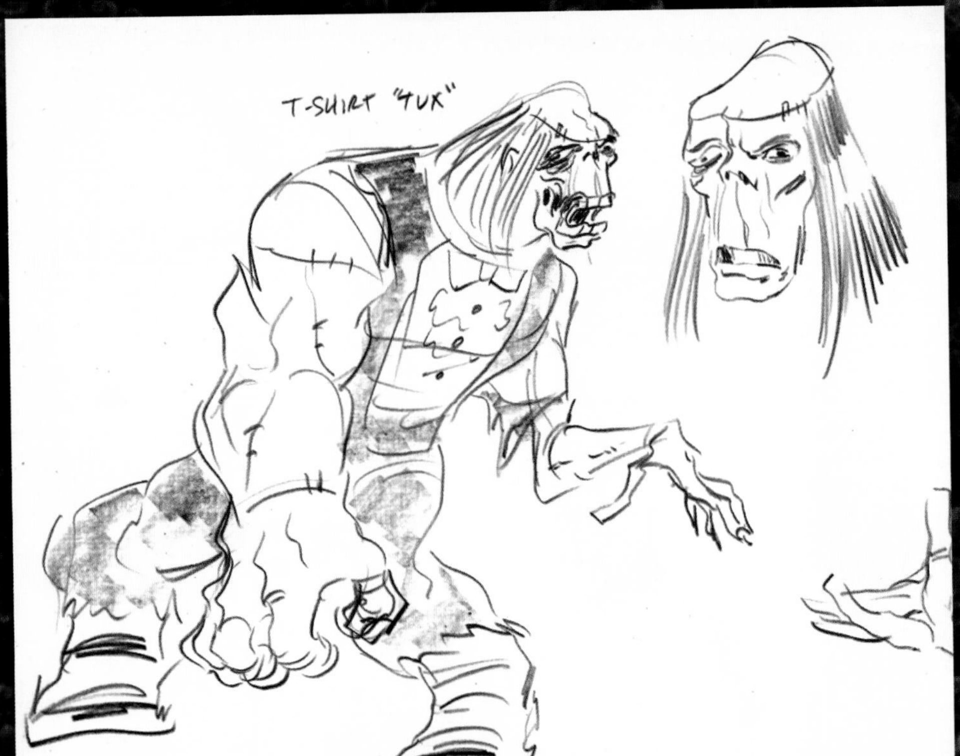
T-SHIRT "TUX"

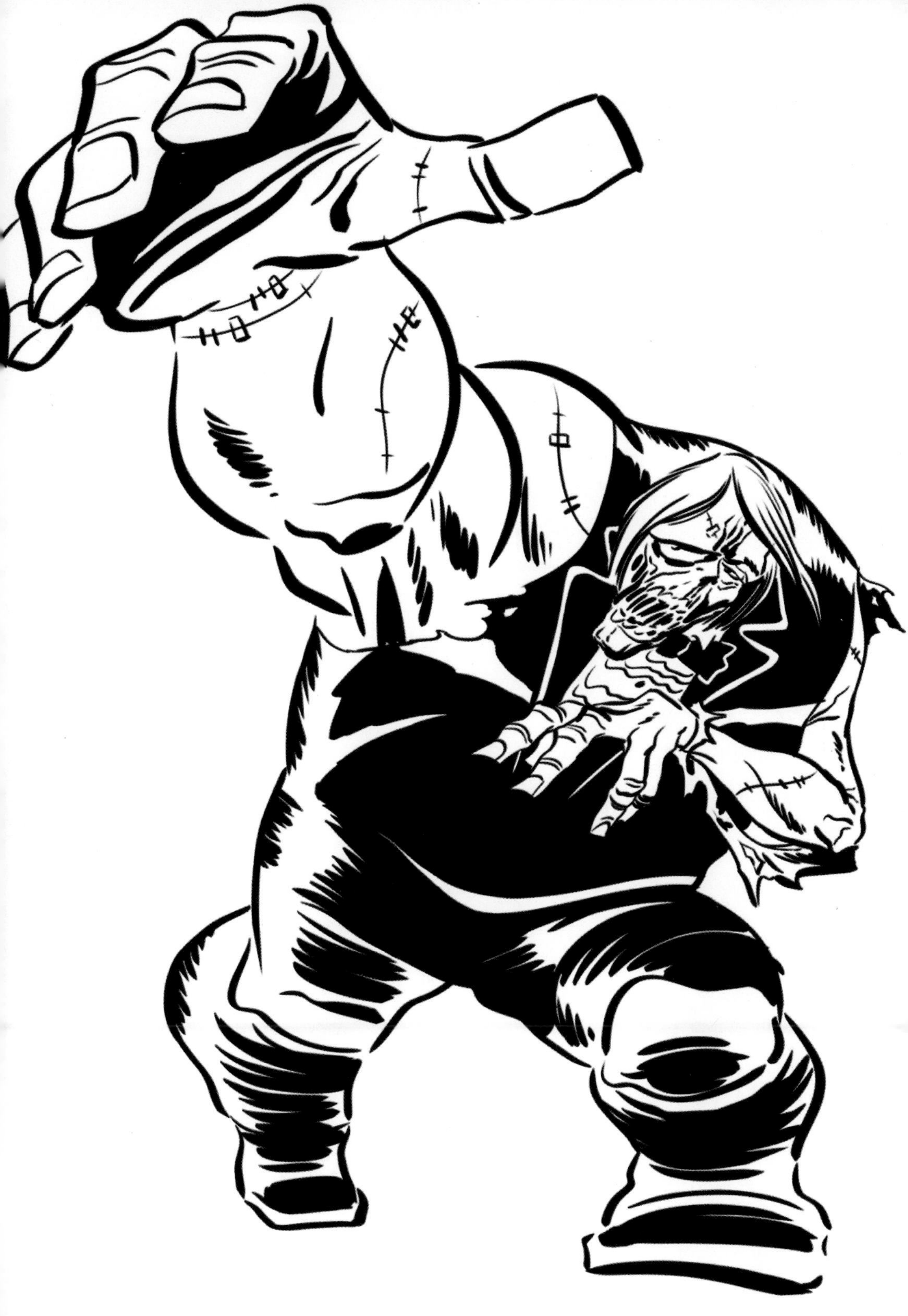

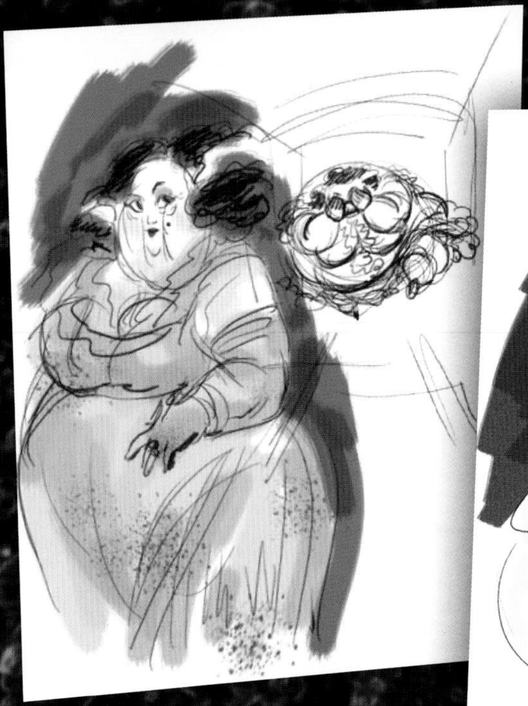
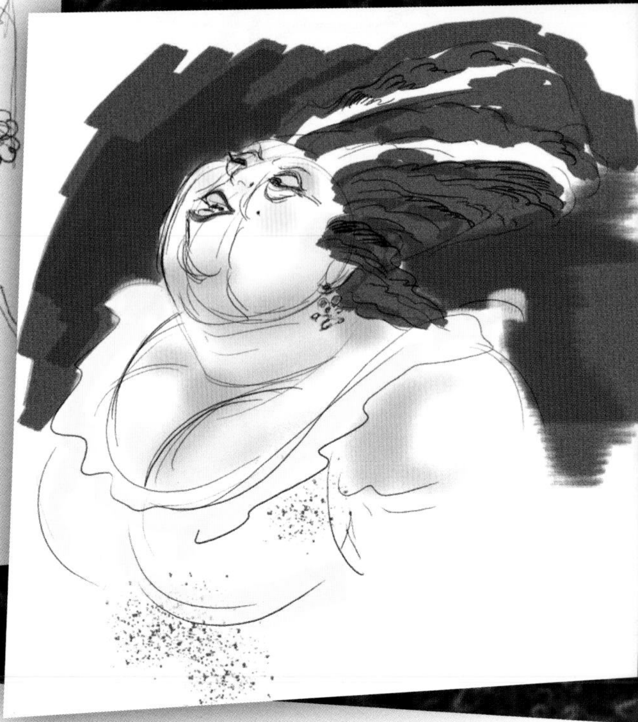
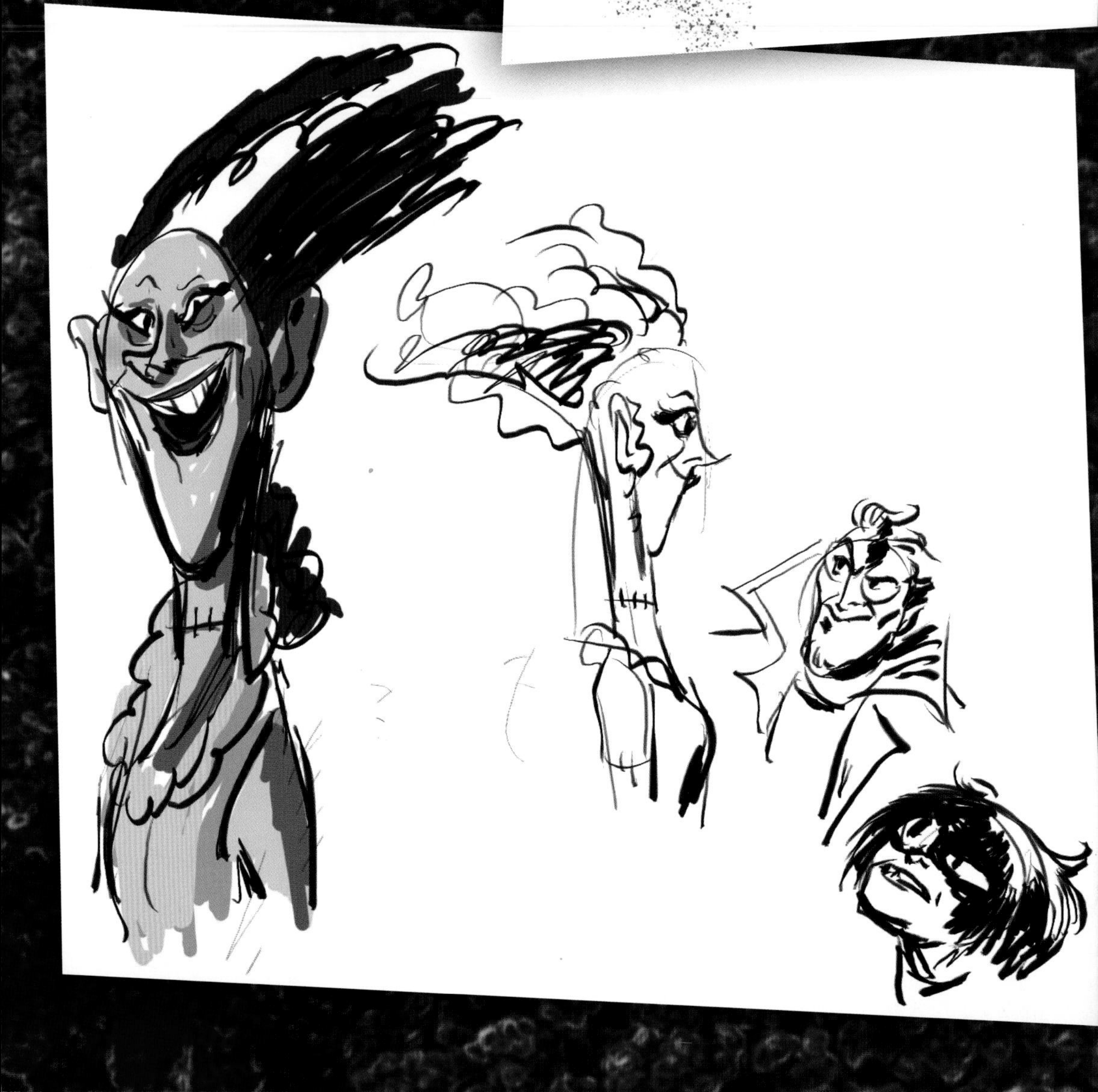

"PARTY ANIMAL"

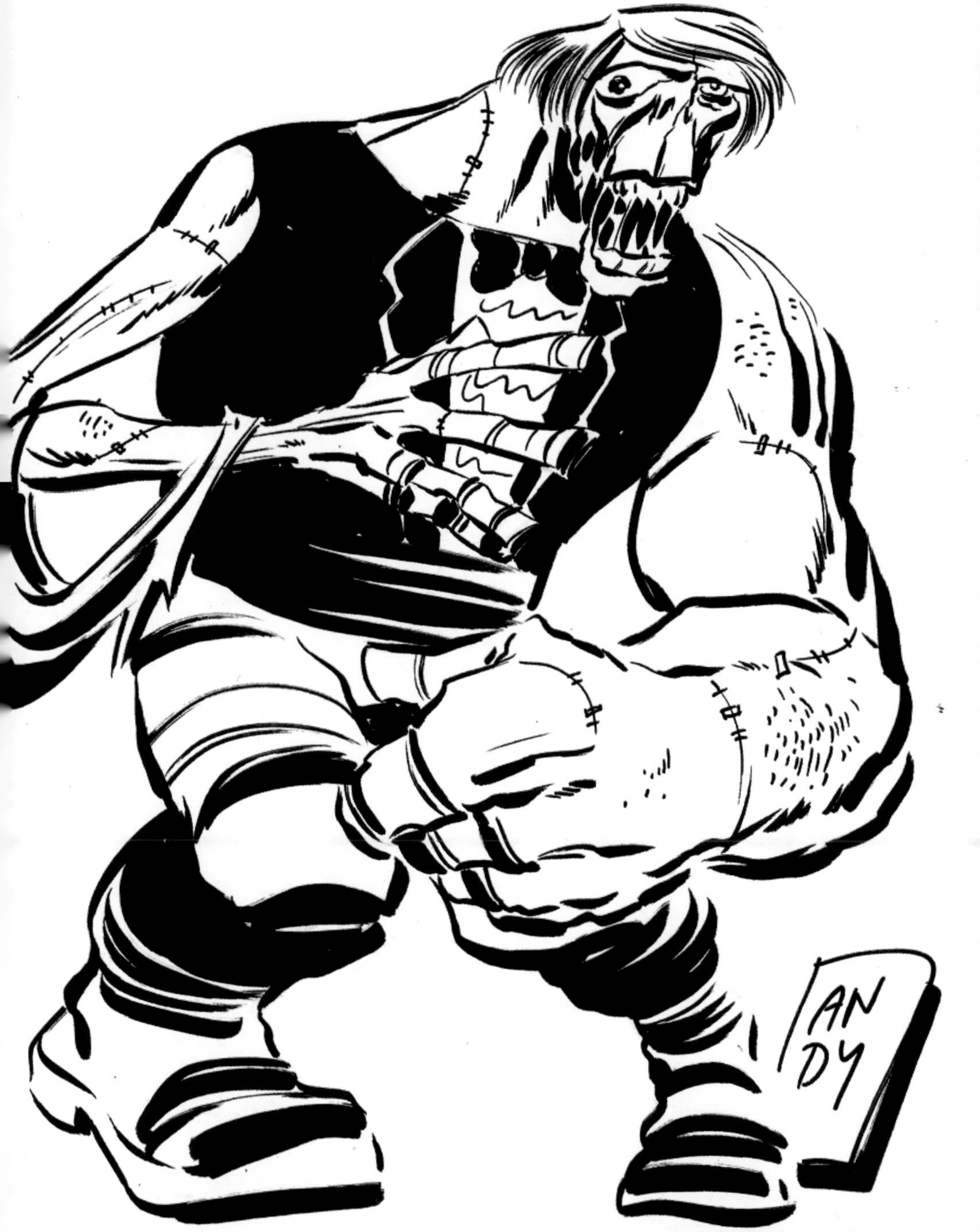
AN
DY

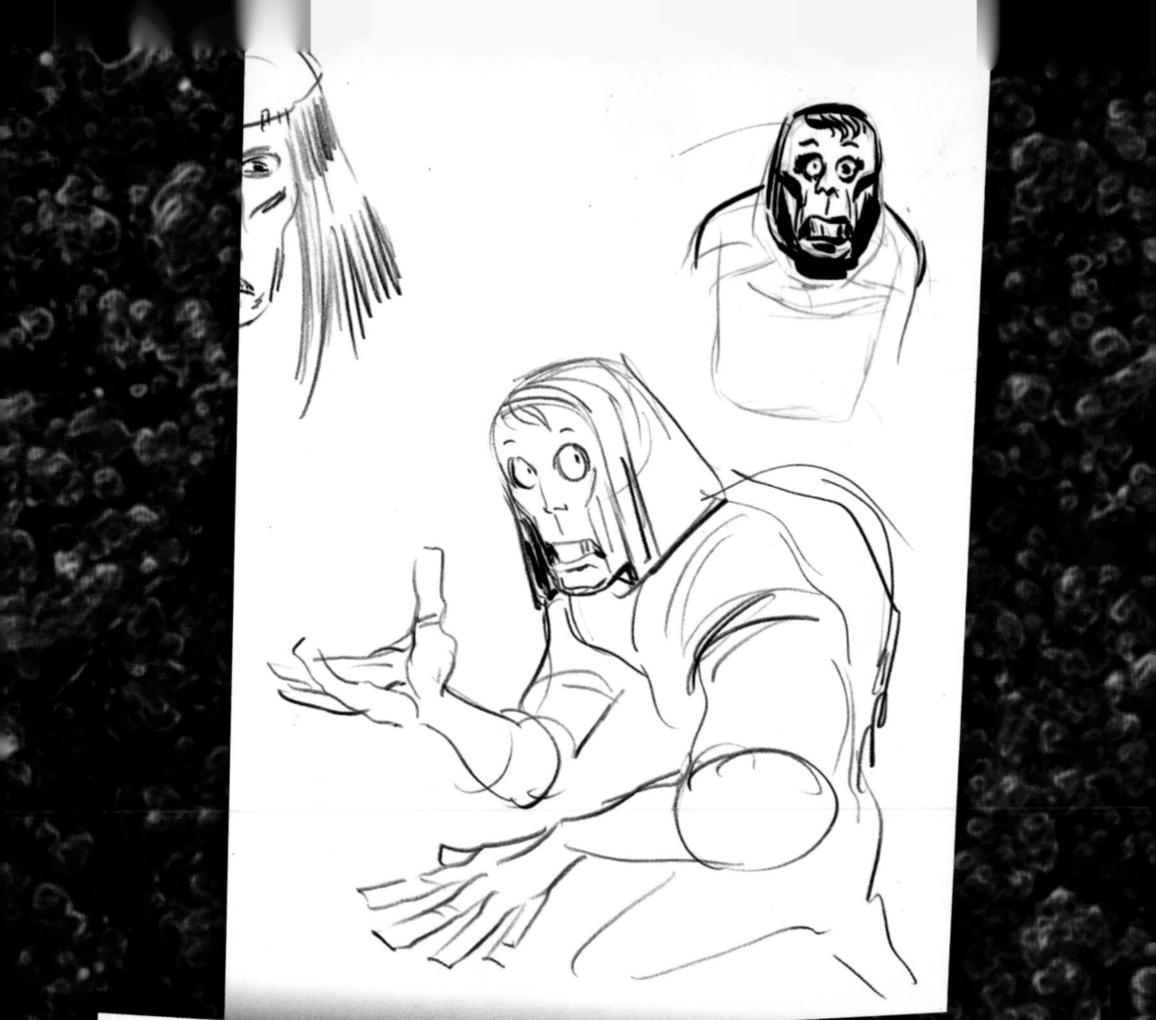

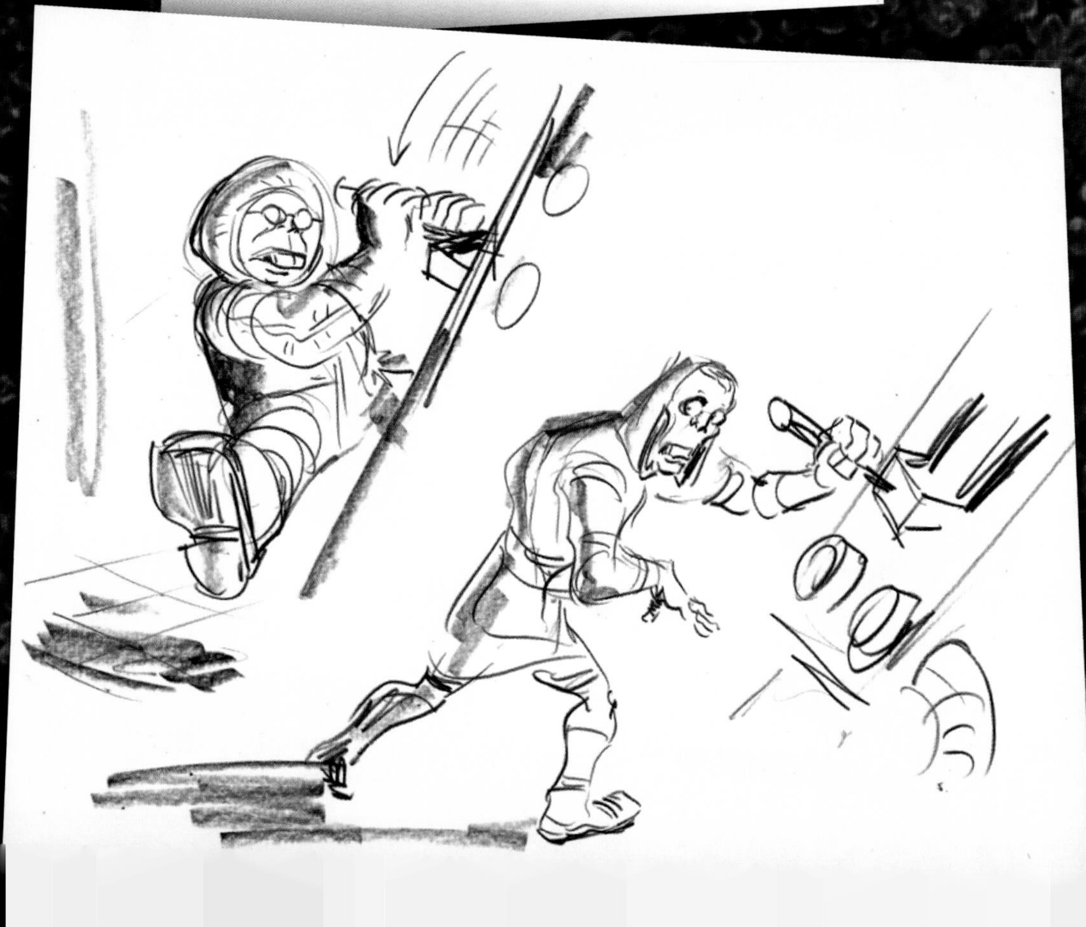

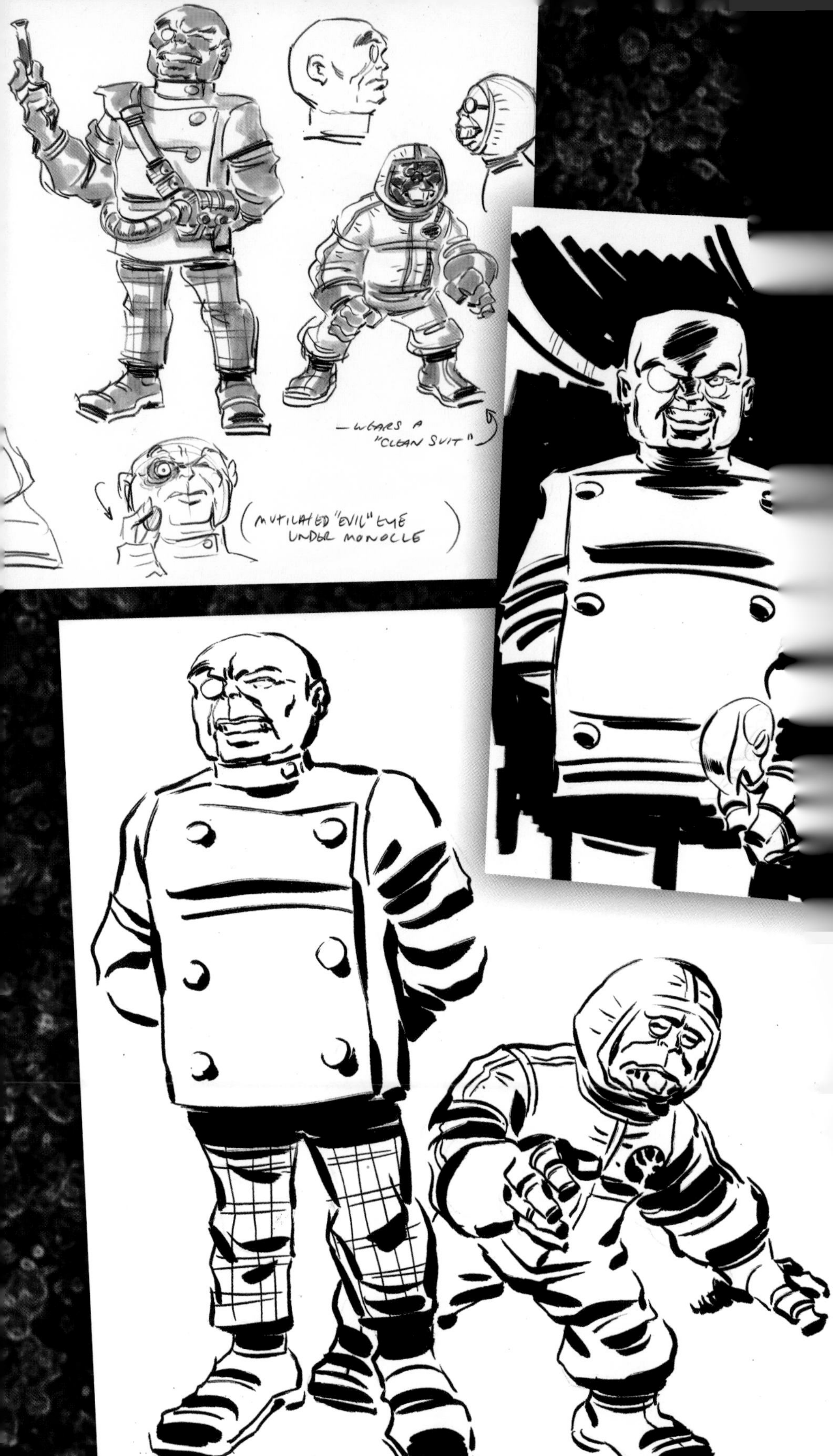
—WEARS A "CLEAN SUIT"
(MUTILATED "EVIL" EYE UNDER MONOCLE)

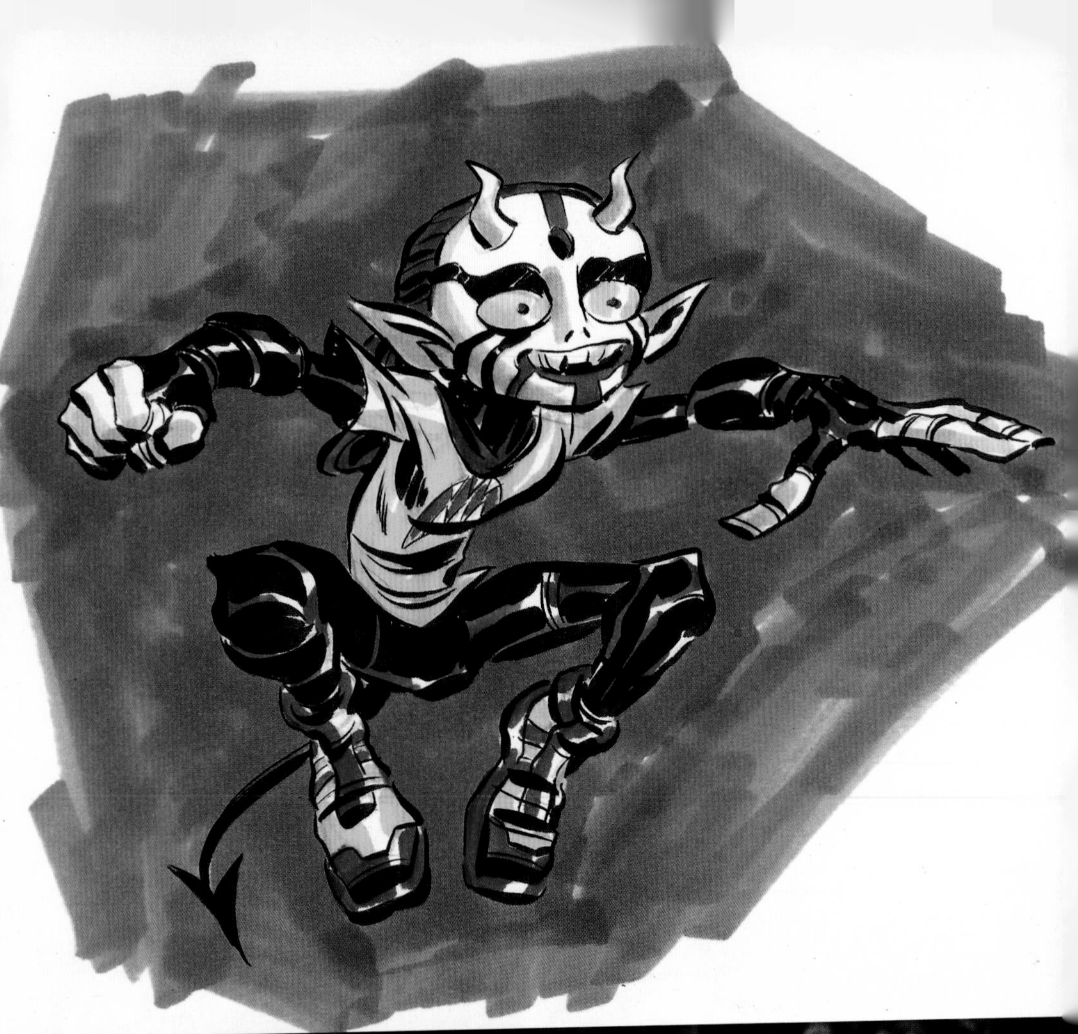

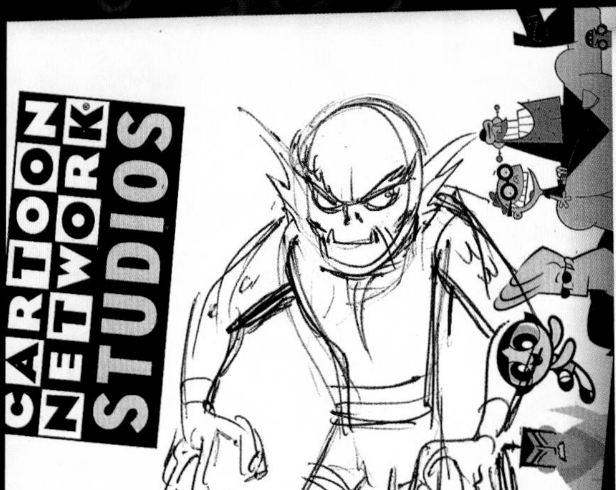
CARTOON NETWORK STUDIOS

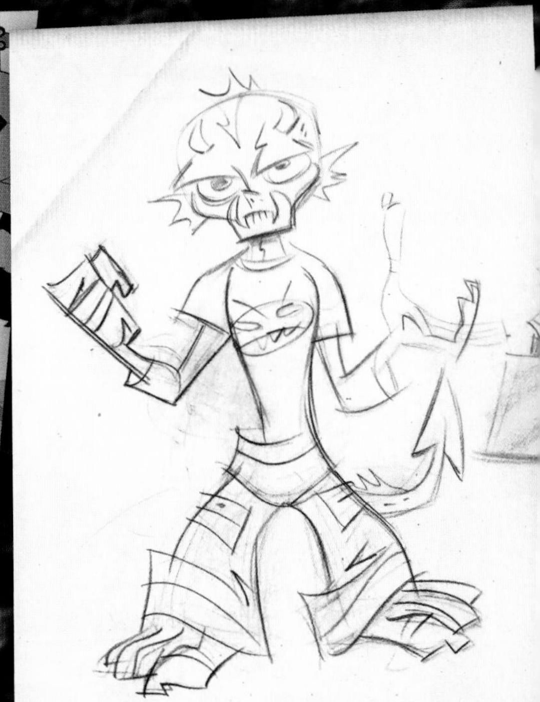

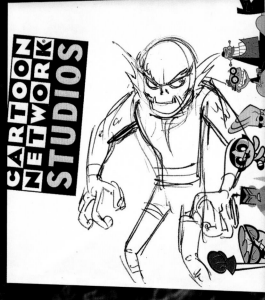

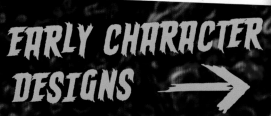

EARLY CHARACTER DESIGNS →

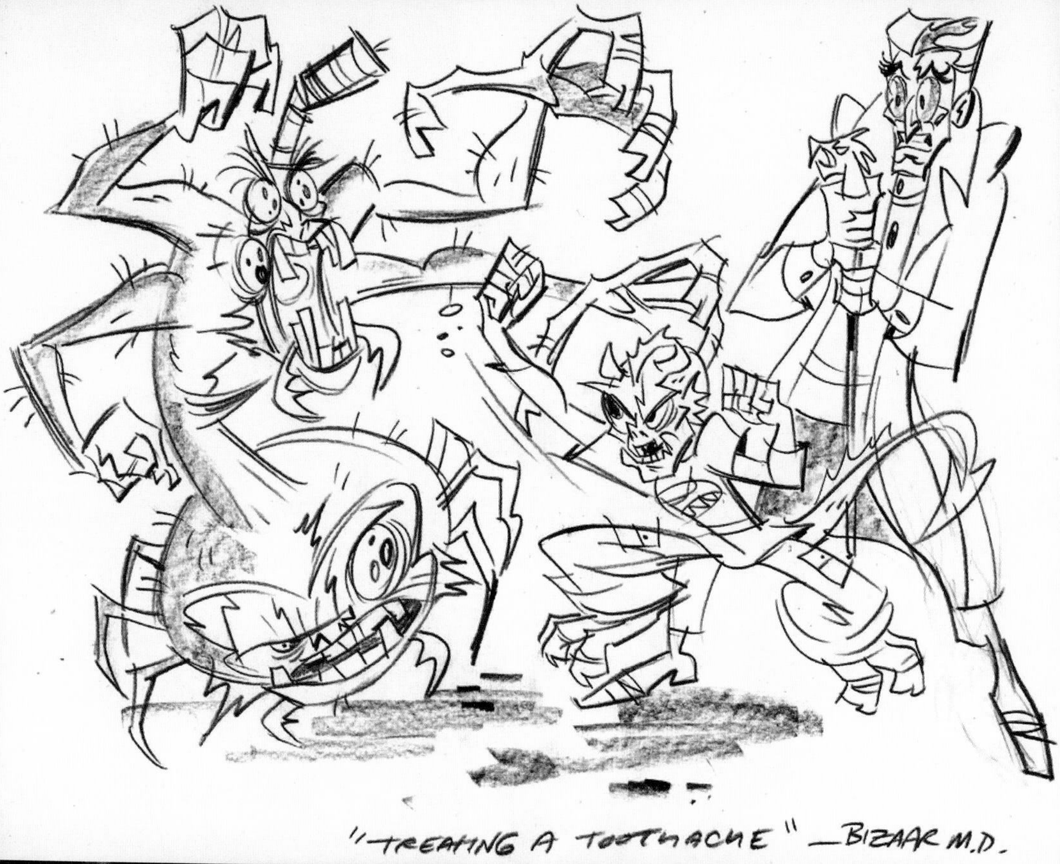
"TREATING A TOOTHACHE" —BIZAAR M.D.

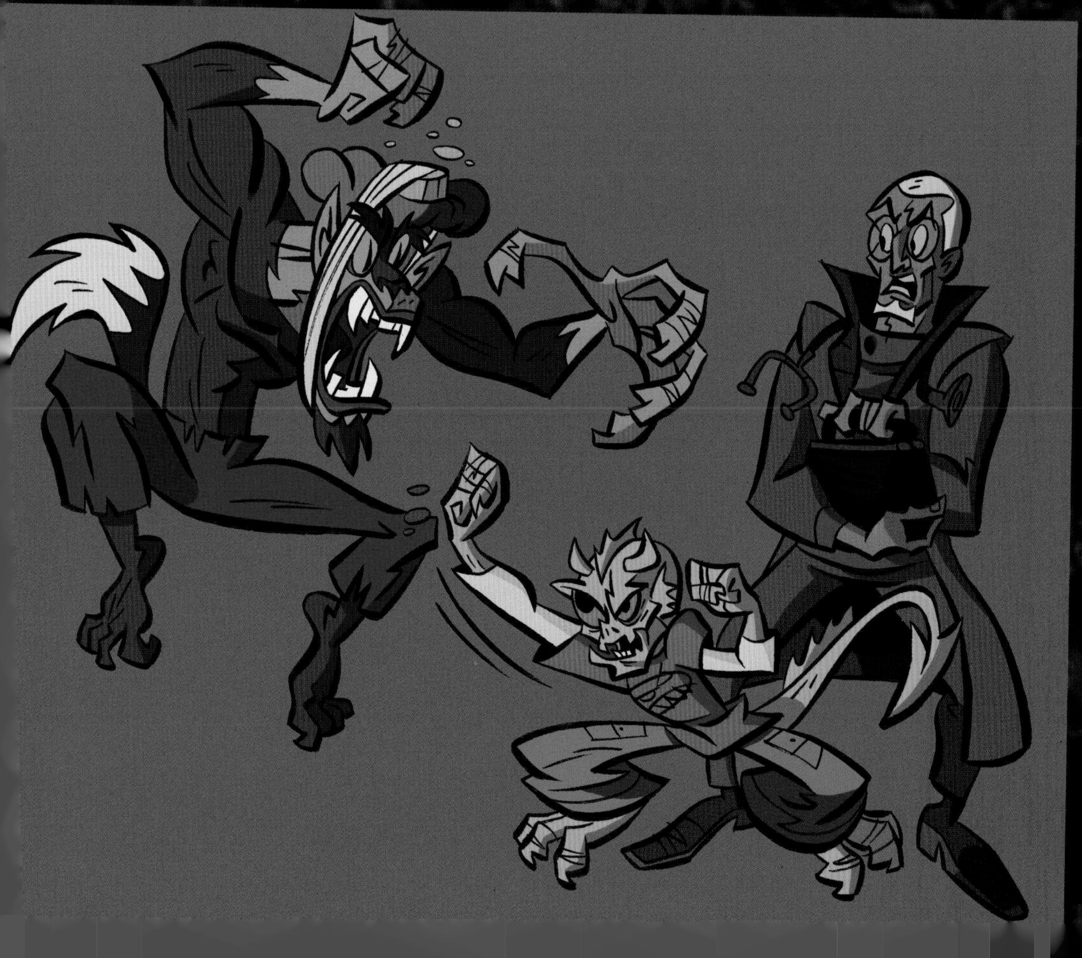

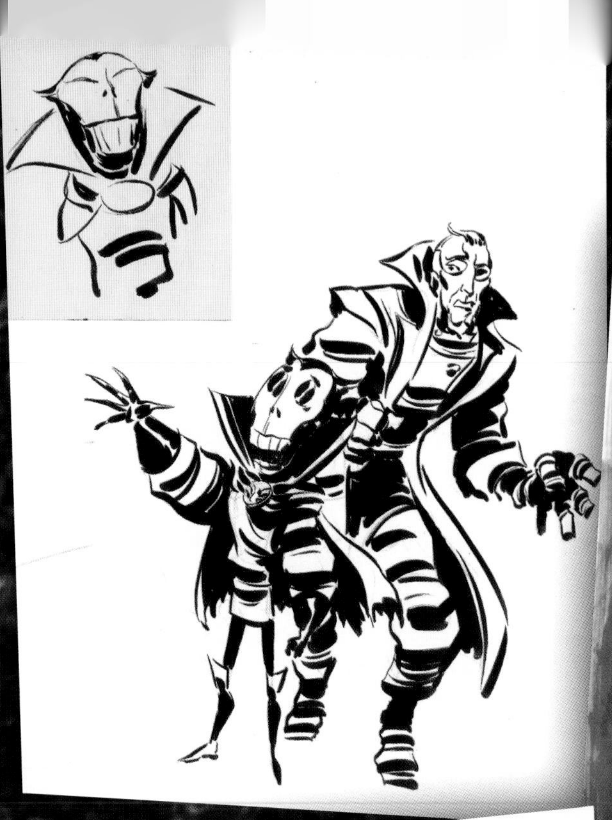
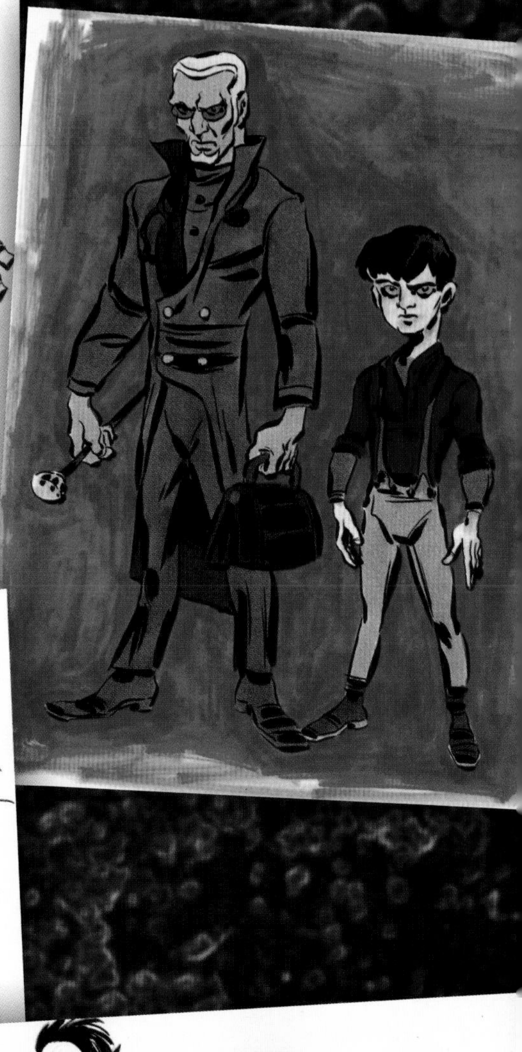
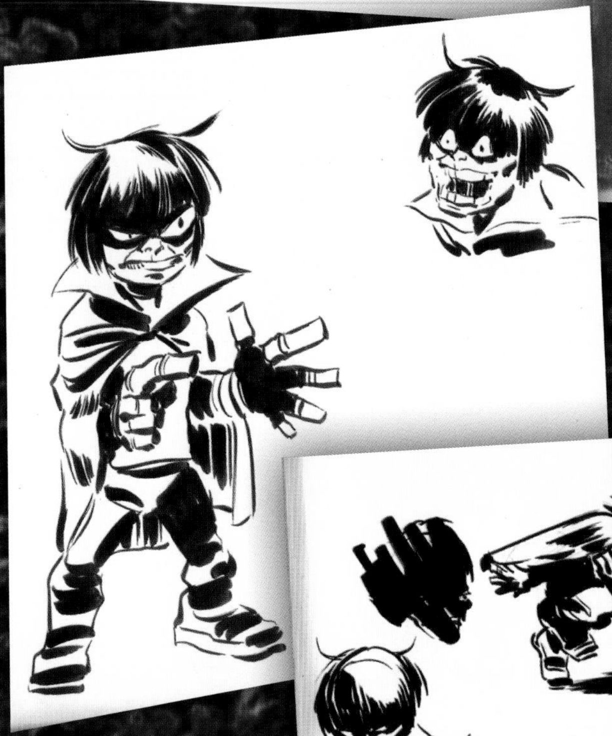
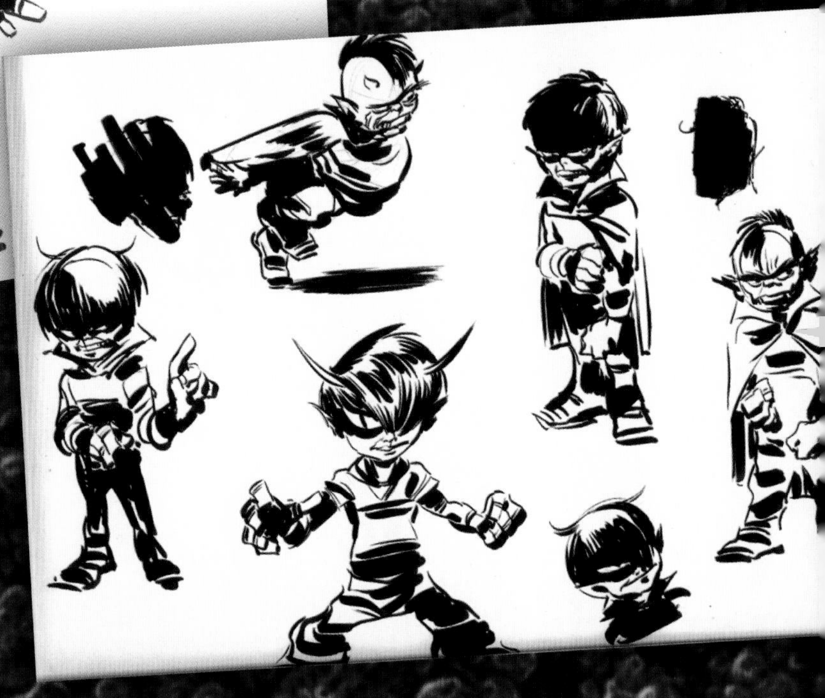

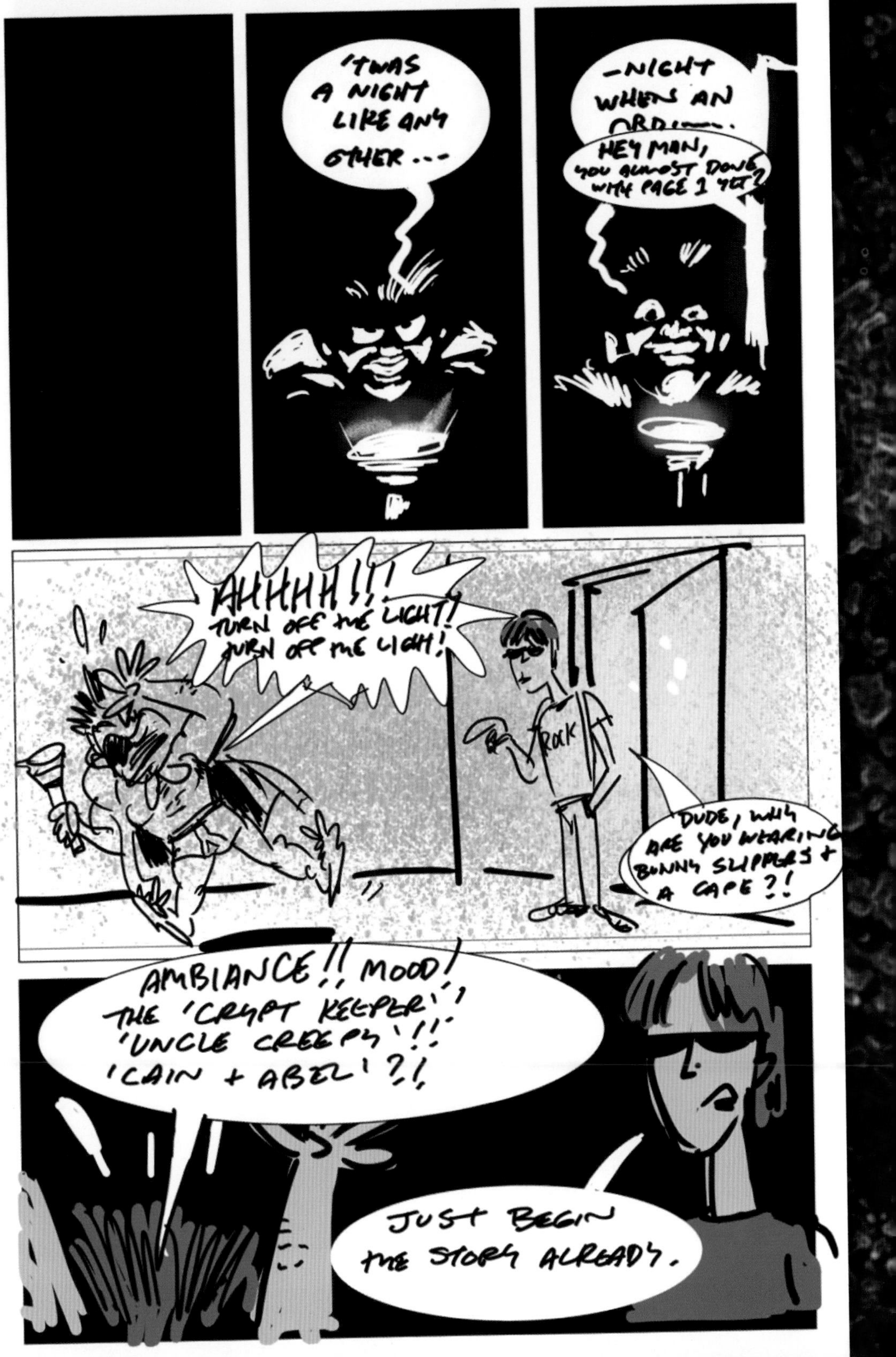
'TWAS A NIGHT LIKE ANY OTHER...
-NIGHT WHEN AN ORDI—
HEY MAN, YOU ALMOST DONE WITH PAGE 1 YET?
AHHHH!!! TURN OFF THE LIGHT! TURN OFF THE LIGHT!
ROCK
DUDE, WHY ARE YOU WEARING BUNNY SLIPPERS + A CAPE?!
AMBIANCE!! MOOD! THE 'CRYPT KEEPER'! 'UNCLE CREEPY'!! 'CAIN + ABEL'?!
JUST BEGIN THE STORY ALREADY.

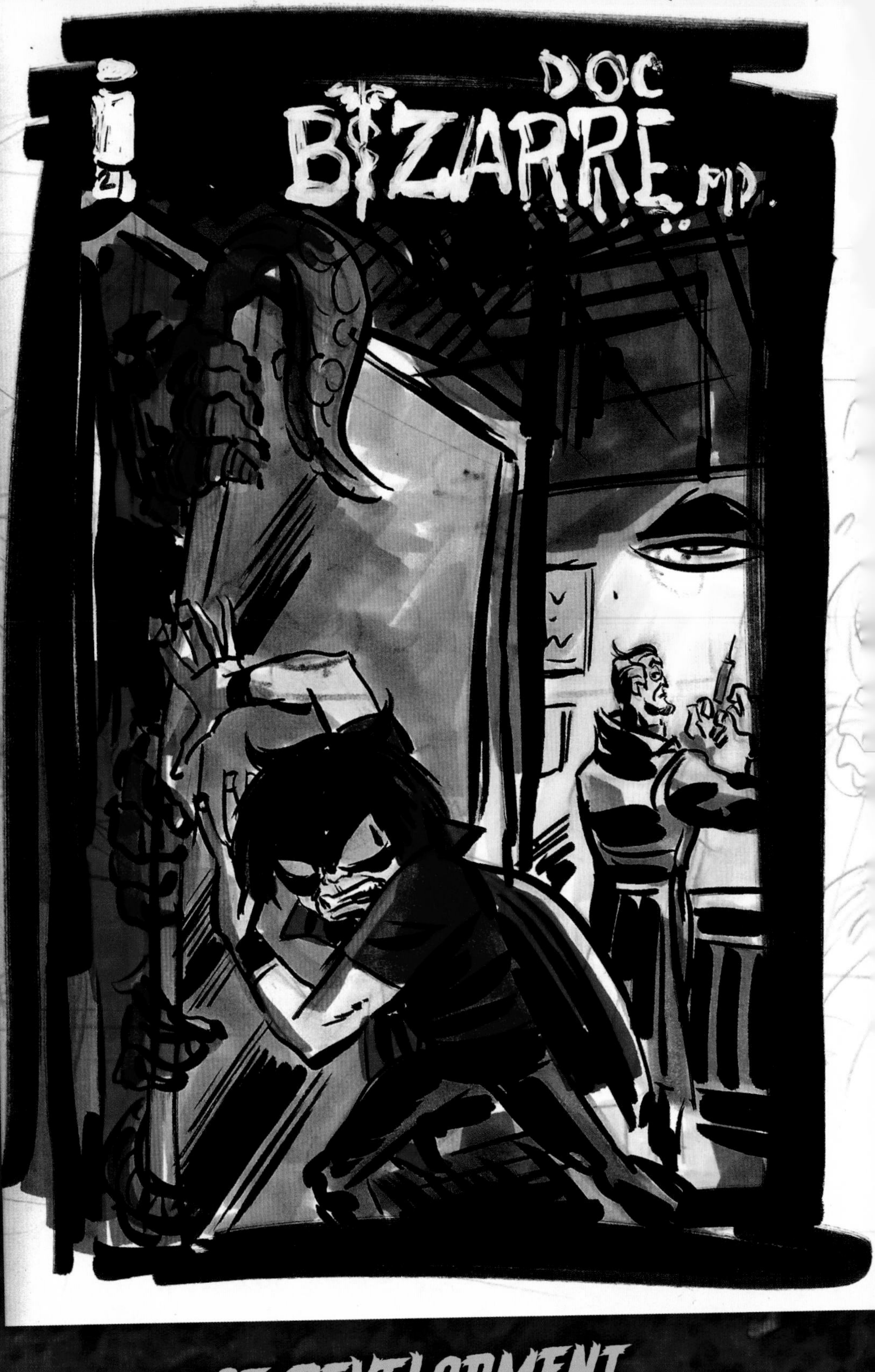
DOC
BIZARRE M.D.

PAGE DEVELOPMENT AND COLOR SCRIPTS →

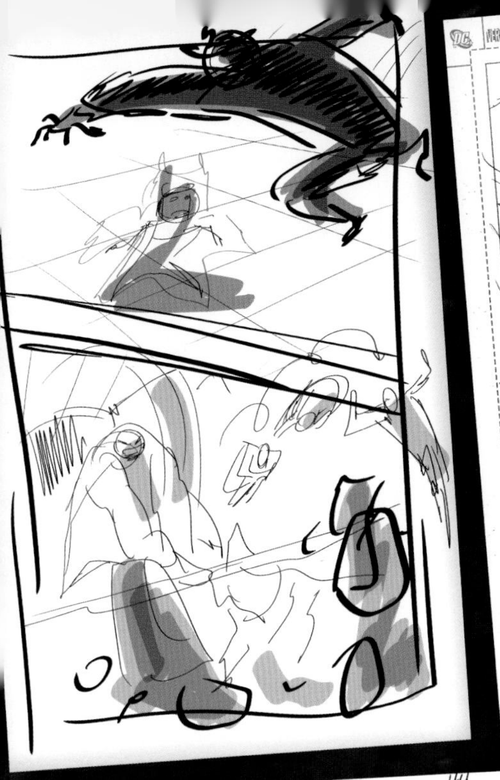

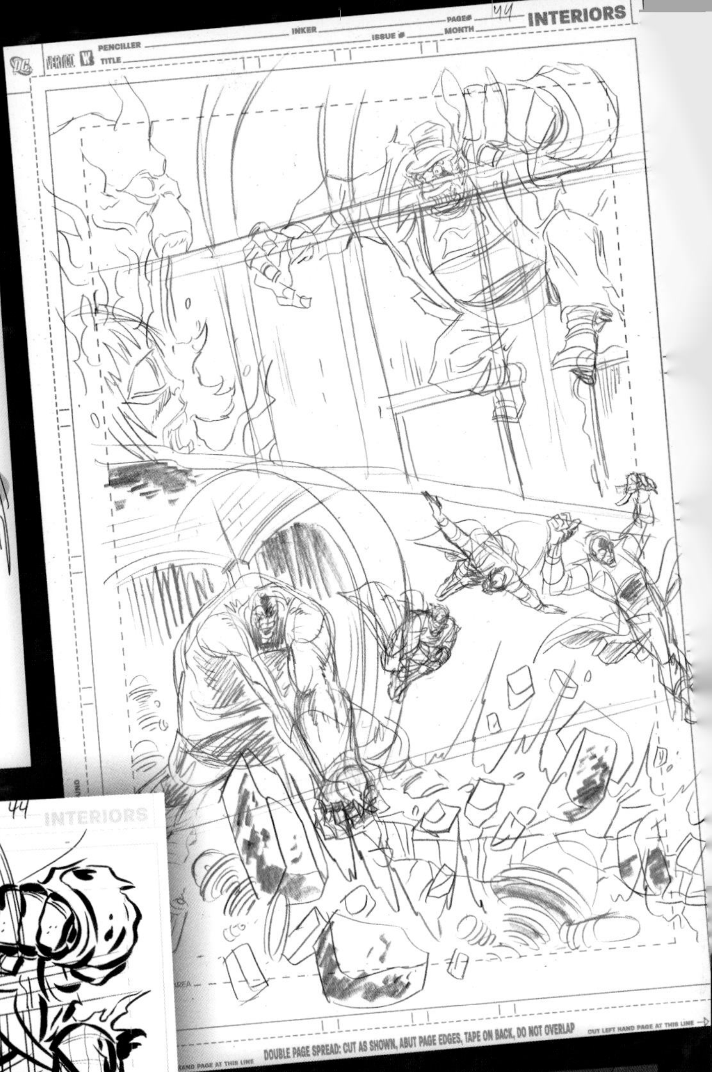
PENCILLER
INKER
ISSUE #
PAGE# 44
MONTH
INTERIORS
TITLE
DOUBLE PAGE SPREAD: CUT AS SHOWN, ABUT PAGE EDGES, TAPE ON BACK, DO NOT OVERLAP
CUT LEFT HAND PAGE AT THIS LINE

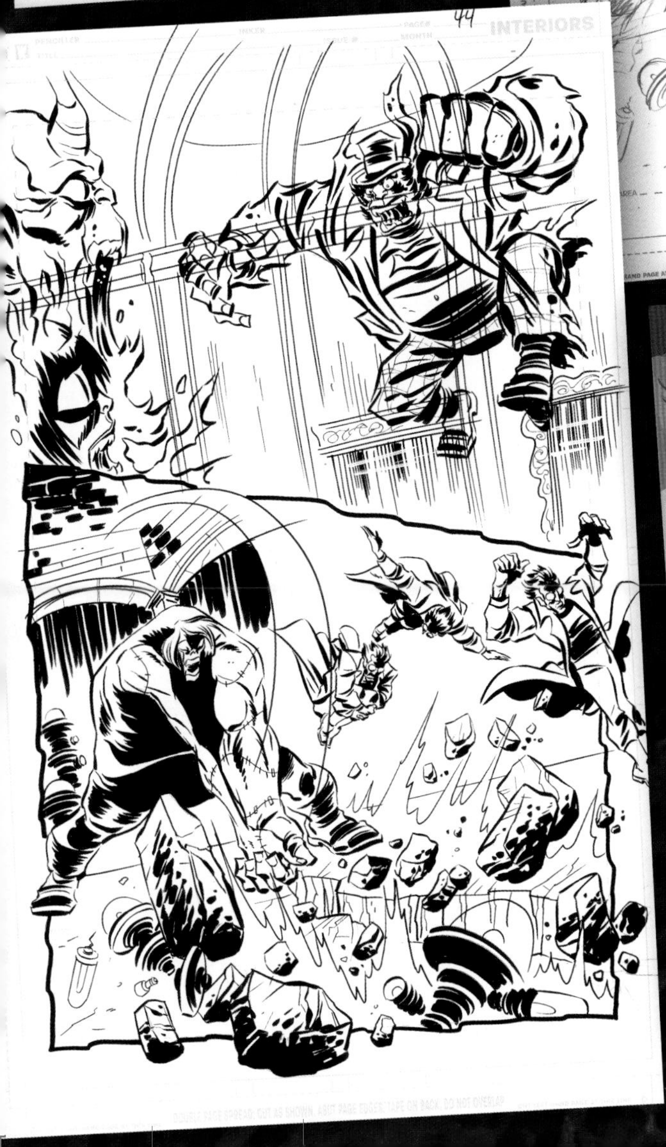
44
INTERIORS

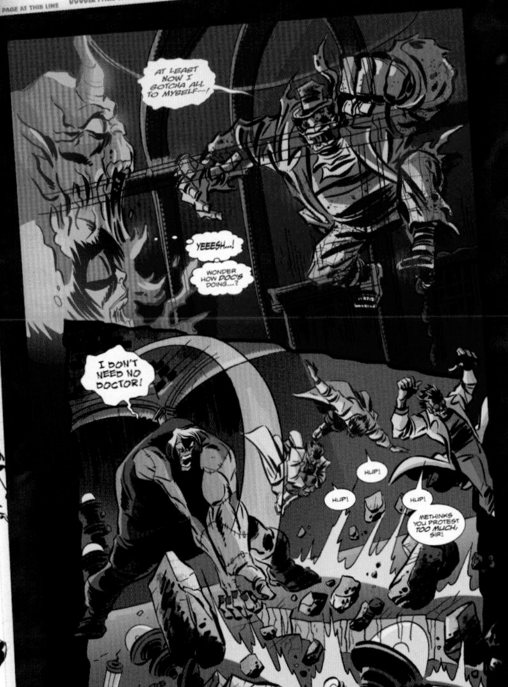
AT LEAST NOW I GOTCHA ALL TO MYSELF--!
YEEESH...!
WONDER HOW DOC'S DOING...?
I DON'T NEED NO DOCTOR!
HUP!
HUP!
HUP!
METHINKS YOU PROTEST TOO MUCH, SIR!

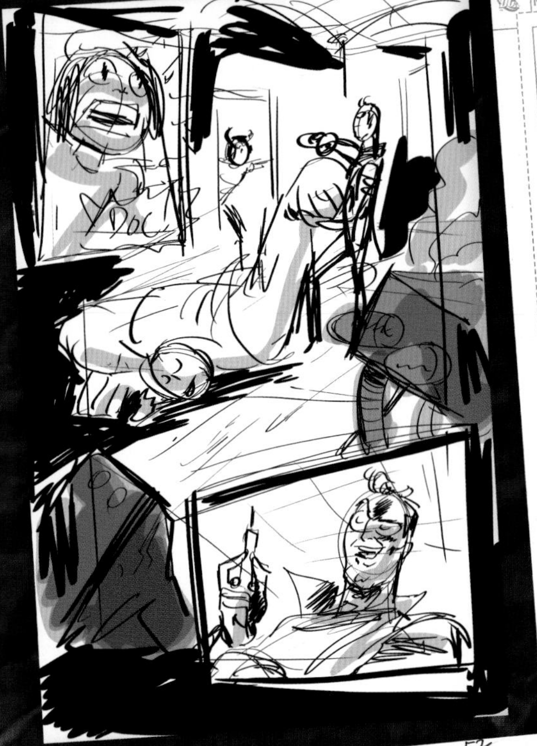

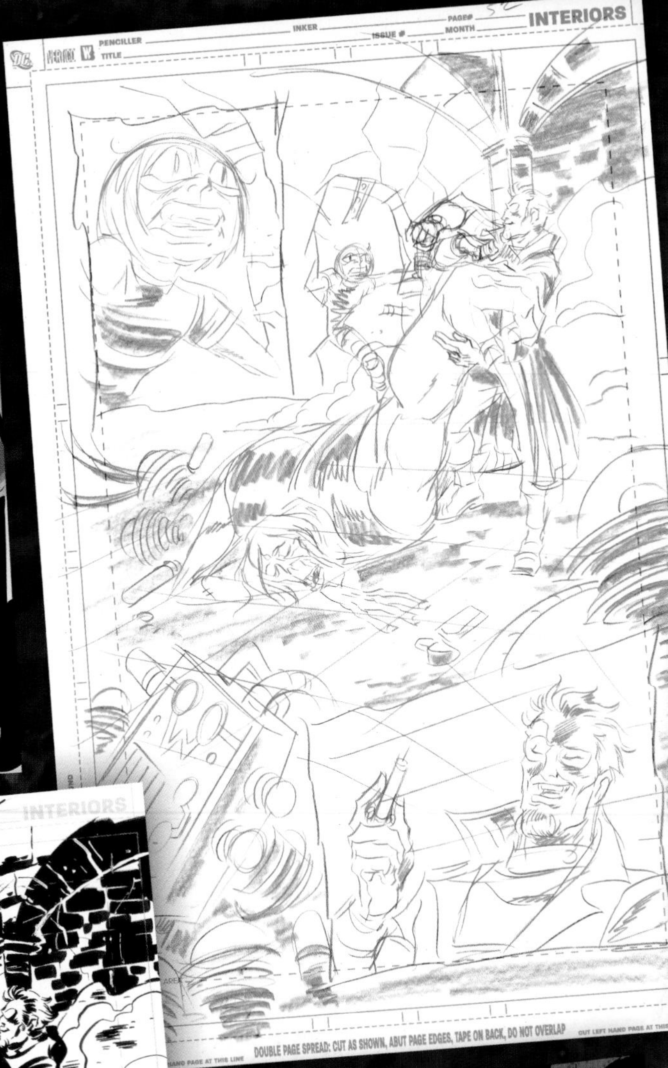
PENCILLER
INKER
ISSUE #
PAGE#
MONTH
INTERIORS
TITLE
DOUBLE PAGE SPREAD: CUT AS SHOWN, ABUT PAGE EDGES, TAPE ON BACK, DO NOT OVERLAP

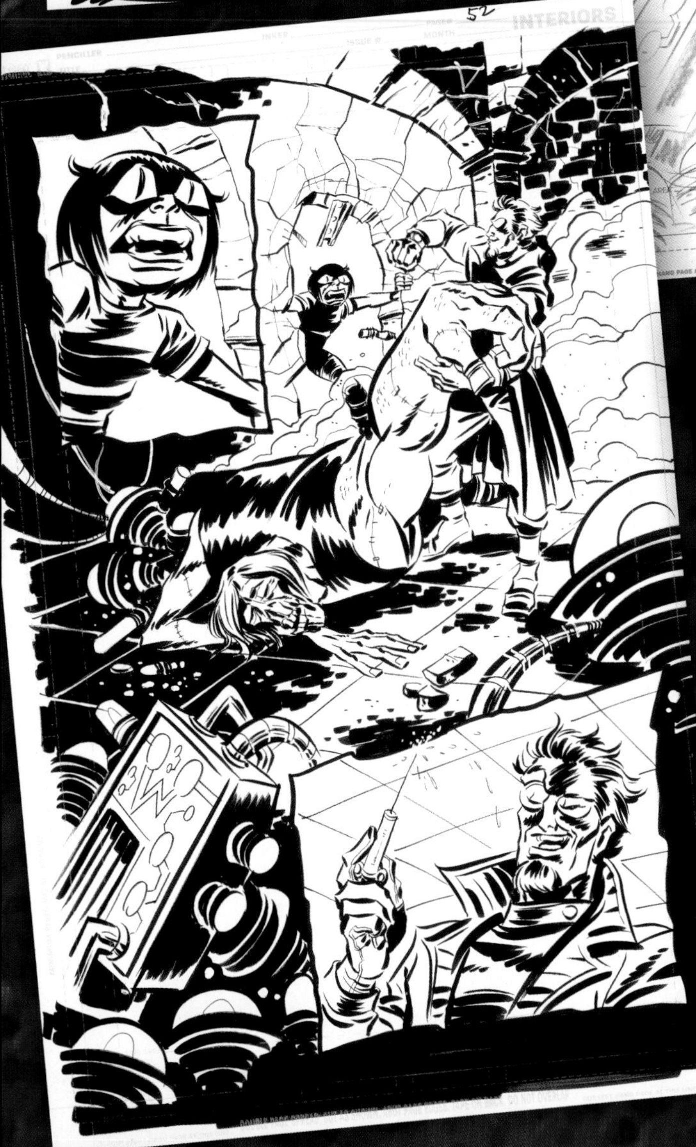
52
INTERIORS

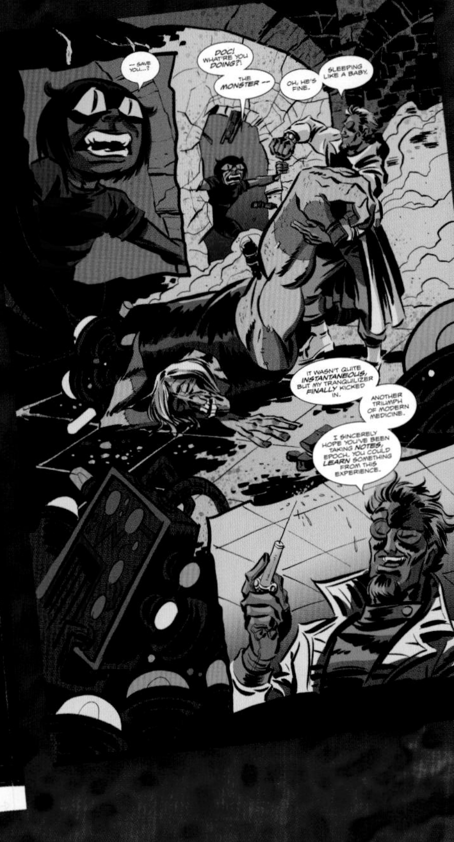
-- SAVE YOU...?
DOC! WHAT'RE YOU DOING?!
THE MONSTER --
OH, HE'S FINE.
SLEEPING LIKE A BABY.
IT WASN'T QUITE INSTANTANEOUS, BUT MY TRANQUILIZER FINALLY KICKED IN.
ANOTHER TRIUMPH OF MODERN MEDICINE.
I SINCERELY HOPE YOU'VE BEEN TAKING NOTES, EPOCH. YOU COULD LEARN SOMETHING FROM THIS EXPERIENCE.

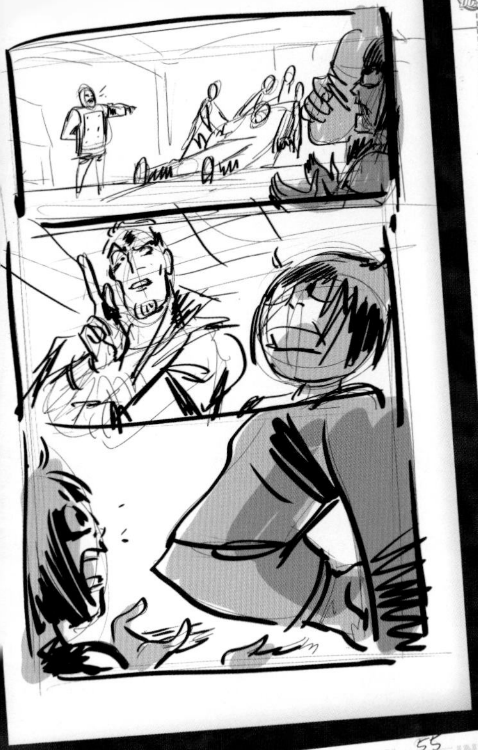

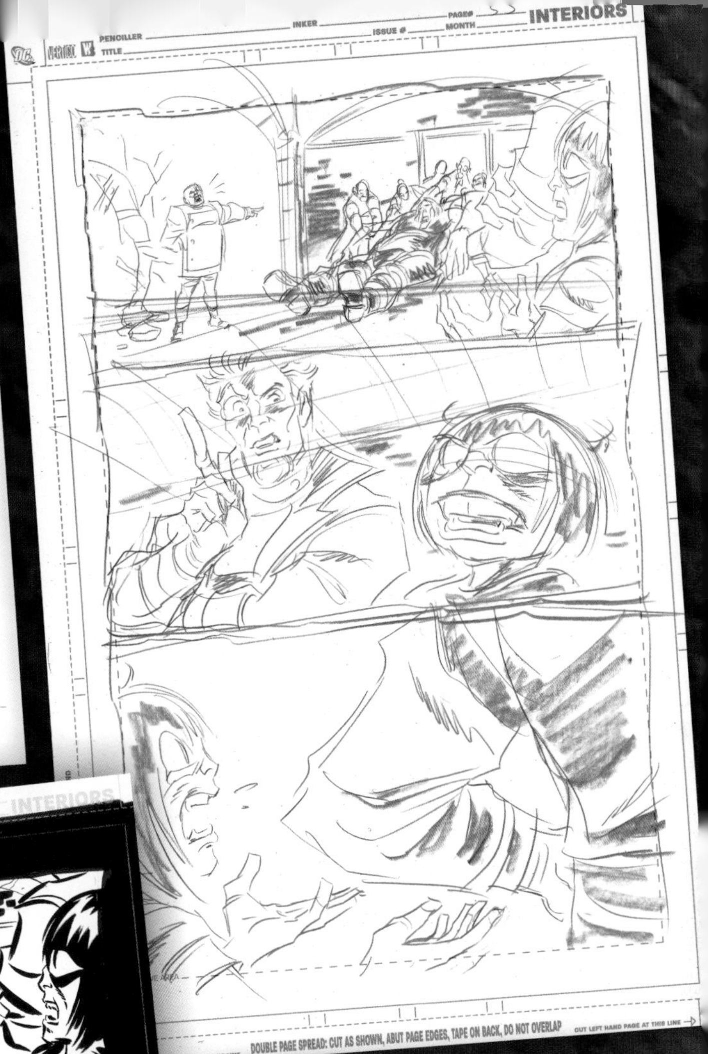
PENCILLER
INKER
PAGE#
INTERIORS
TITLE
ISSUE #
MONTH
DOUBLE PAGE SPREAD: CUT AS SHOWN, ABUT PAGE EDGES, TAPE ON BACK, DO NOT OVERLAP
CUT LEFT HAND PAGE AT THIS LINE

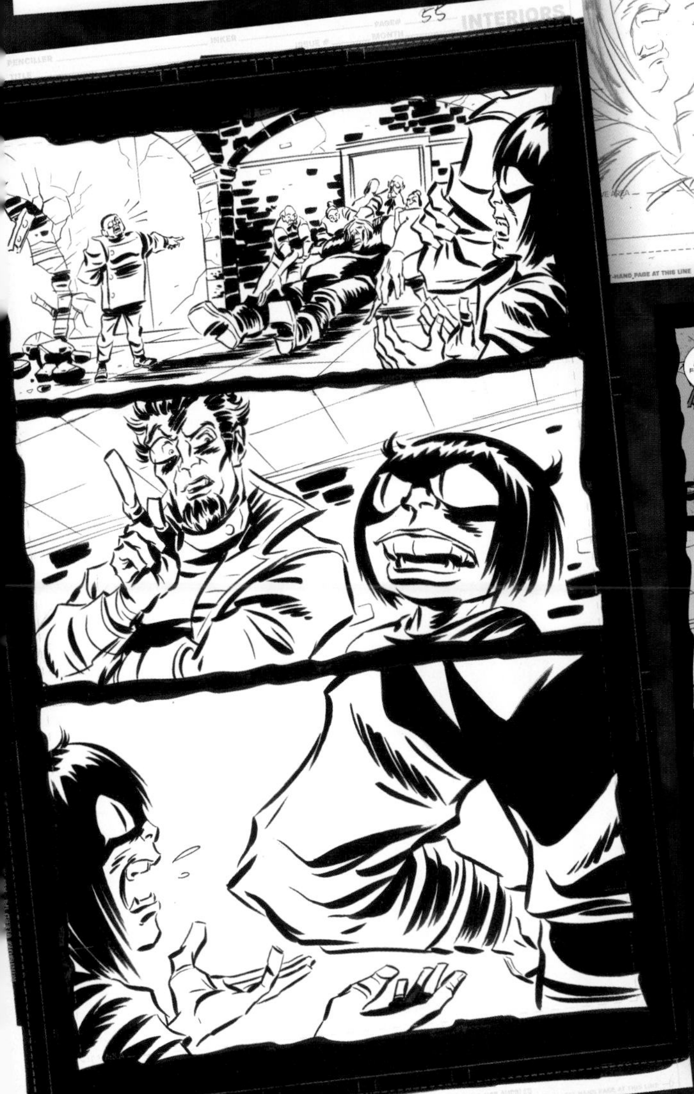
55
INTERIORS

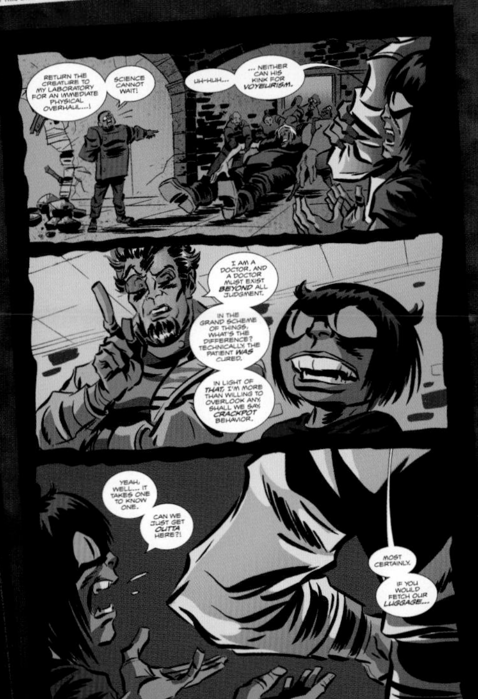
RETURN THE CREATURE TO MY LABORATORY FOR AN IMMEDIATE PHYSICAL OVERHAUL...!
SCIENCE CANNOT WAIT!
UH-HUH...
... NEITHER CAN HIS KINK FOR *VOYEURISM.*
I AM A DOCTOR, AND A DOCTOR MUST EXIST *BEYOND* ALL JUDGMENT.
IN THE GRAND SCHEME OF THINGS, WHAT'S THE DIFFERENCE? TECHNICALLY, THE PATIENT *WAS* CURED.
IN LIGHT OF *THAT,* I'M MORE THAN WILLING TO OVERLOOK ANY, SHALL WE SAY, *CRACKPOT* BEHAVIOR.
YEAH, WELL... IT TAKES ONE TO KNOW ONE.
CAN WE JUST GET *OUTTA* HERE?!
MOST CERTAINLY.
IF YOU WOULD FETCH OUR *LUGGAGE...*

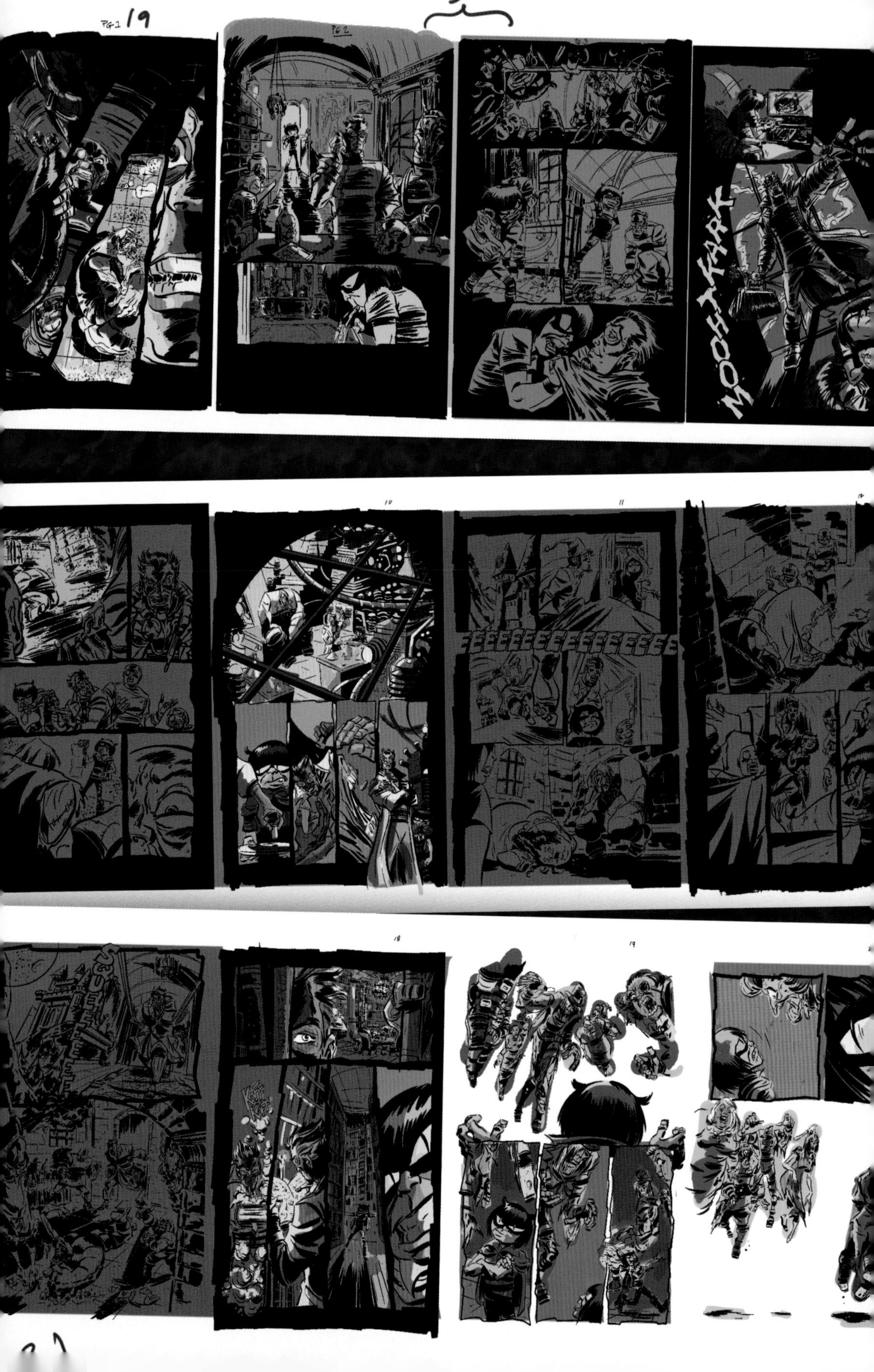

PG 1 19
3
PG 2
10
11
EEEEEEEEEEEEEEEE
18
19

4 (PG 116 ??)

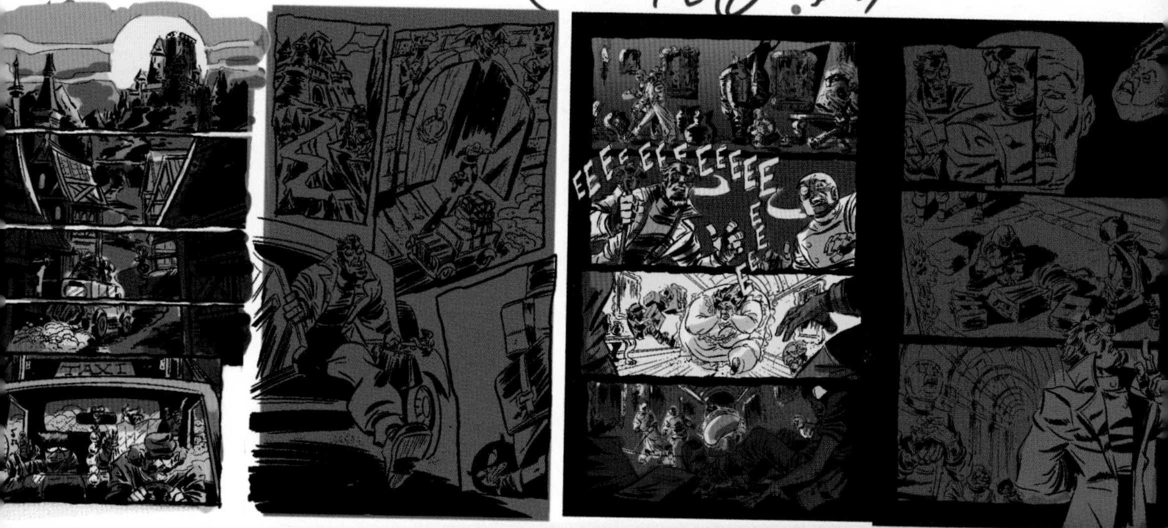
TAXI
EEEEEEEEEEEE

13 14 15 16

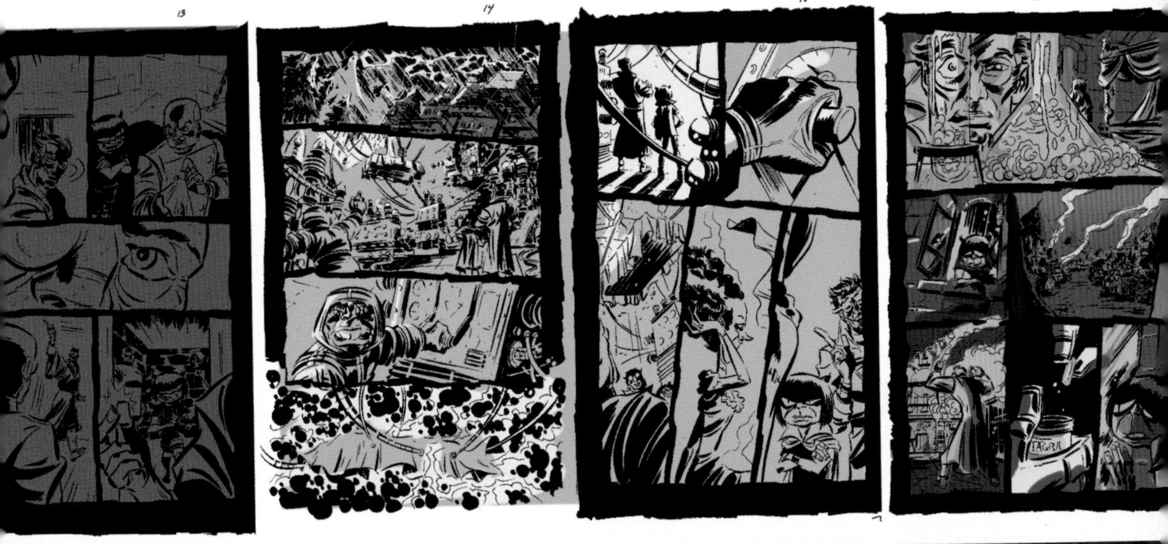

21 22 23 20 + 16 24

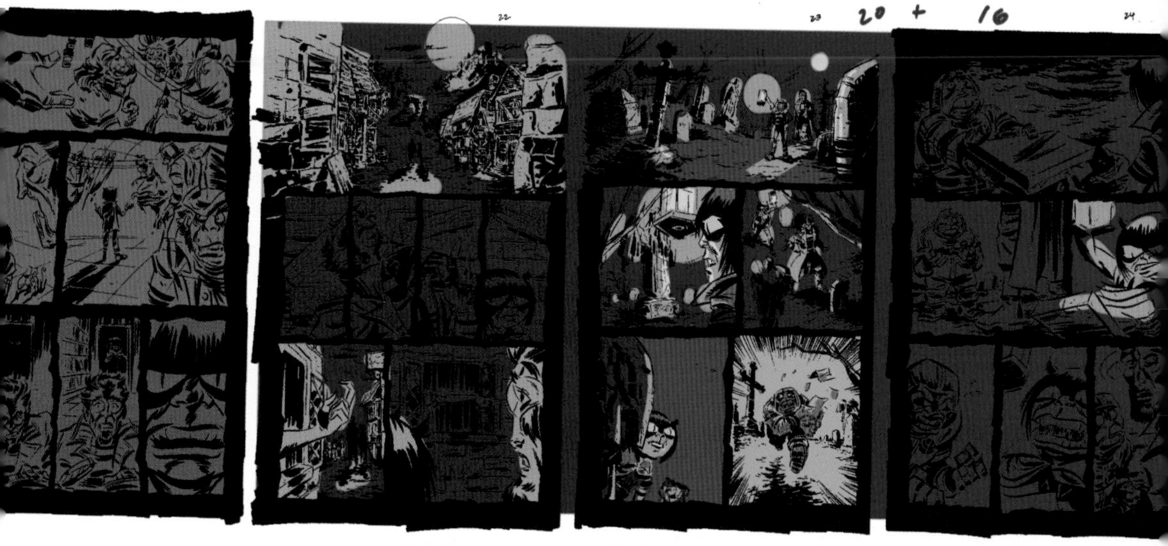

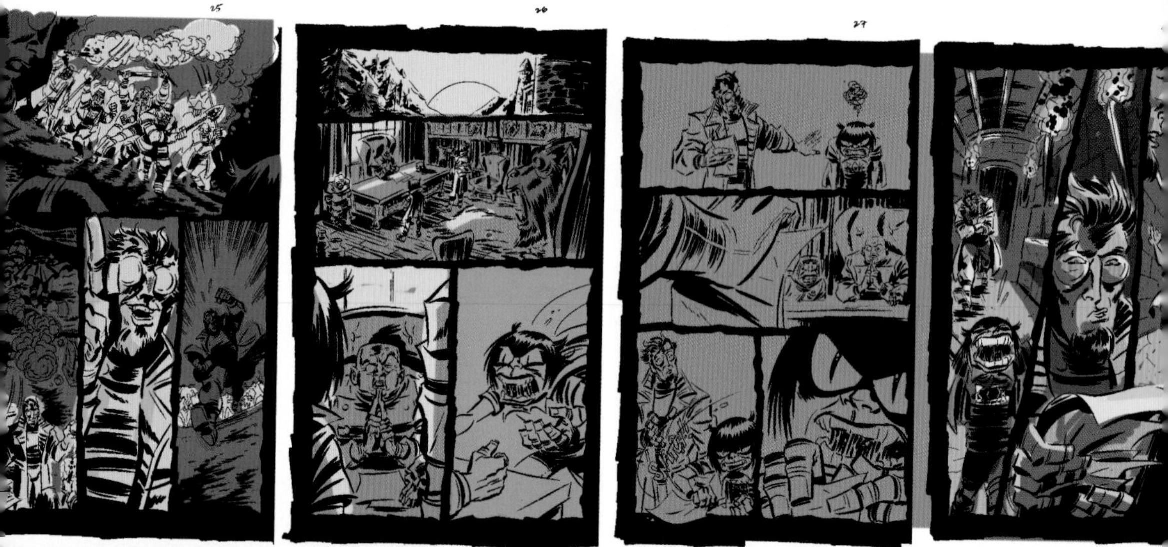

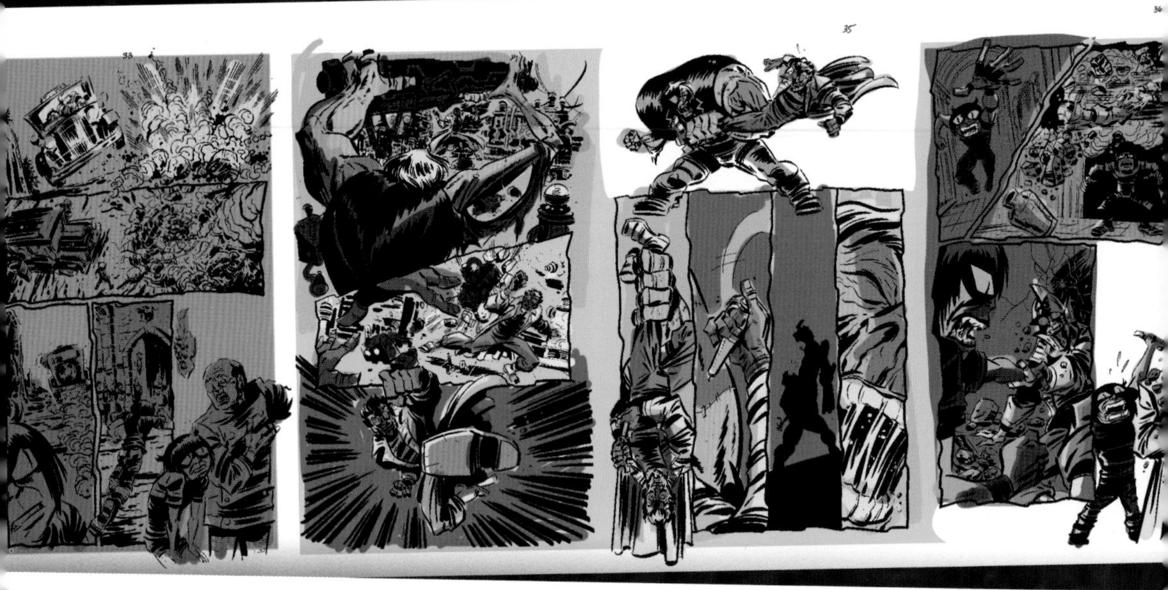

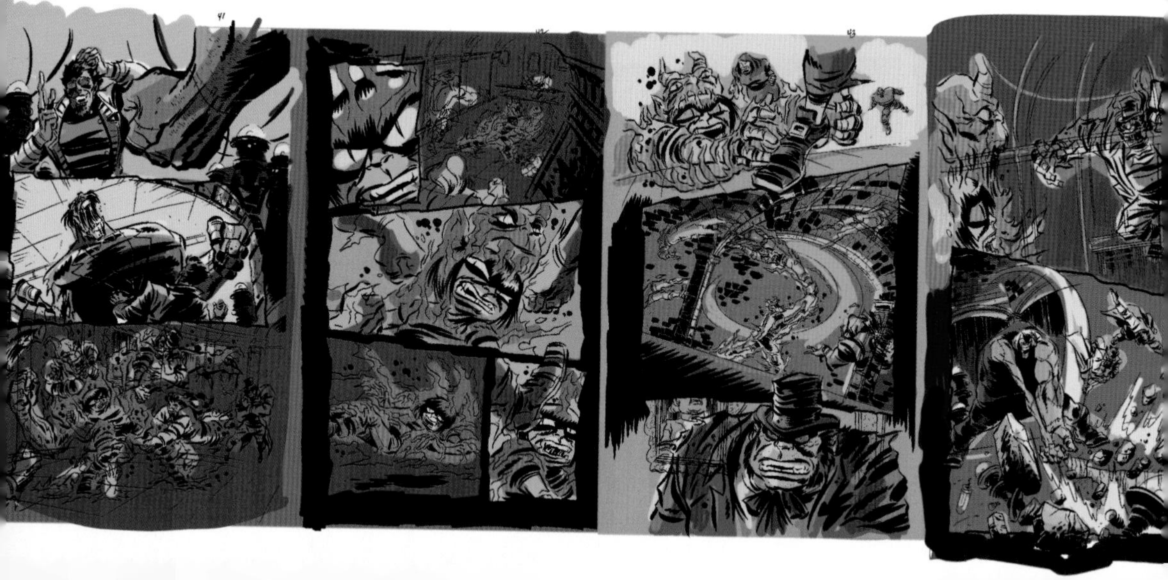

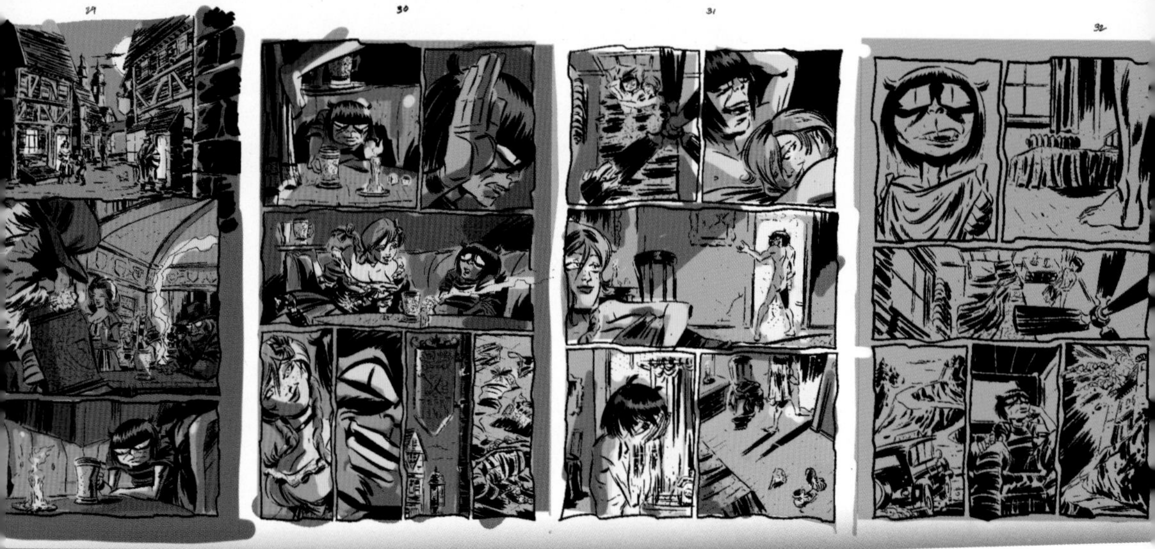

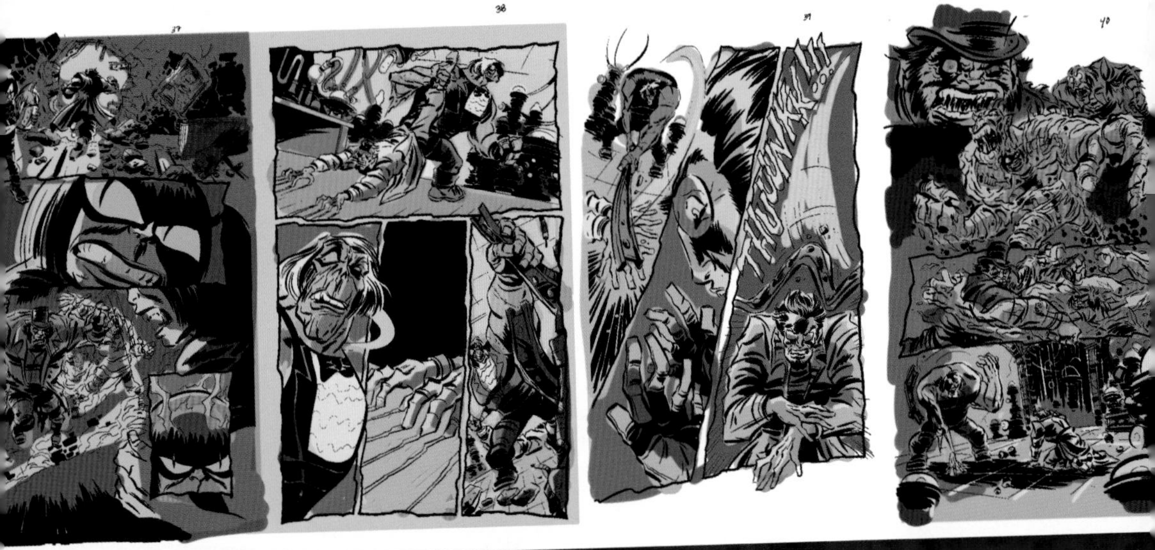

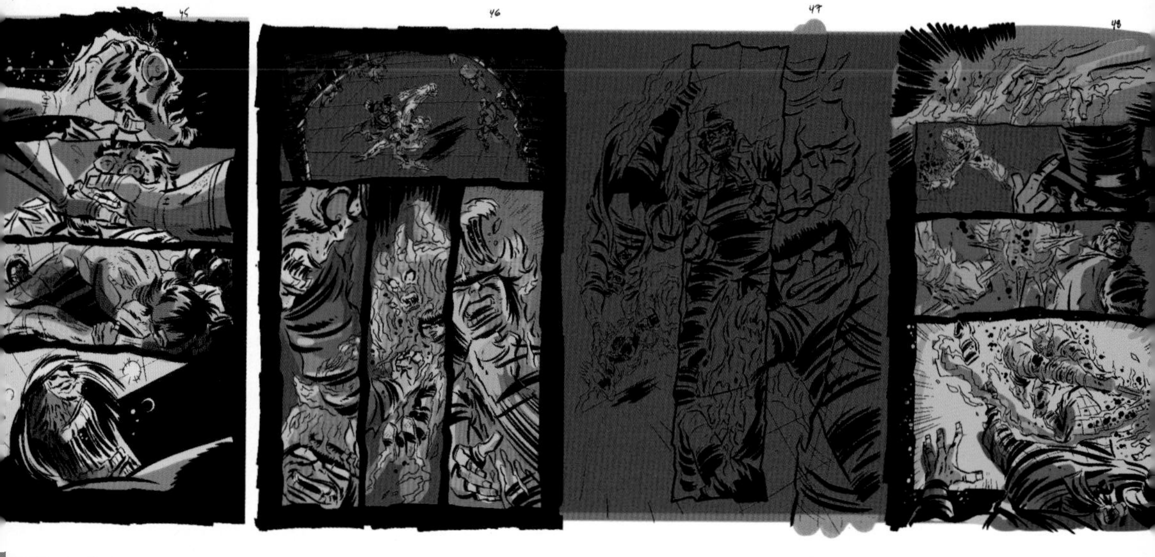

49

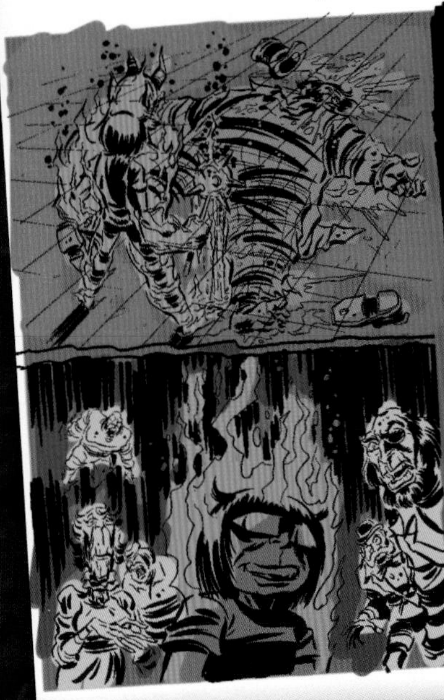

50

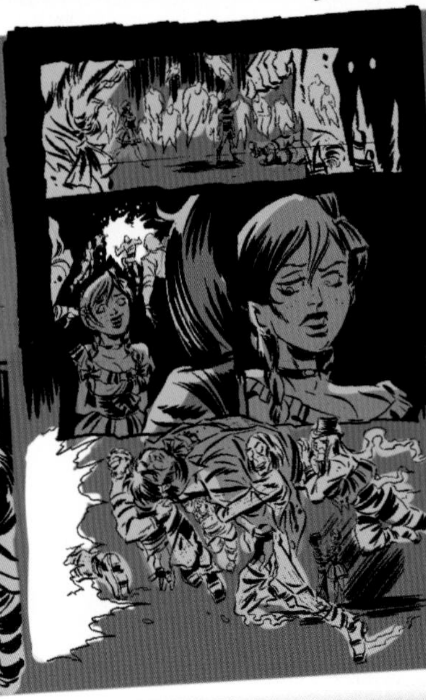

51

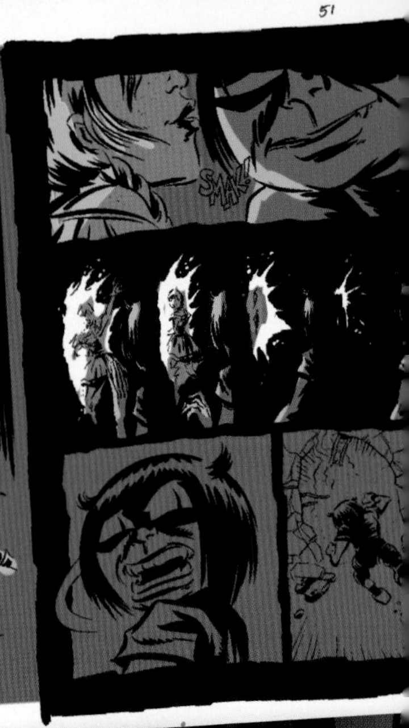

52

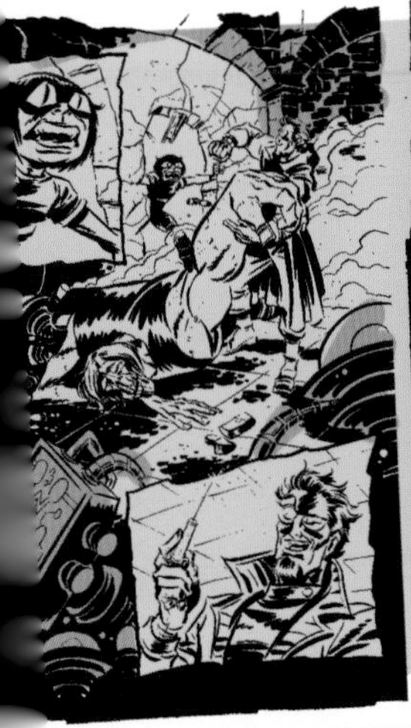

53

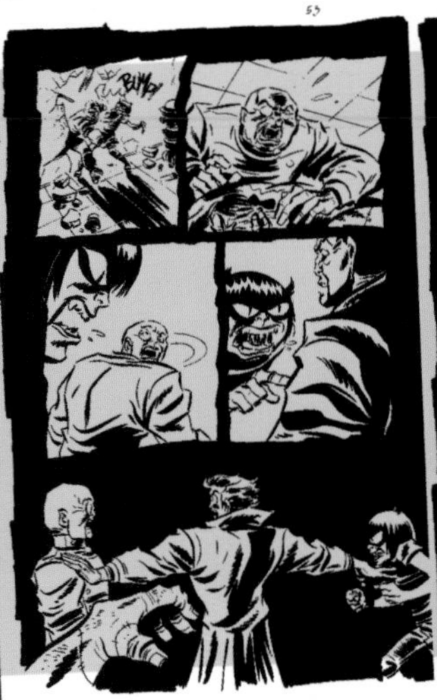

54

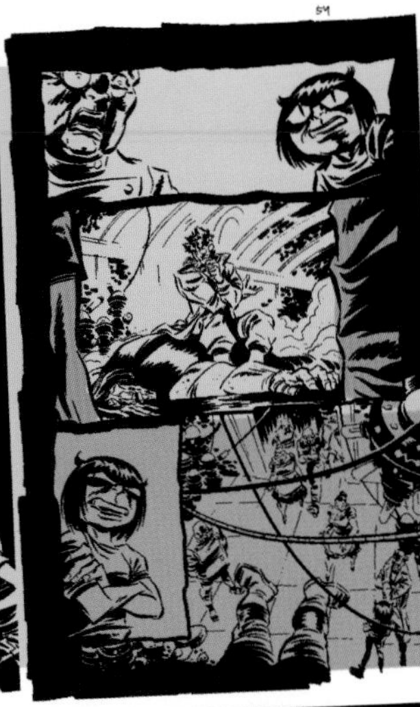

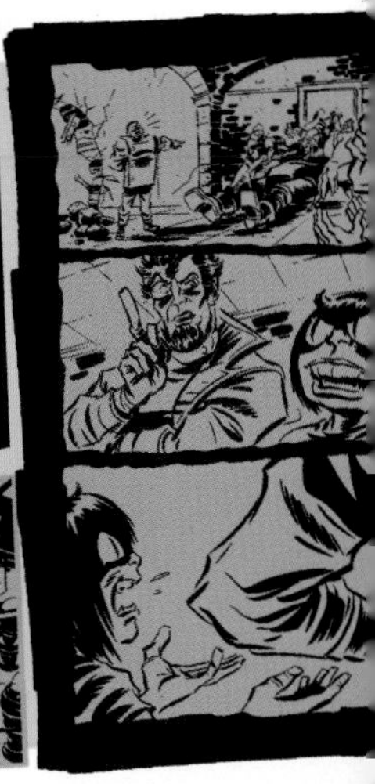

56

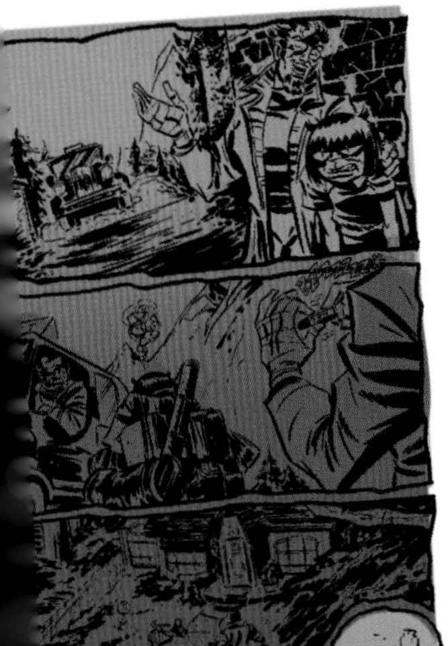

57

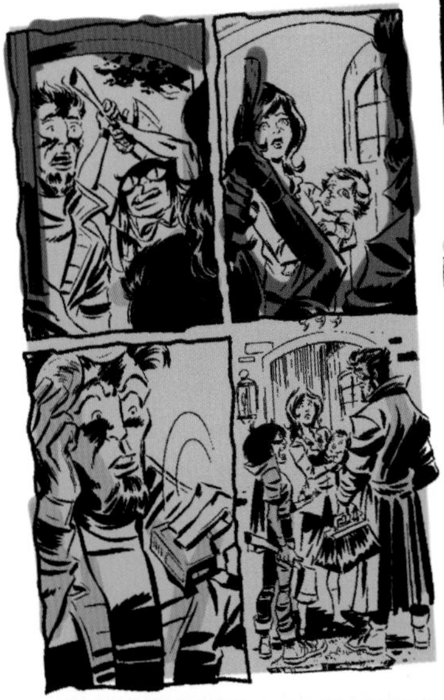

58

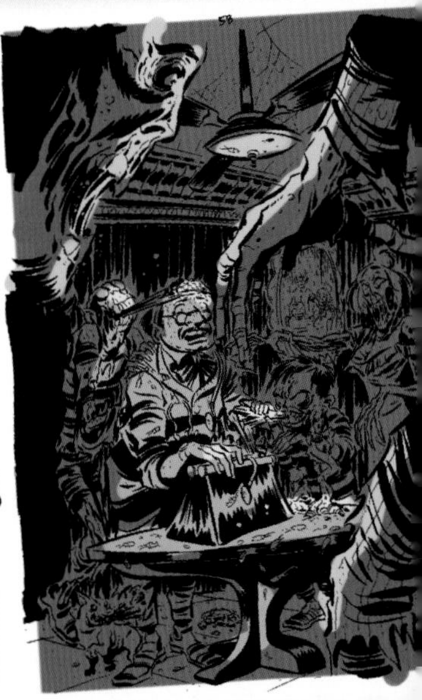

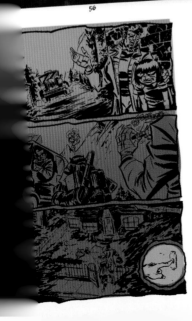

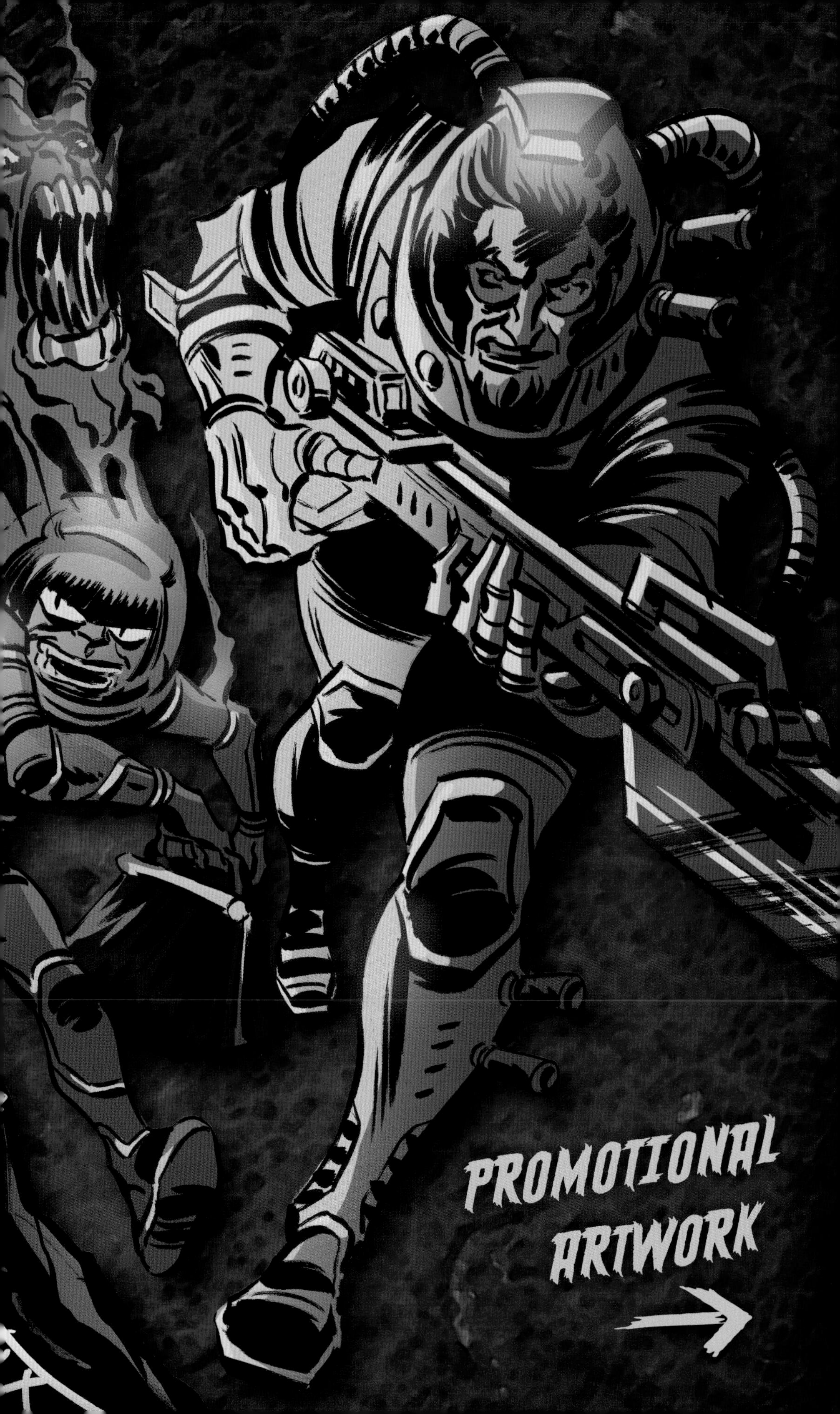
PROMOTIONAL
ARTWORK

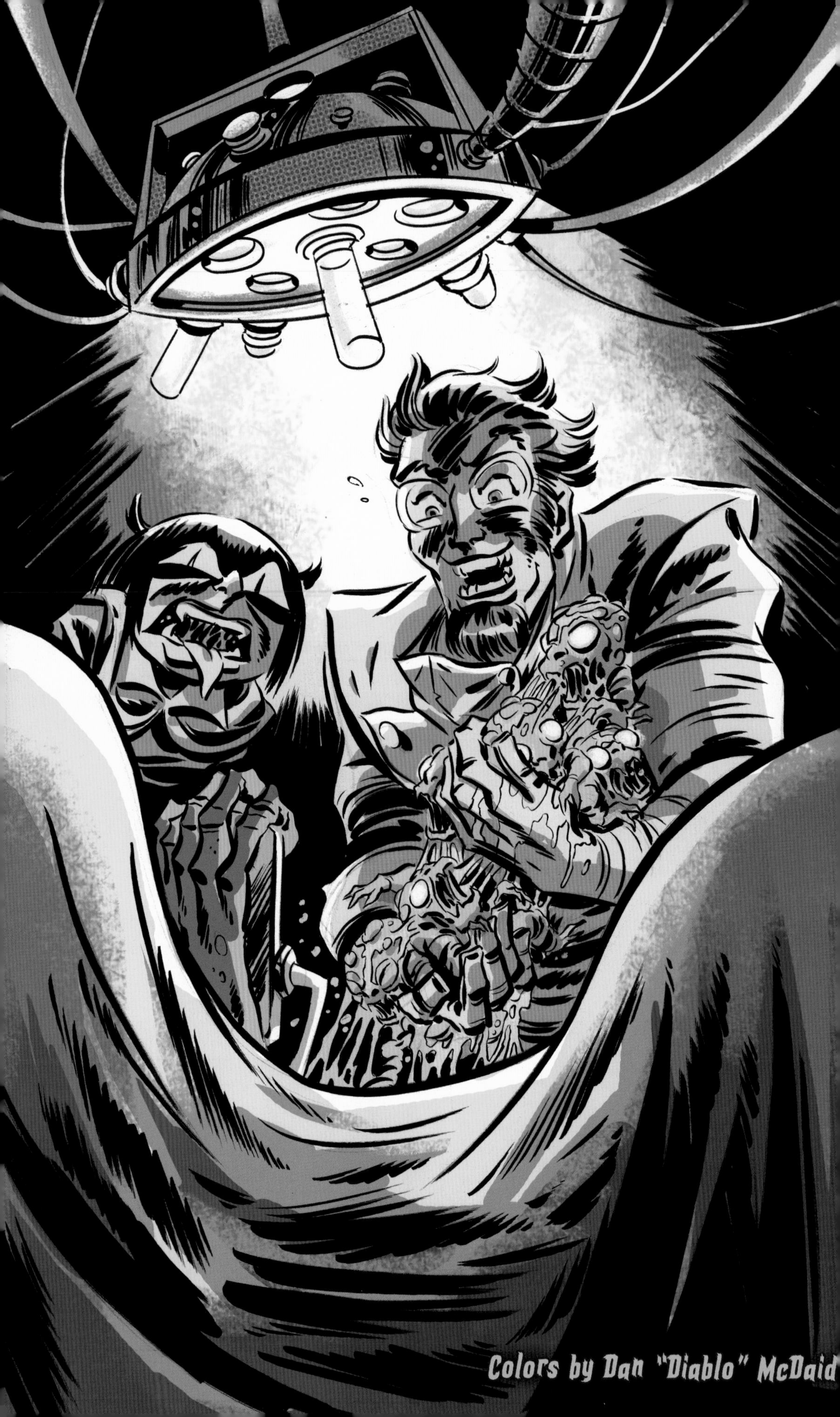
Colors by Dan "Diablo" McDaid

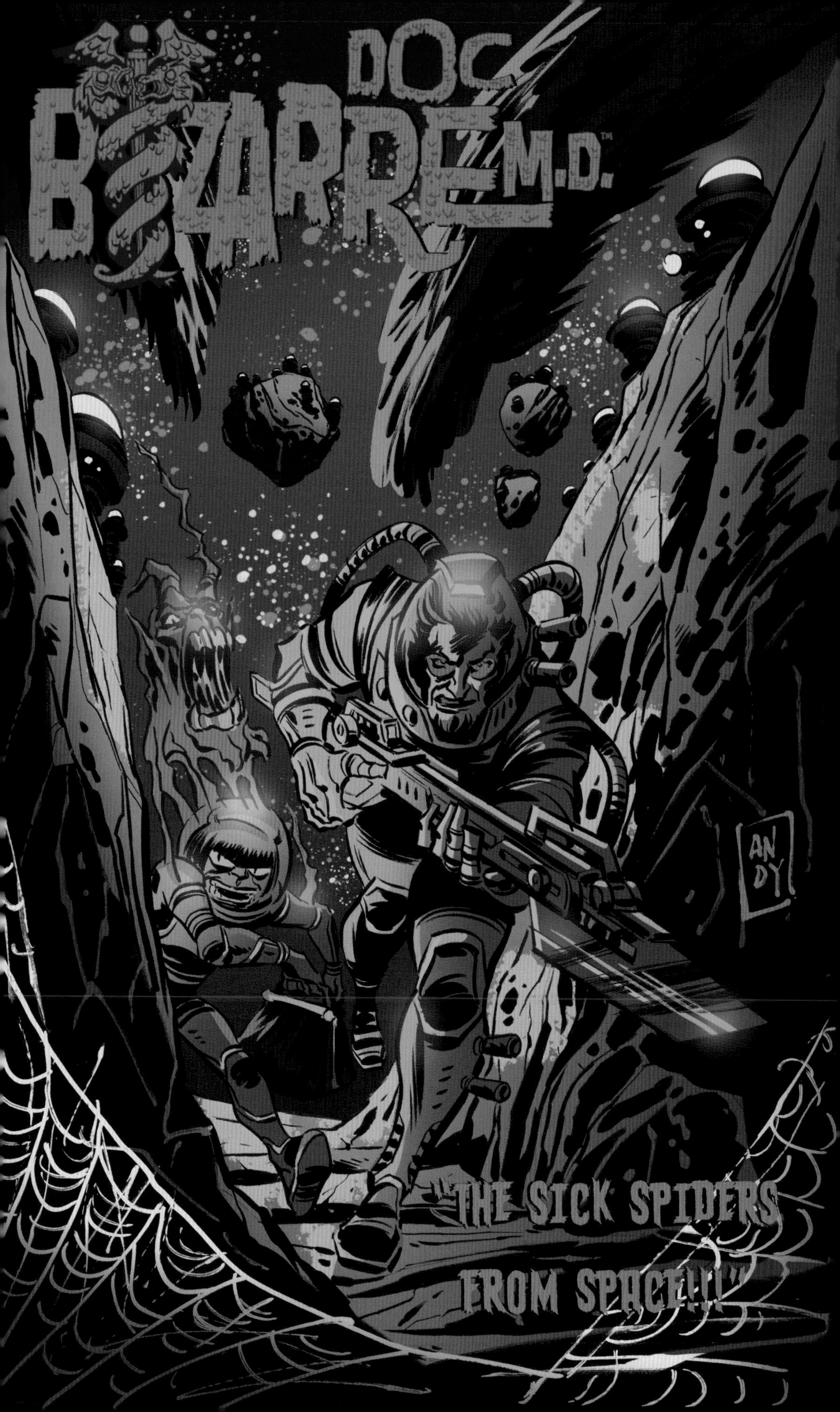
DOC BIZARRE M.D.™
ANDY
"THE SICK SPIDERS
FROM SPACE!!!"

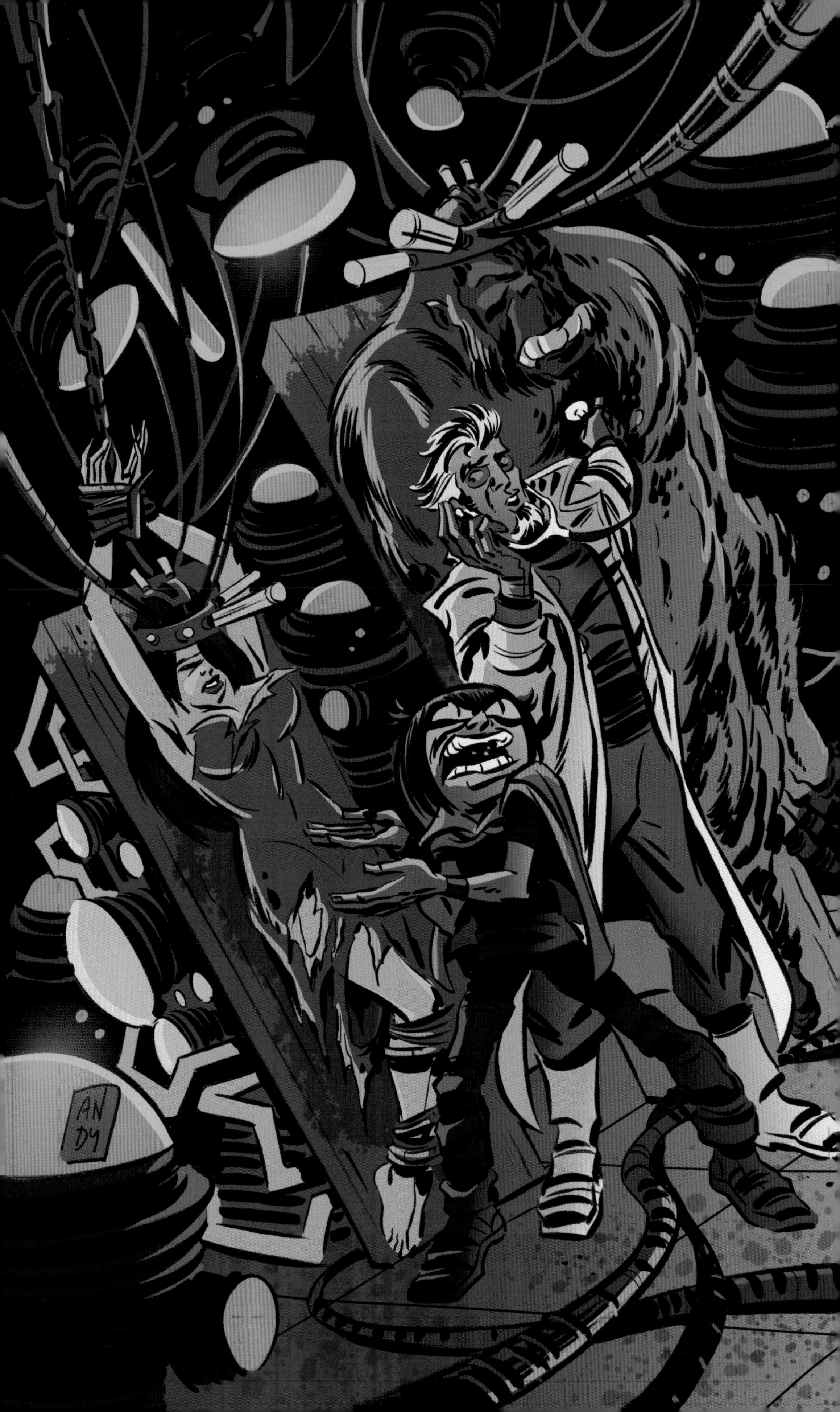
AN
DY

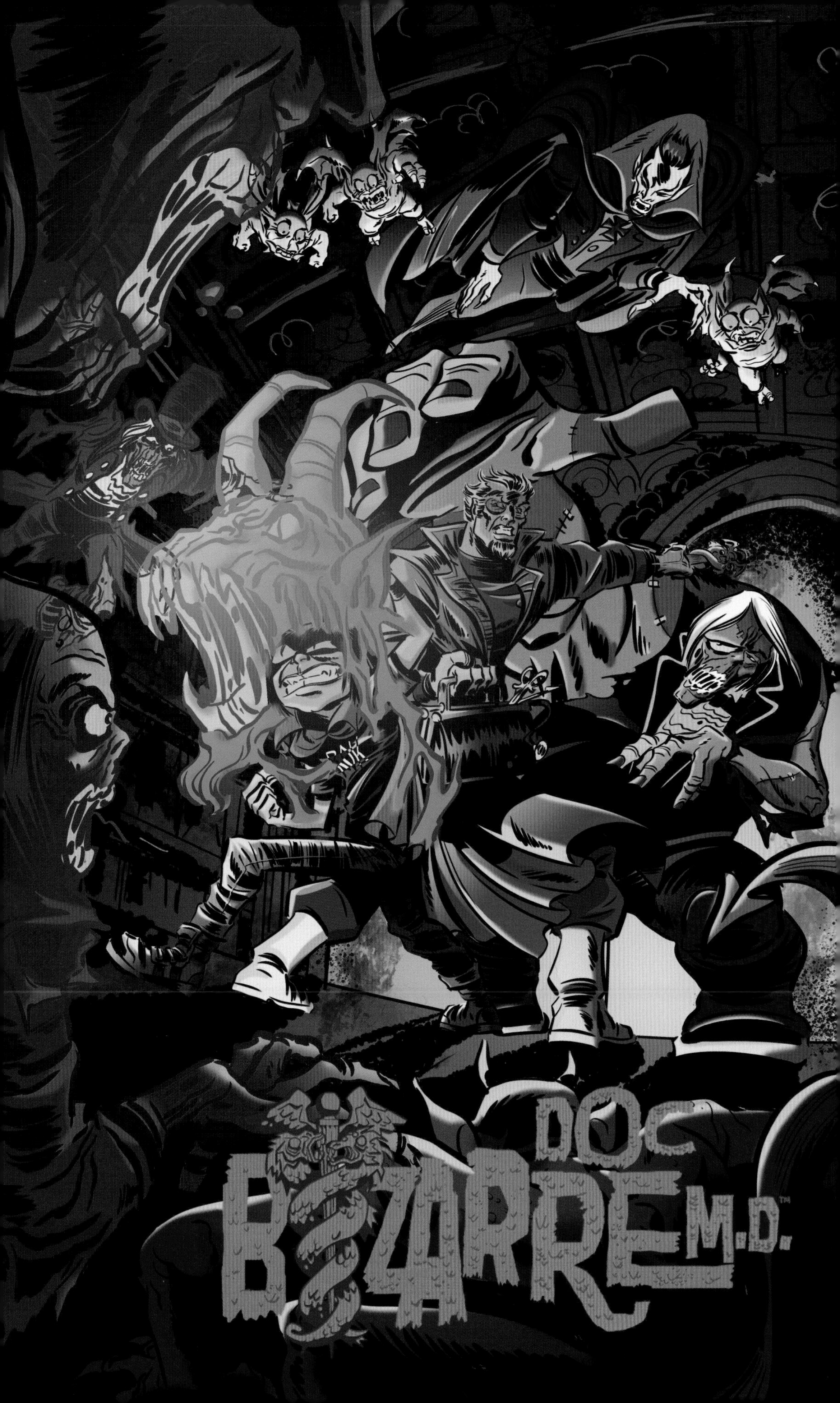
DOC
BIZARRE M.D.™

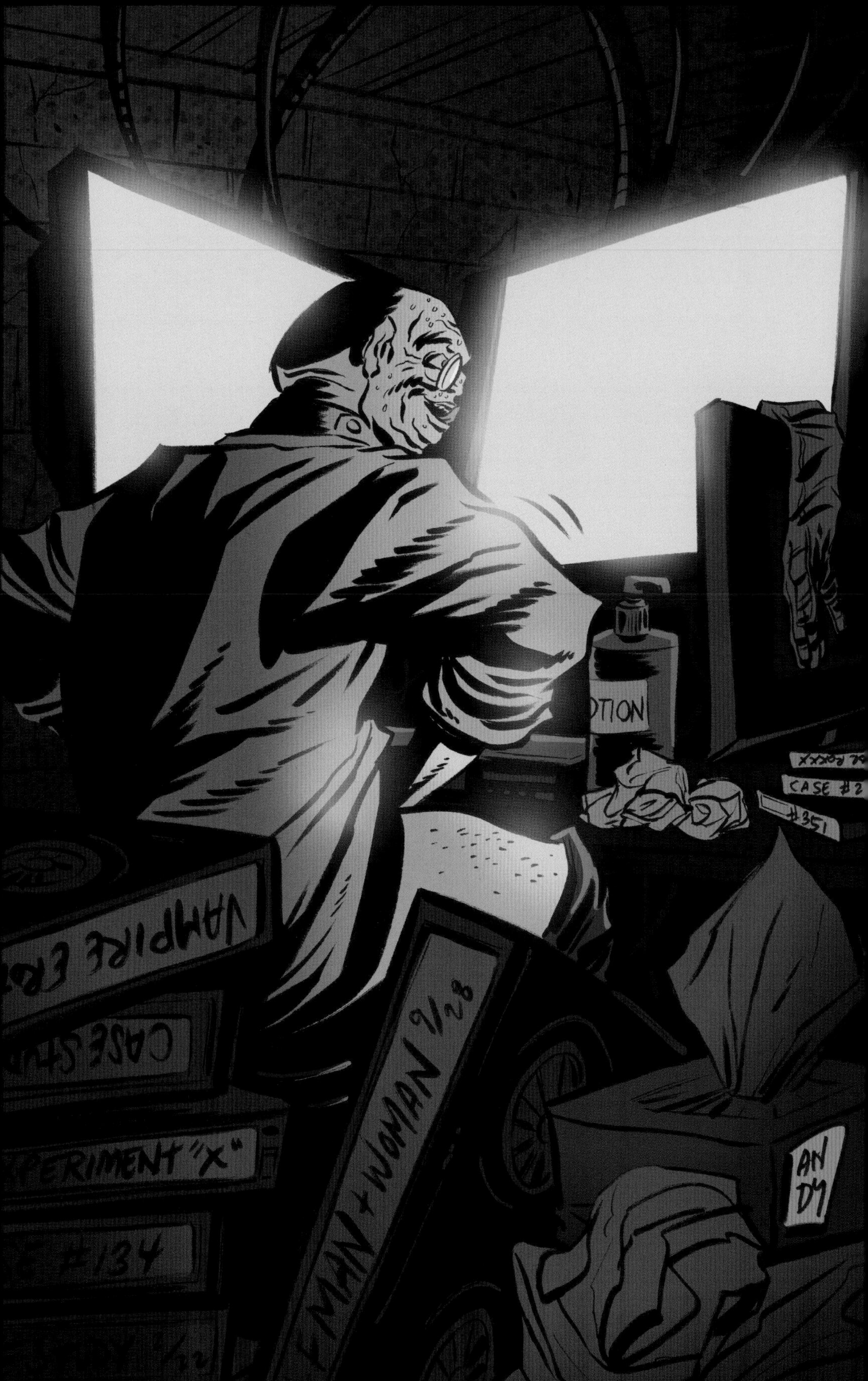
OTION
CASE #2
#351
VAMPIRE ER
CASE STU
PERIMENT "X"
#134
MAN + WOMAN 9/28
AN
DY

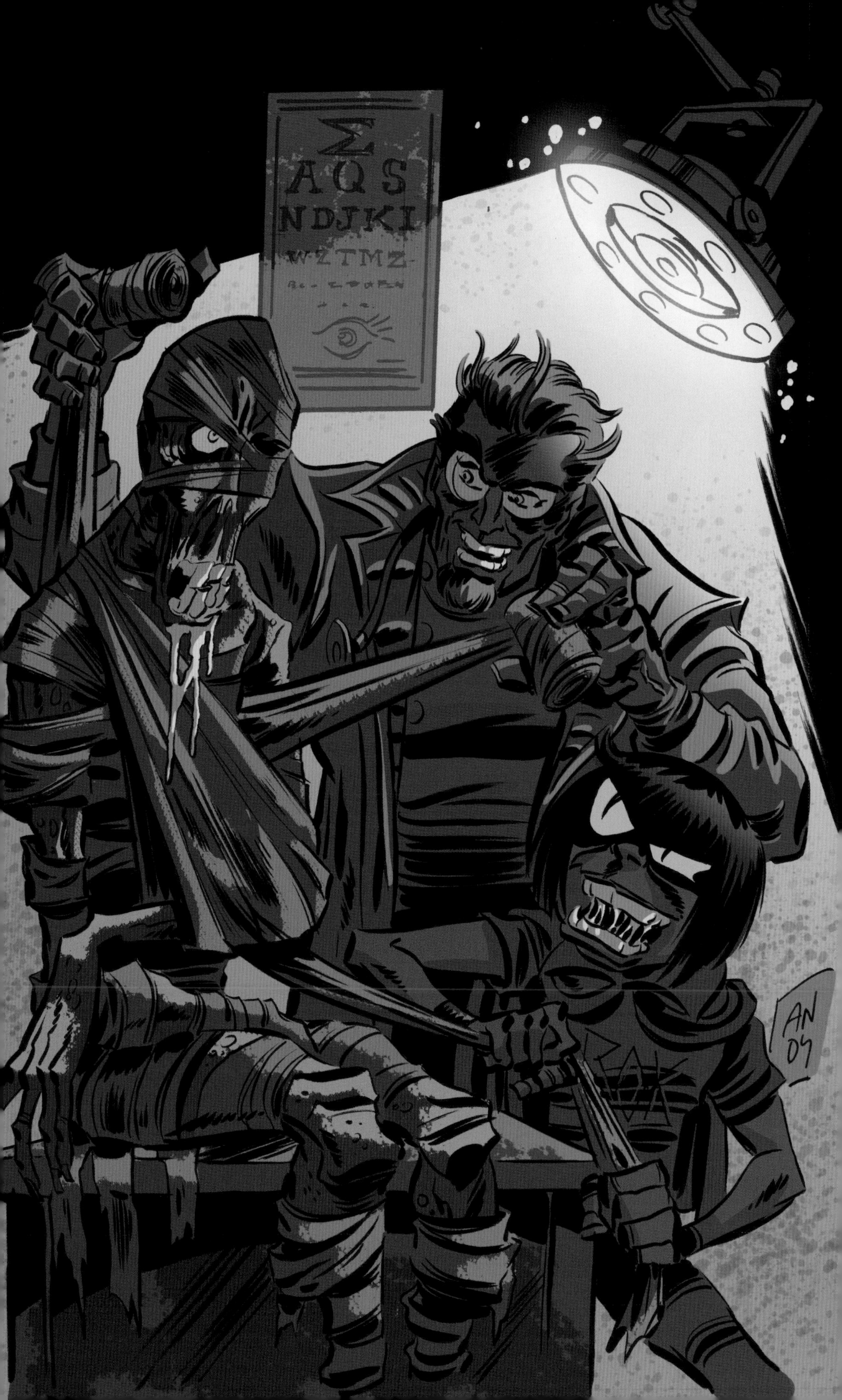
Σ
AQS
NDJKI
WZTMZ

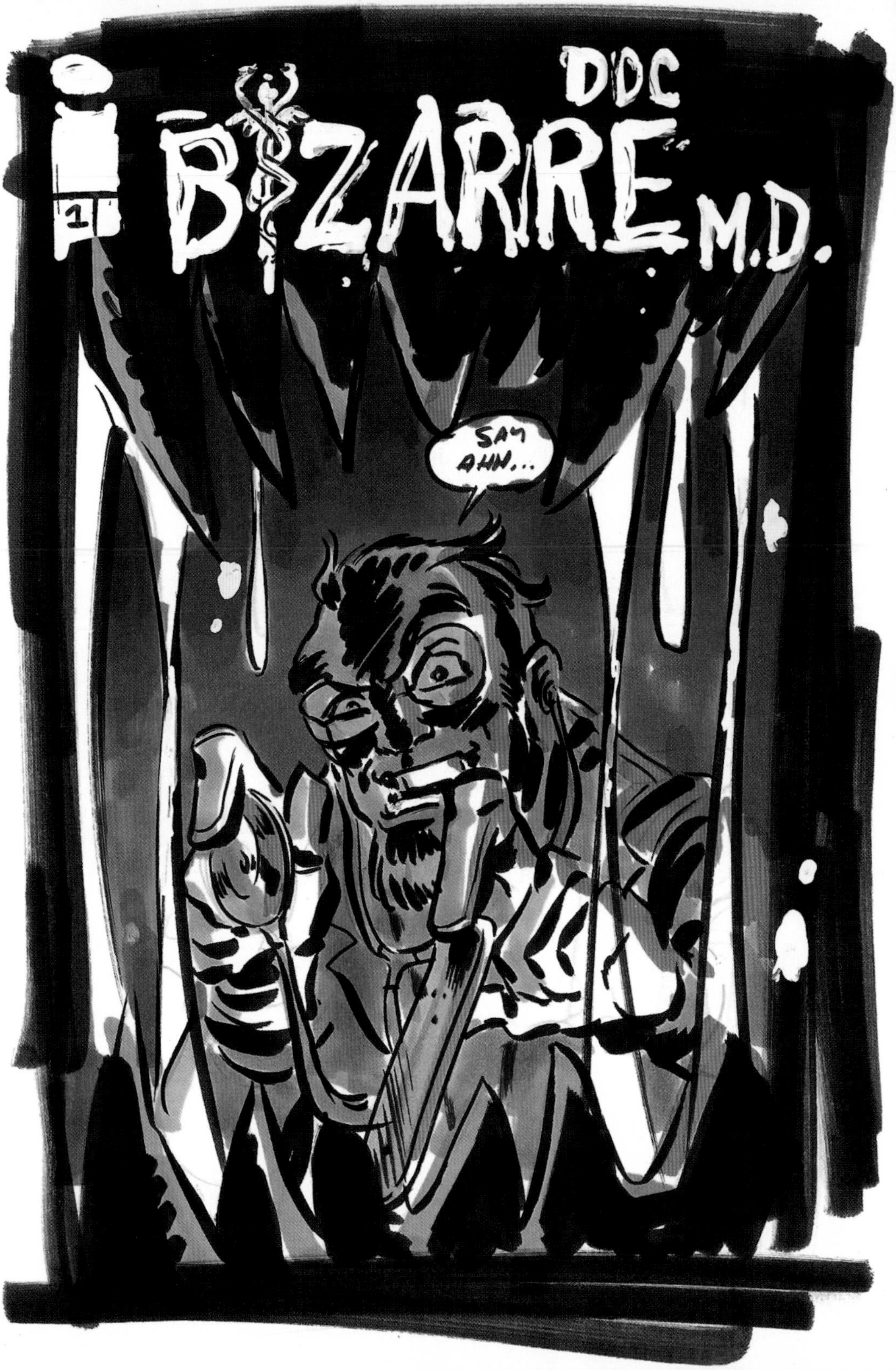
1
DOC
BIZARRE M.D.
SAM AHN...

A MACABRE MEDICAL MYSTERY
FROM THE TWISTED MINDS OF

JOE CASEY & ANDY SURIANO...

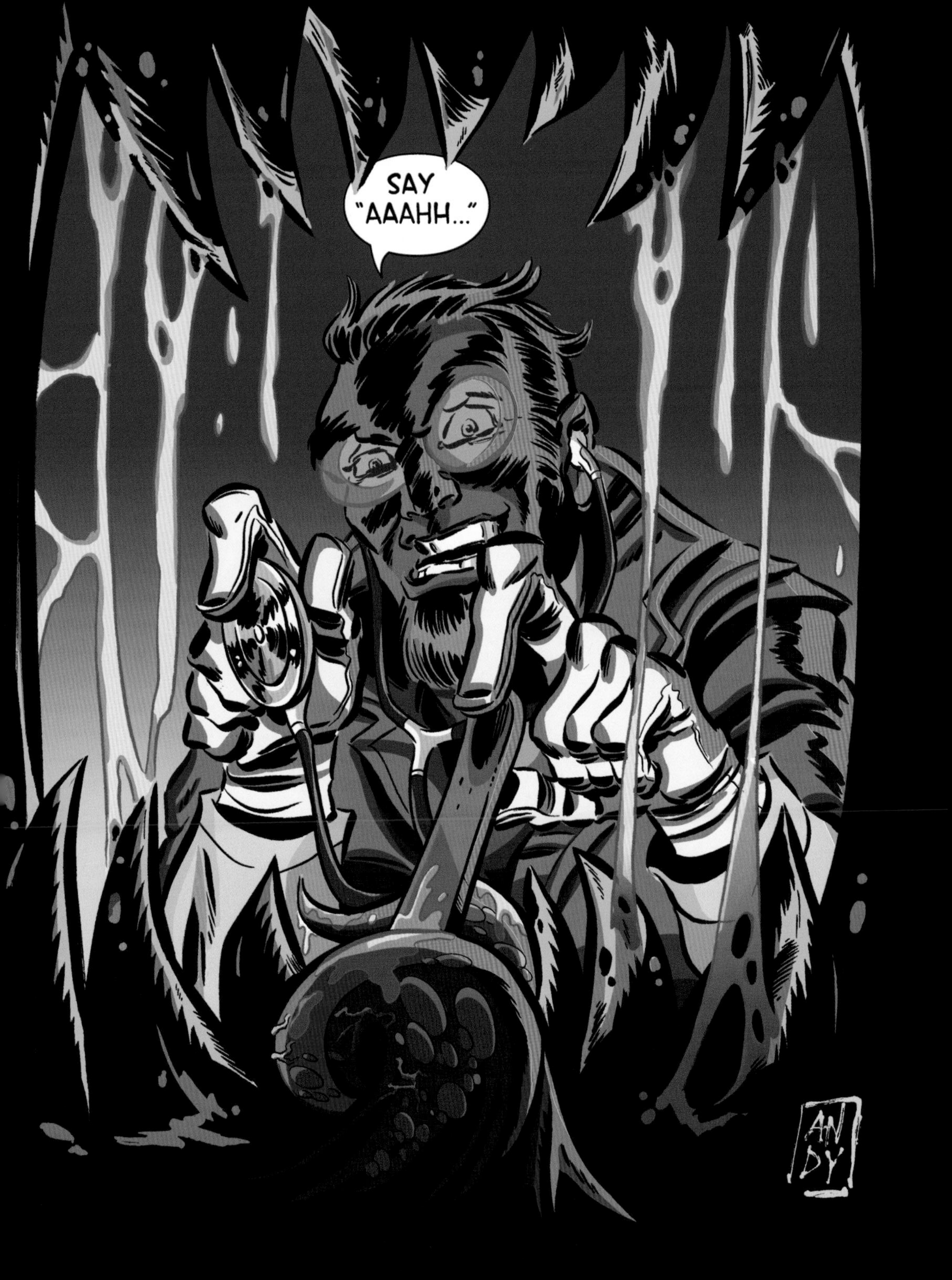
SAY "AAAHH..."
ANDY

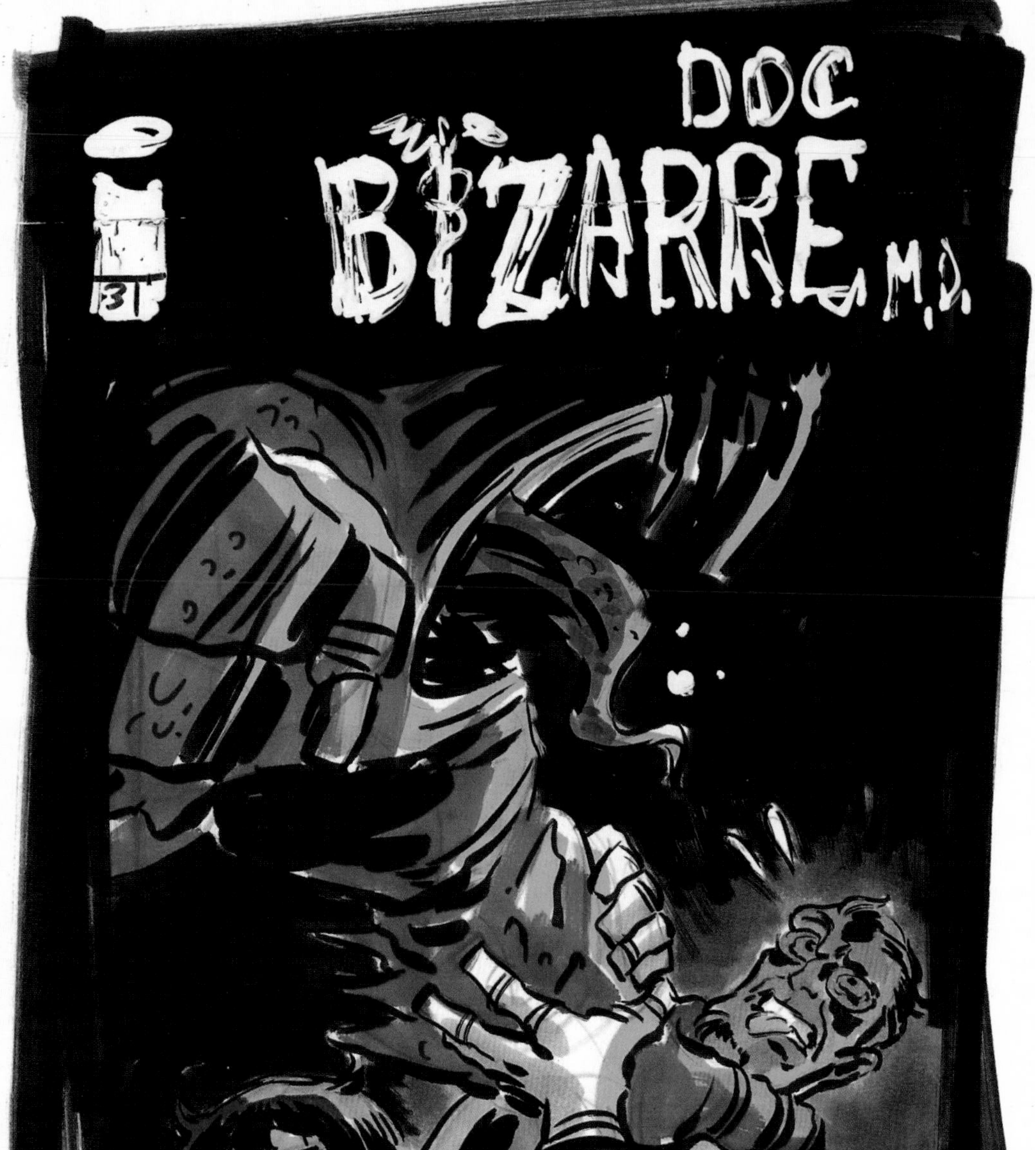
DOC
BIZARRE M.D.
3

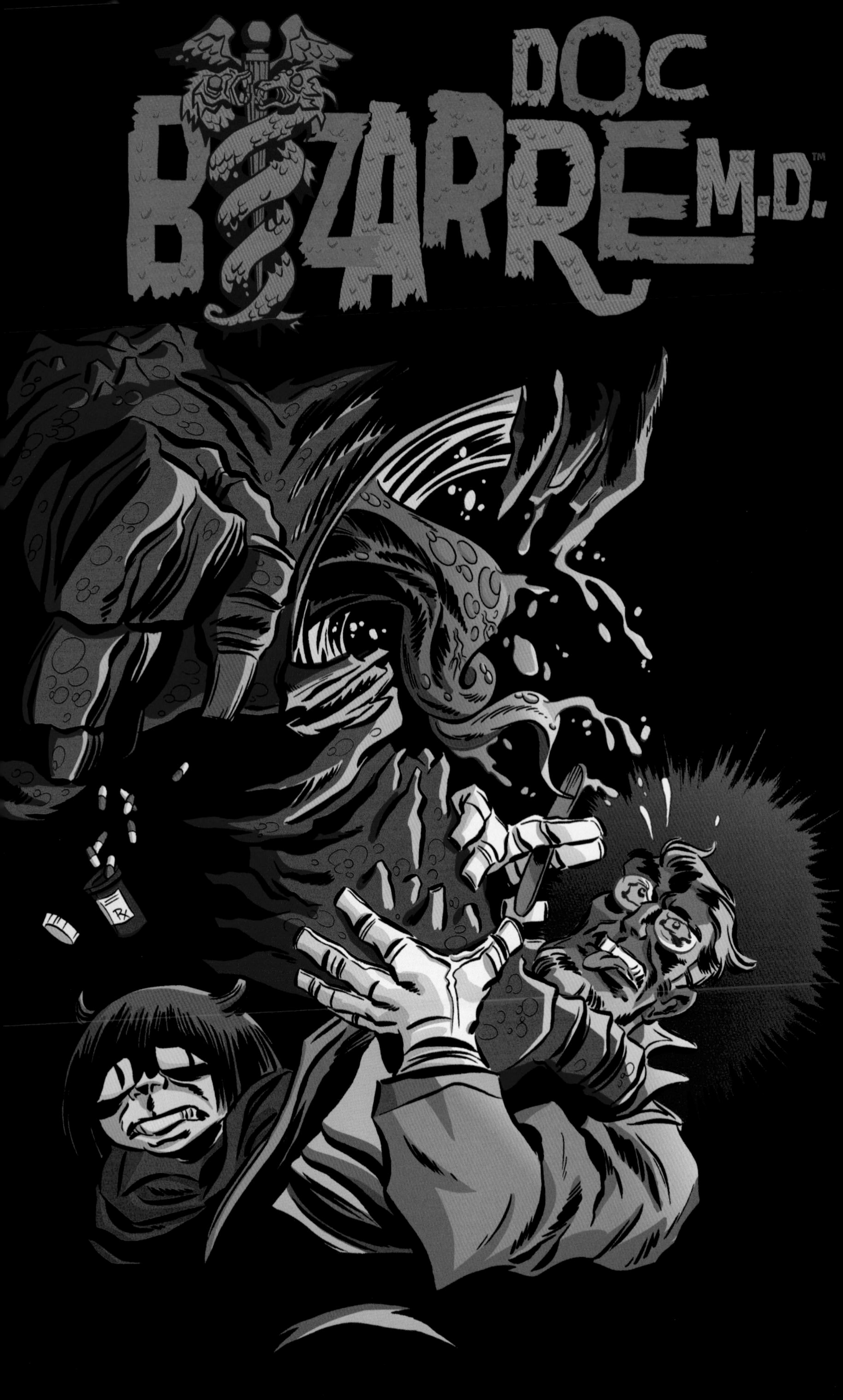
DOC
BIZARRE M.D.™
Rx

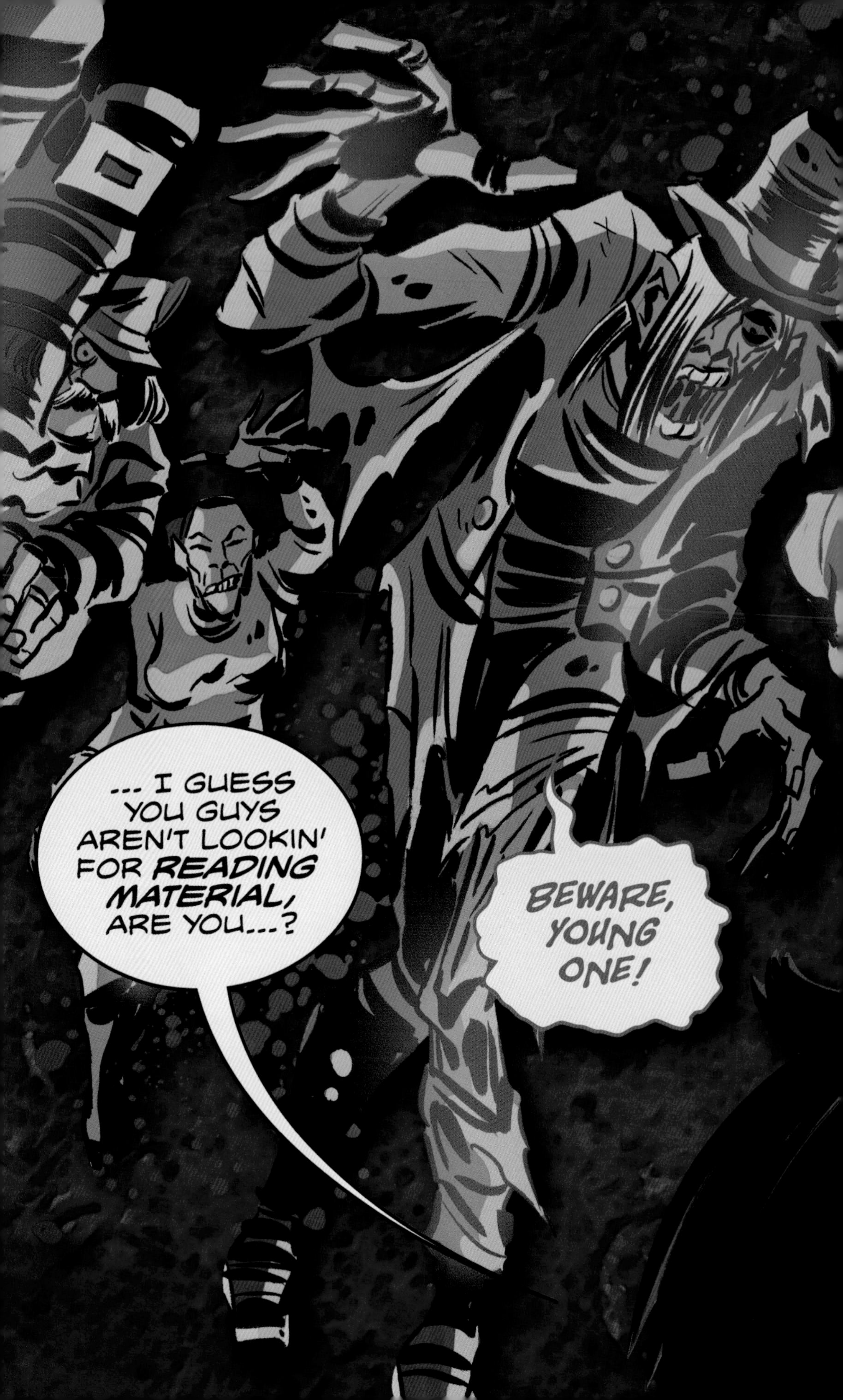
... I GUESS YOU GUYS AREN'T LOOKIN' FOR *READING MATERIAL*, ARE YOU...?
BEWARE, YOUNG ONE!

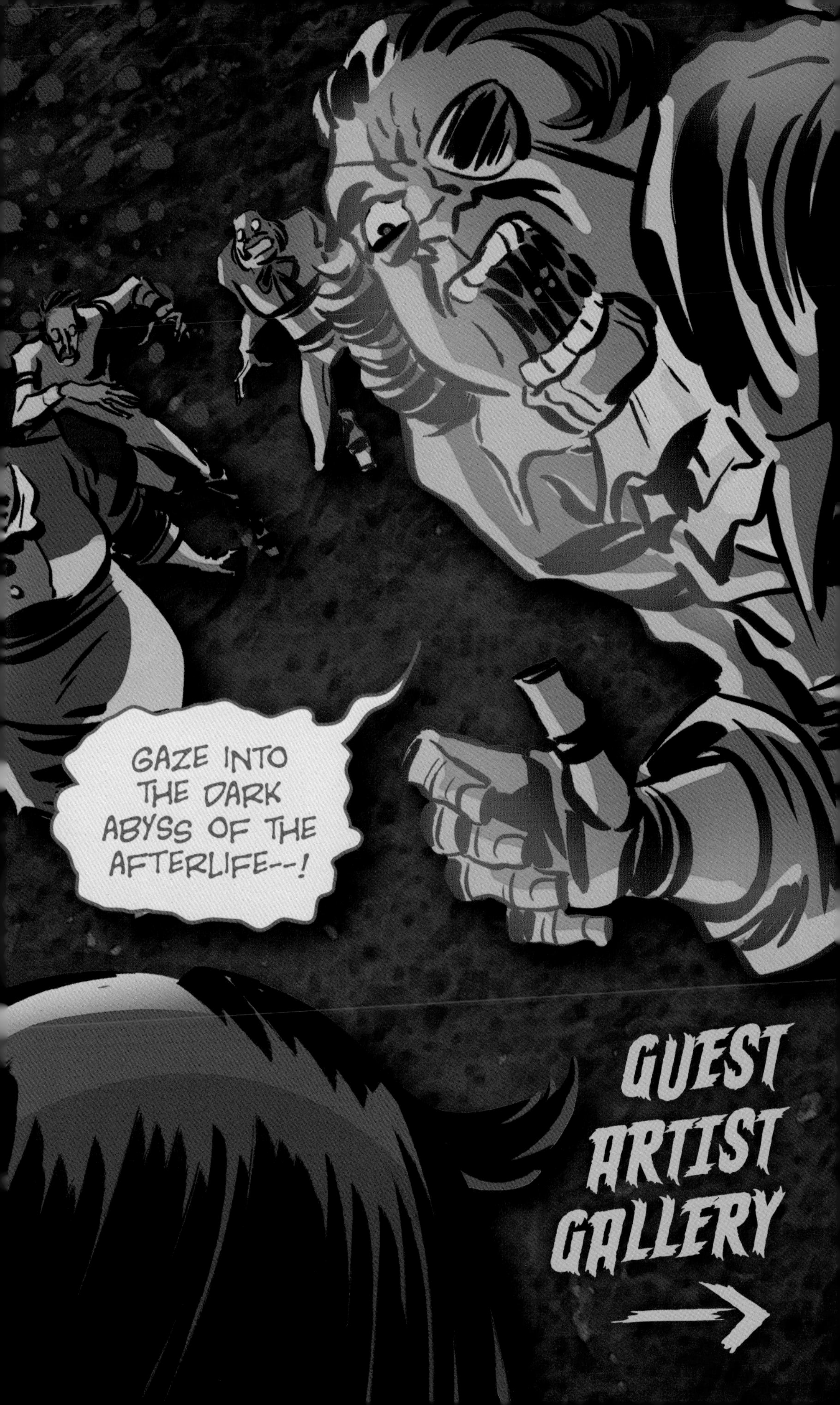
GAZE INTO THE DARK ABYSS OF THE AFTERLIFE--!
GUEST ARTIST GALLERY

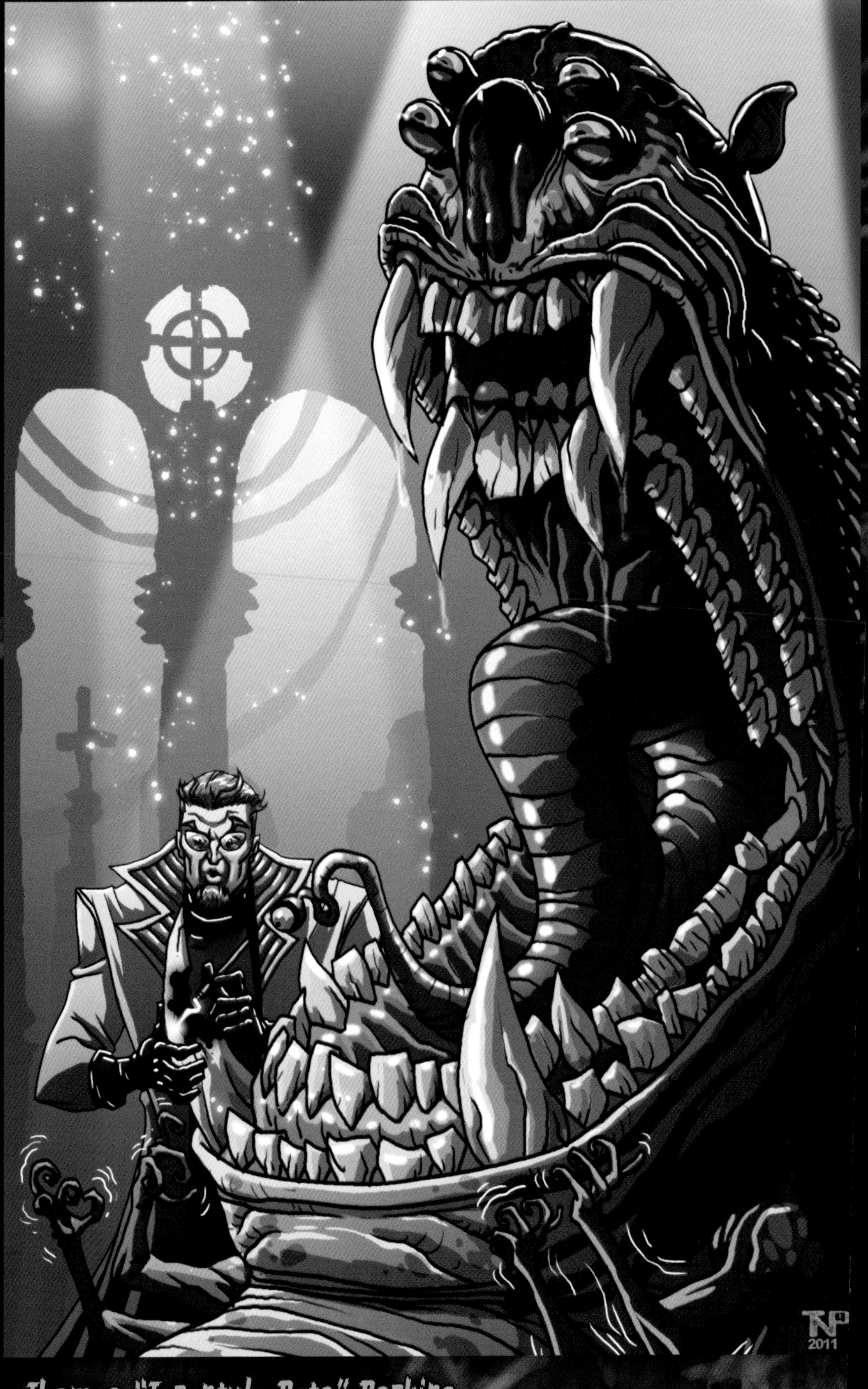
TNP
2011

Thomas "Tarantula Pate" Perkins

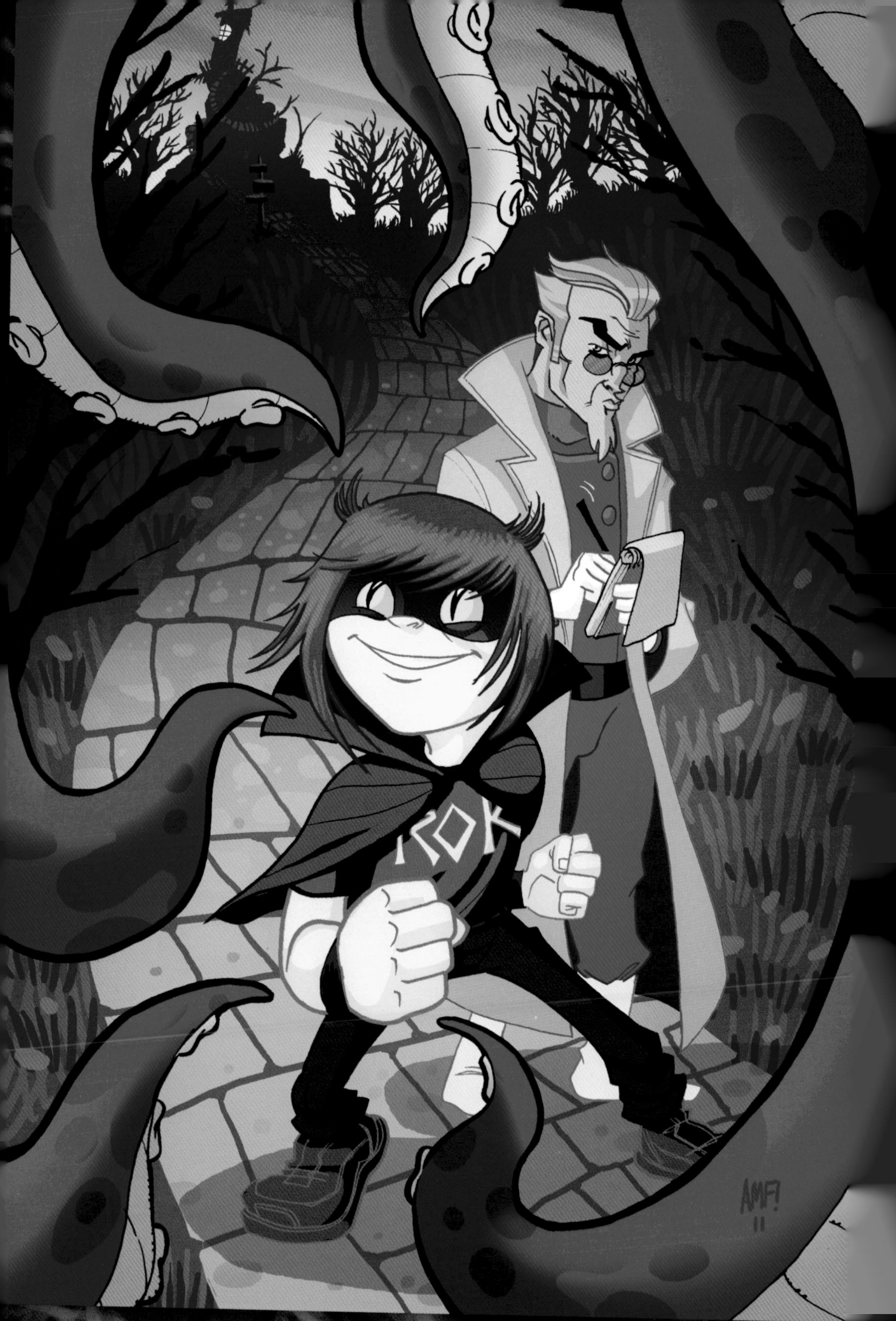

Tony "You Will Flee" Fleecs

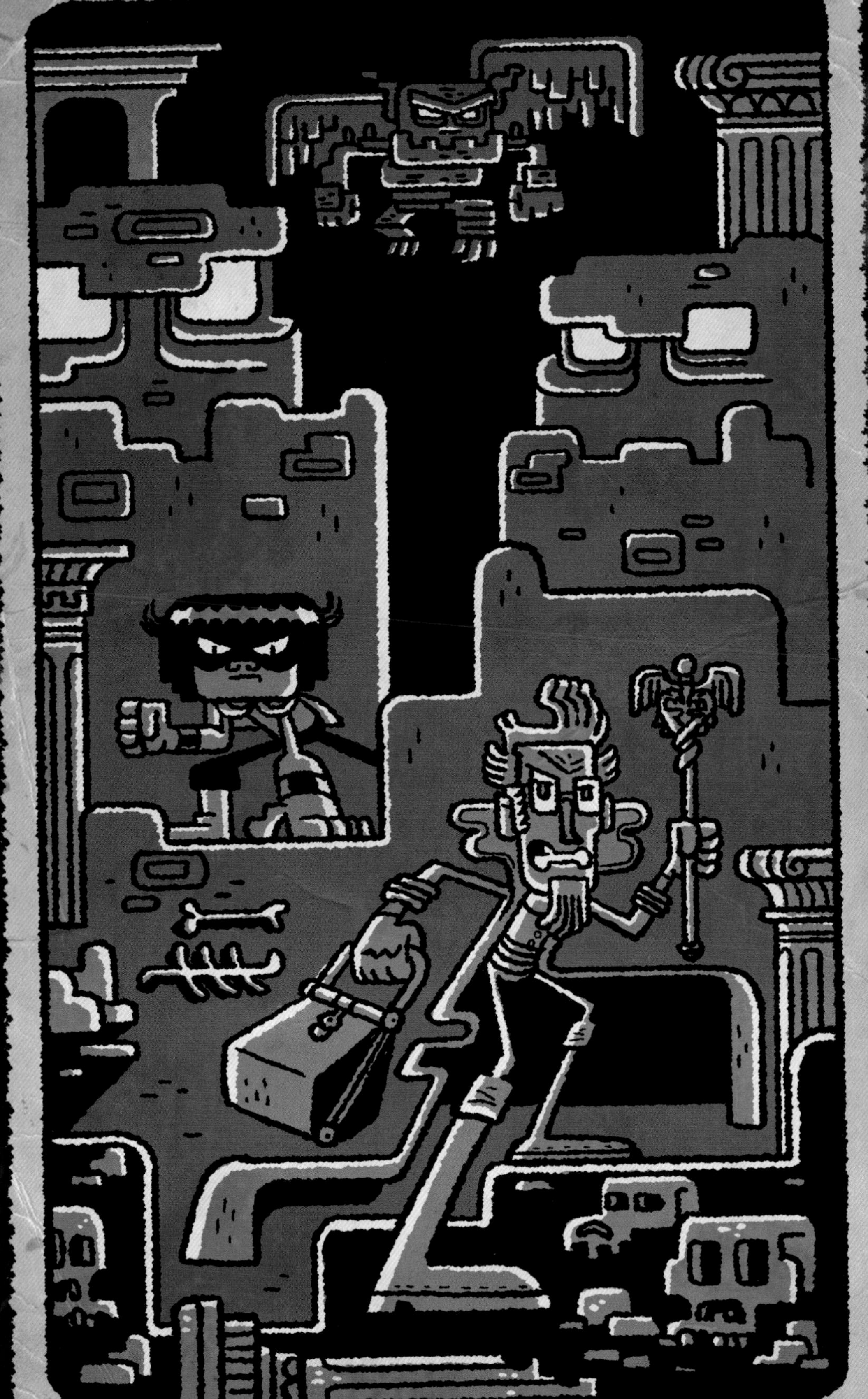

Bob "Witch's" Boyle

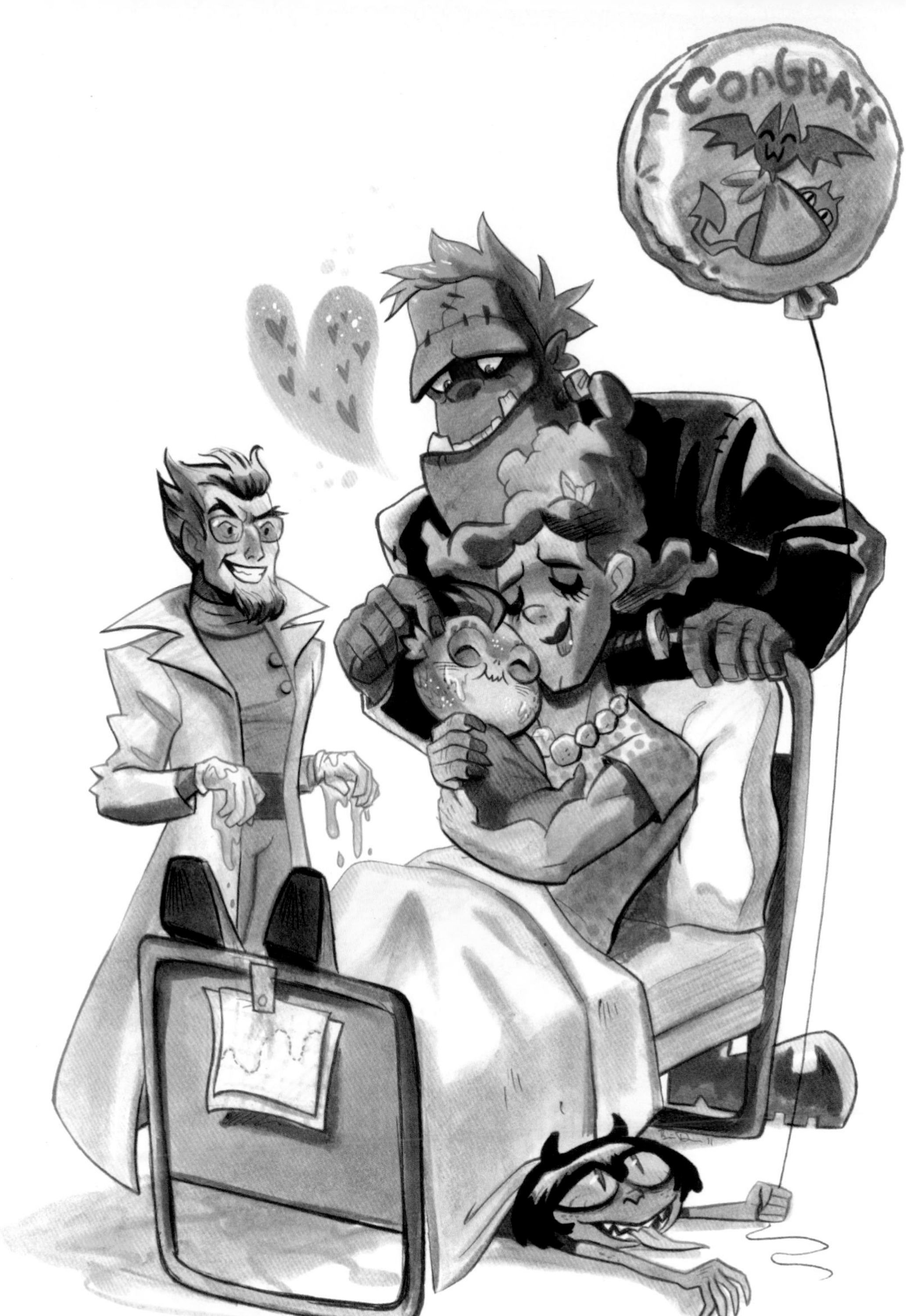
CONGRATS

Brianne "Drooling" Drouhard

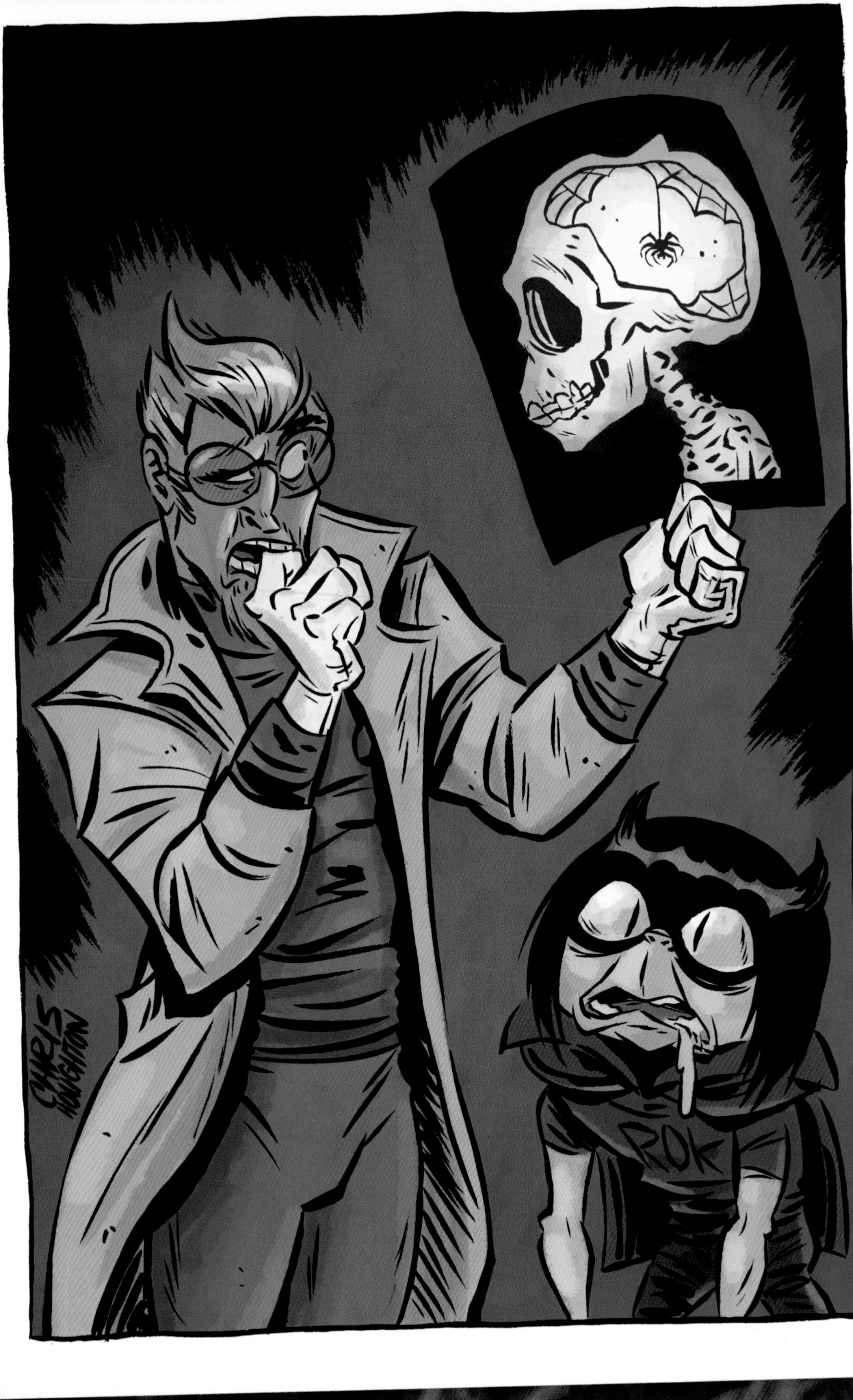
CHRIS HOUGHTON
ROK

"Howling" Chris Houghton

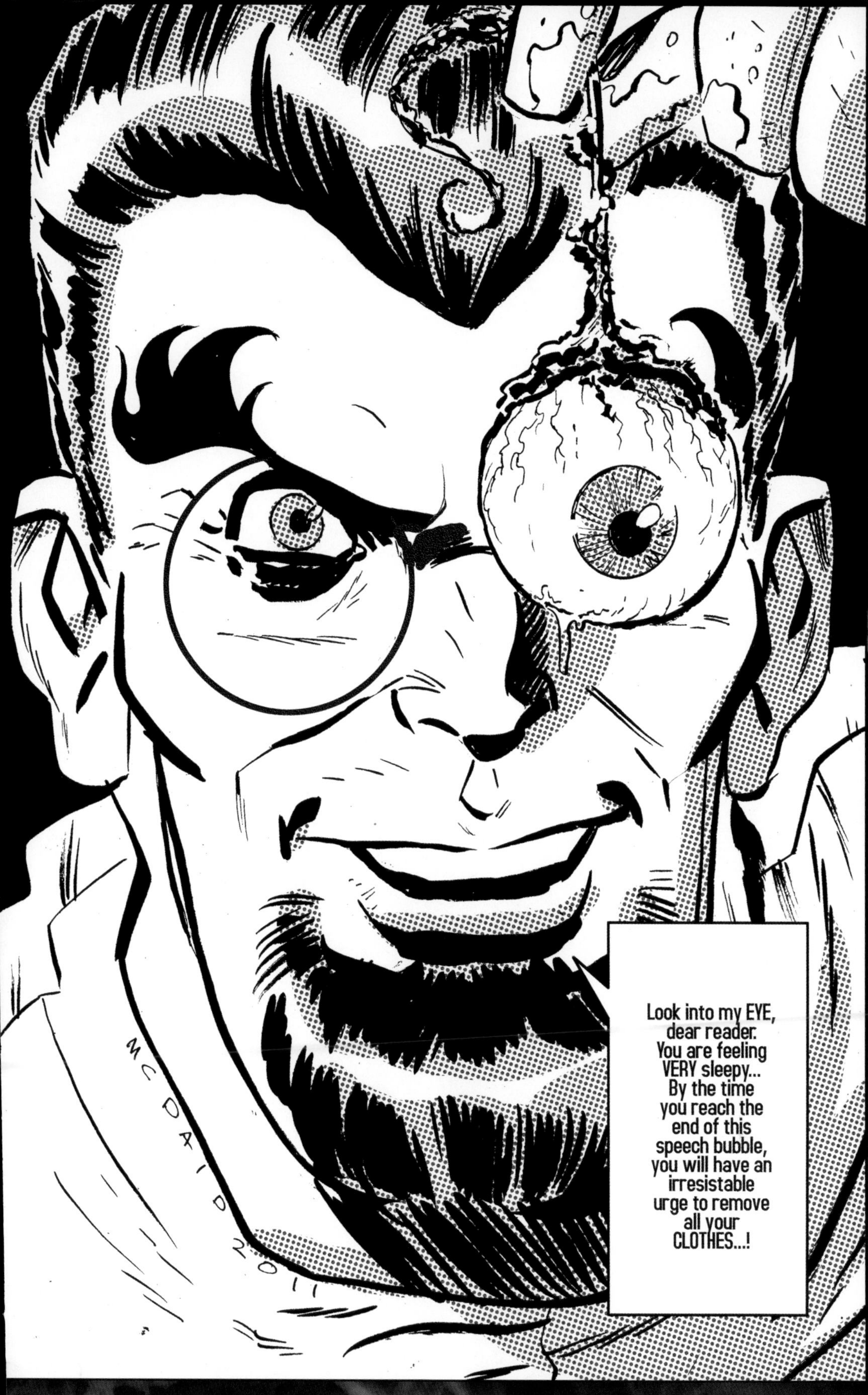
Look into my EYE, dear reader. You are feeling VERY sleepy... By the time you reach the end of this speech bubble, you will have an irresistable urge to remove all your CLOTHES...!
MCDAID 2011

Dan "McDead" McDaid

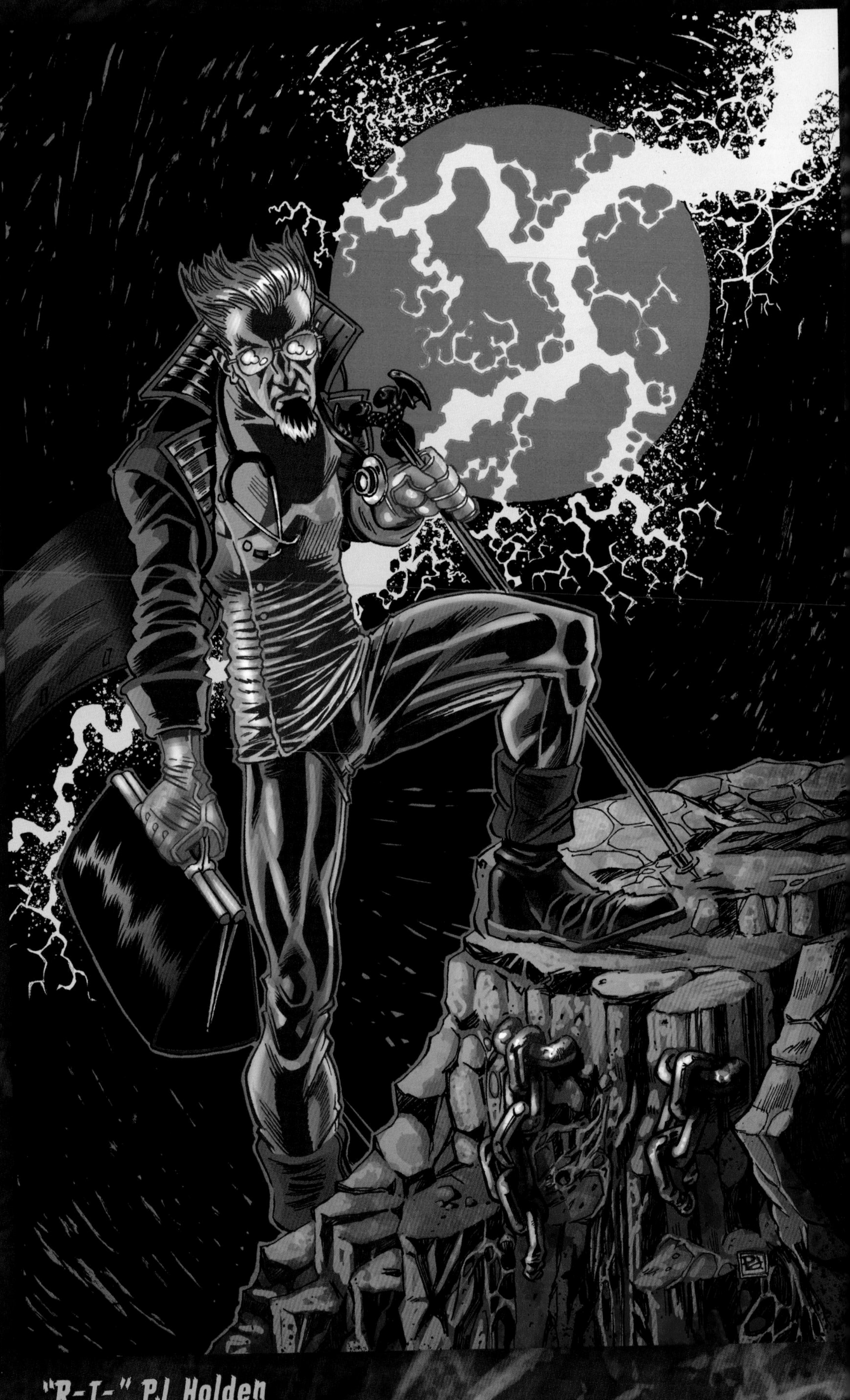

"R-I-" PJ Holden

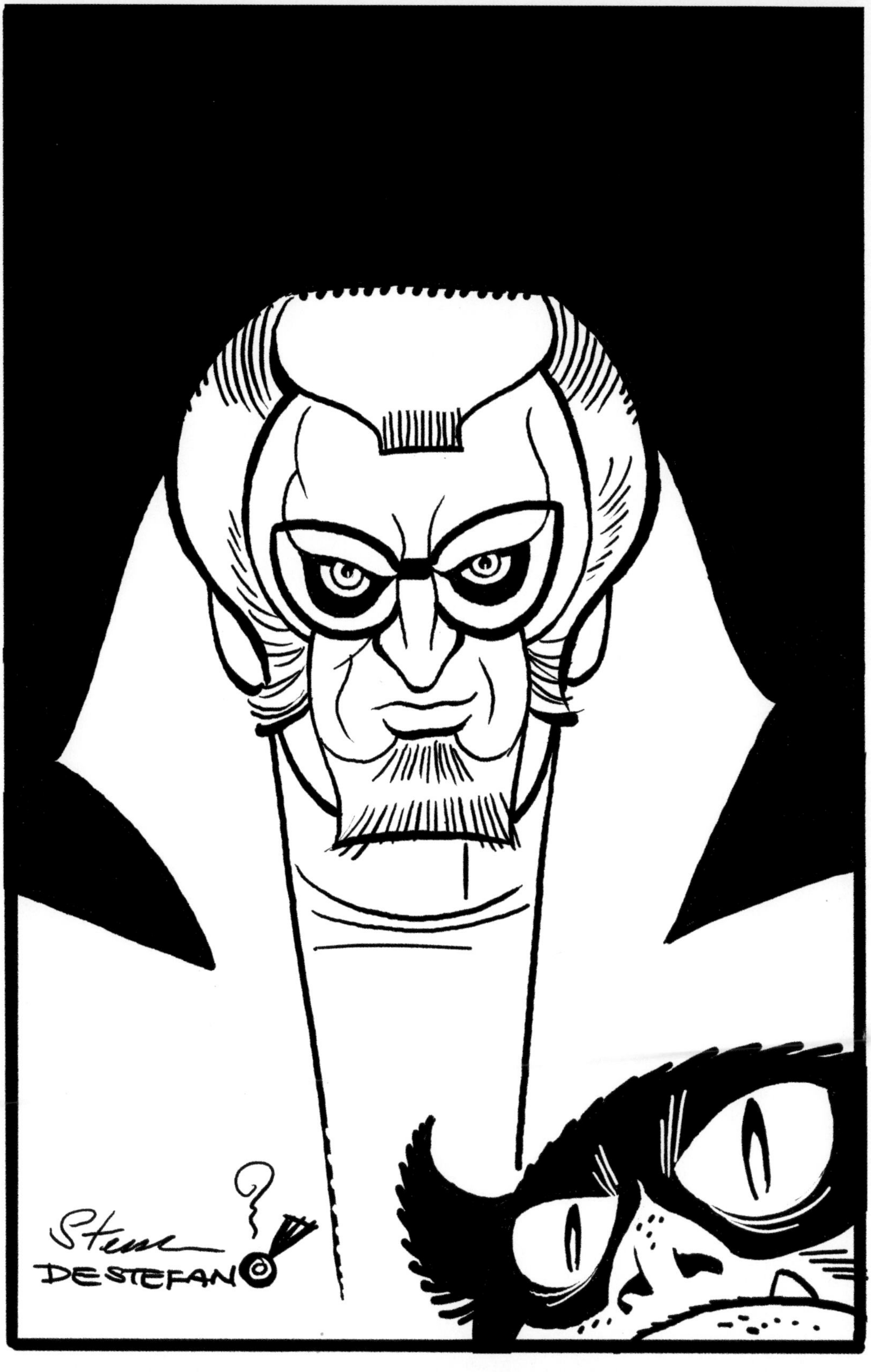
Steve
DESTEFANO

"Nefarious" Stephen DeStefano

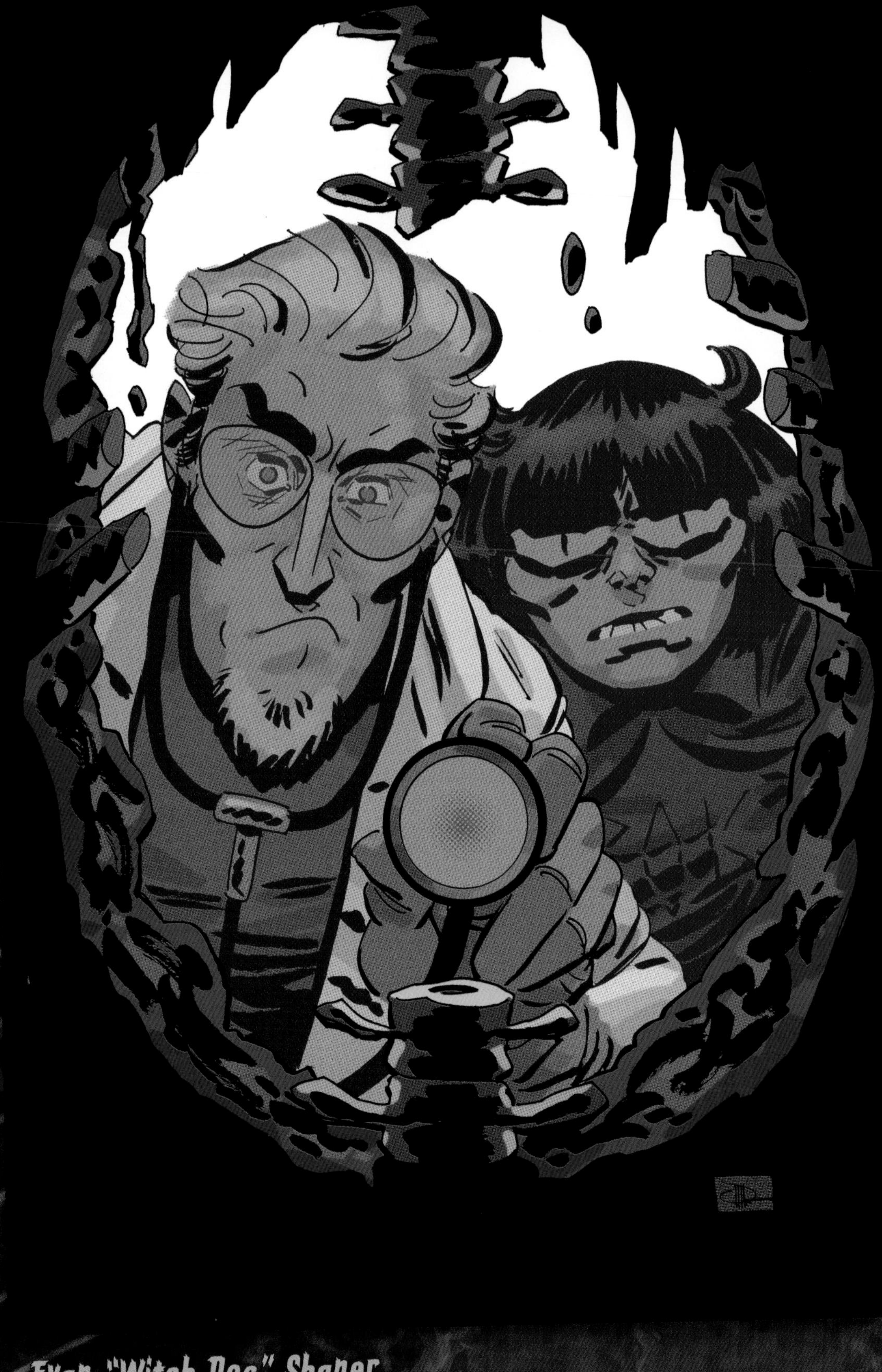

Evan "Witch Doc" Shaner

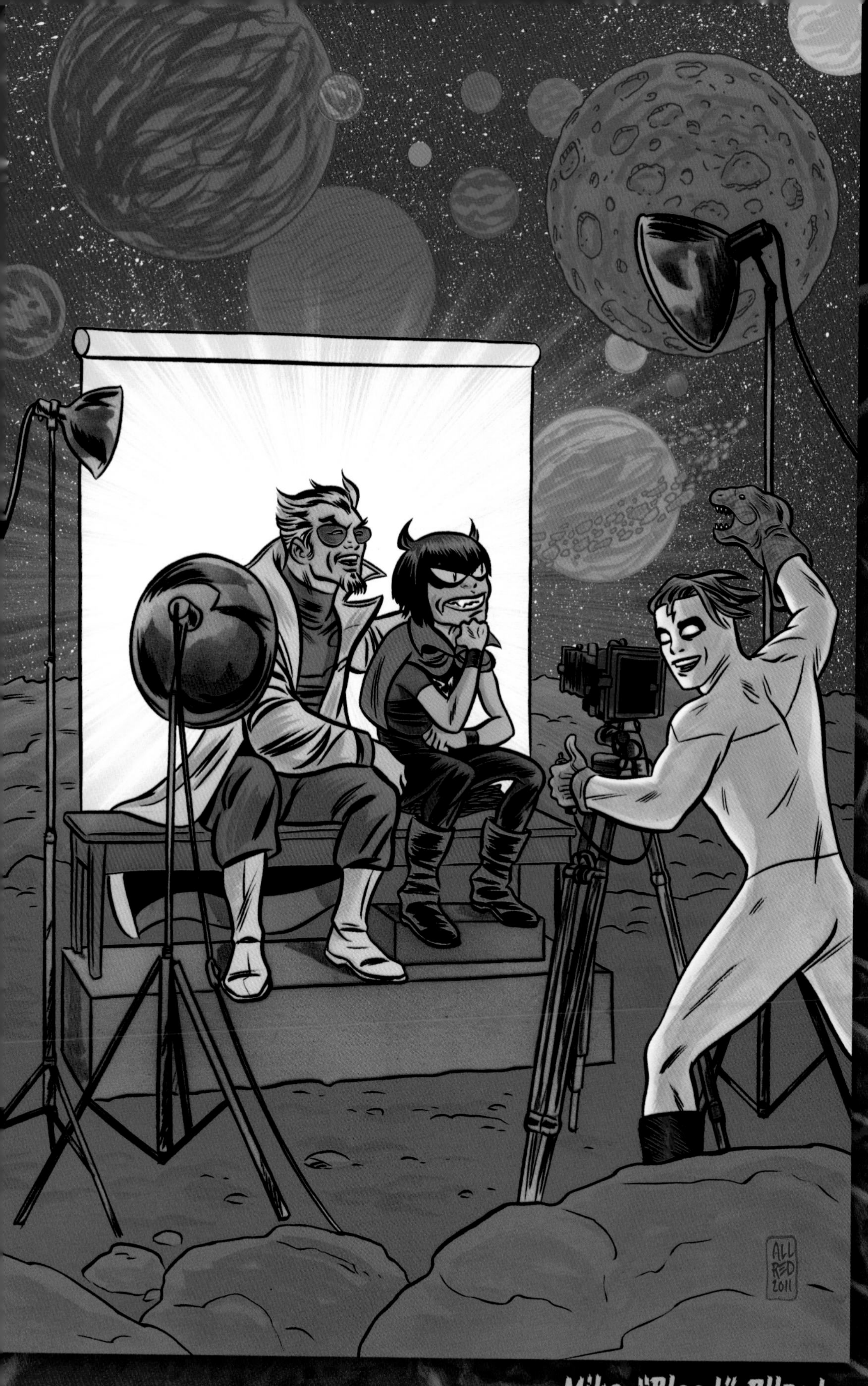
ALL
RED
2011

Mike "Blood" Allred

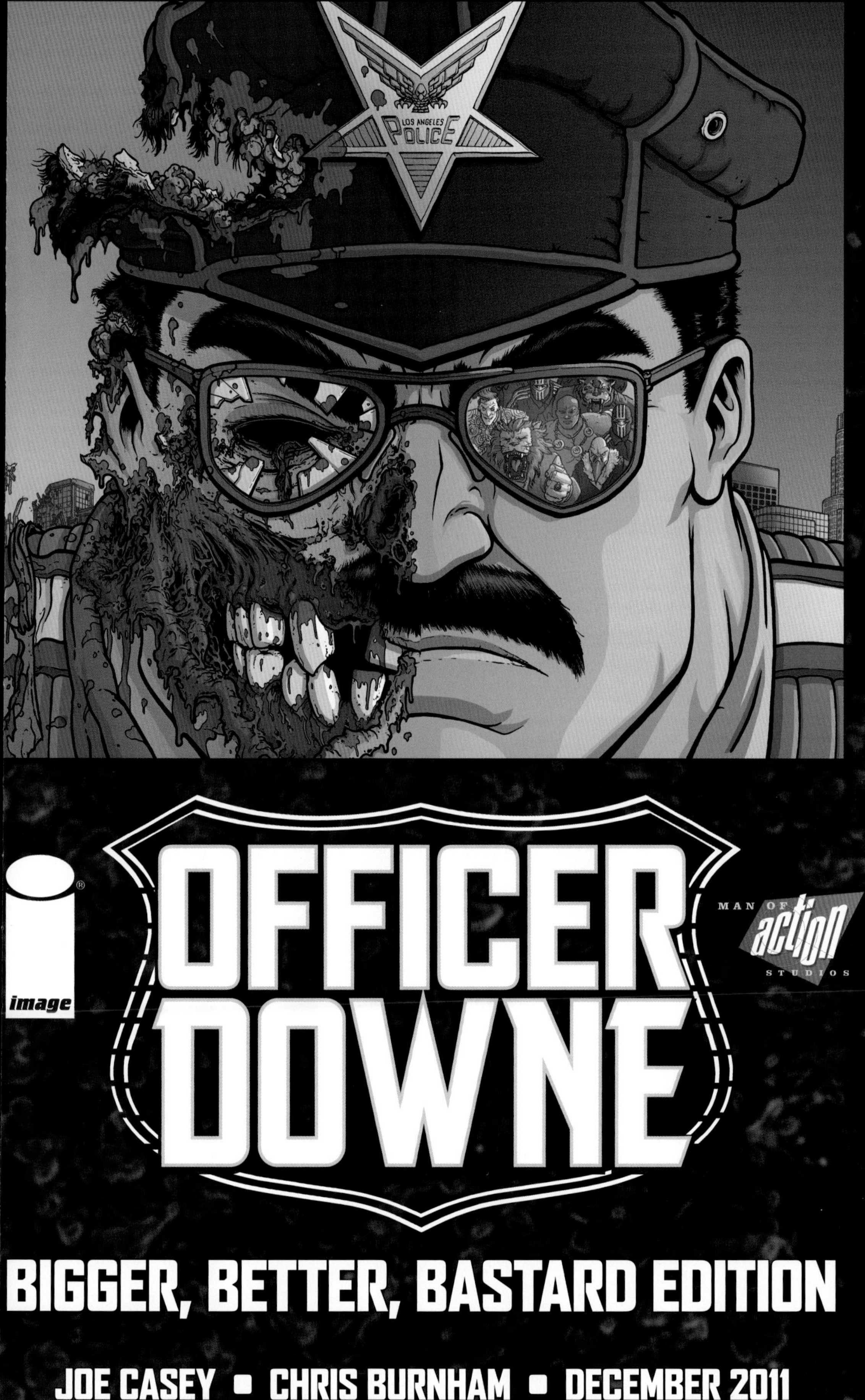
LOS ANGELES
POLICE

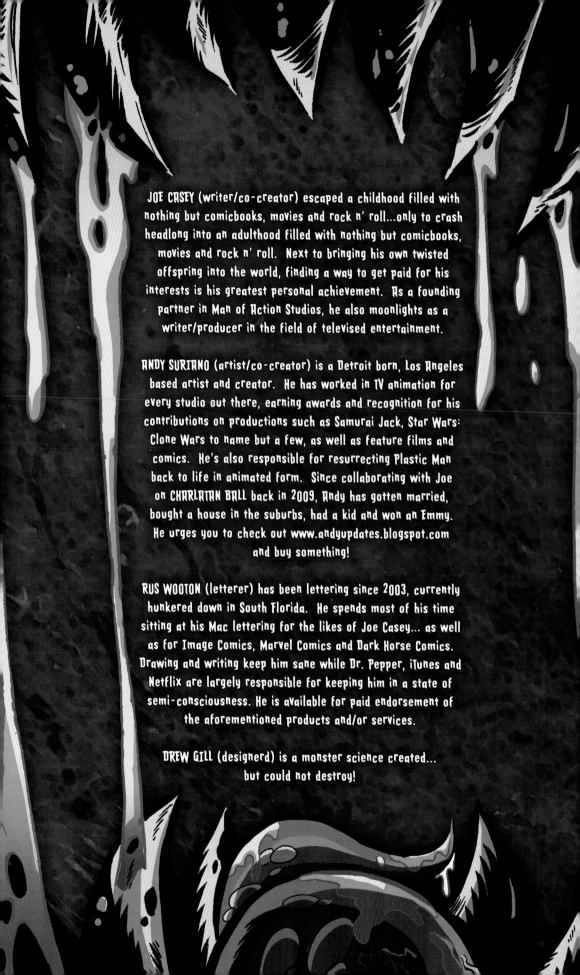

JOE CASEY (writer/co-creator) escaped a childhood filled with nothing but comicbooks, movies and rock n' roll...only to crash headlong into an adulthood filled with nothing but comicbooks, movies and rock n' roll. Next to bringing his own twisted offspring into the world, finding a way to get paid for his interests is his greatest personal achievement. As a founding partner in Man of Action Studios, he also moonlights as a writer/producer in the field of televised entertainment.

ANDY SURIANO (artist/co-creator) is a Detroit born, Los Angeles based artist and creator. He has worked in TV animation for every studio out there, earning awards and recognition for his contributions on productions such as Samurai Jack, Star Wars: Clone Wars to name but a few, as well as feature films and comics. He's also responsible for resurrecting Plastic Man back to life in animated form. Since collaborating with Joe on CHARLATAN BALL back in 2009, Andy has gotten married, bought a house in the suburbs, had a kid and won an Emmy. He urges you to check out www.andyupdates.blogspot.com and buy something!

RUS WOOTON (letterer) has been lettering since 2003, currently hunkered down in South Florida. He spends most of his time sitting at his Mac lettering for the likes of Joe Casey... as well as for Image Comics, Marvel Comics and Dark Horse Comics. Drawing and writing keep him sane while Dr. Pepper, iTunes and Netflix are largely responsible for keeping him in a state of semi-consciousness. He is available for paid endorsement of the aforementioned products and/or services.

DREW GILL (designerd) is a monster science created... but could not destroy!

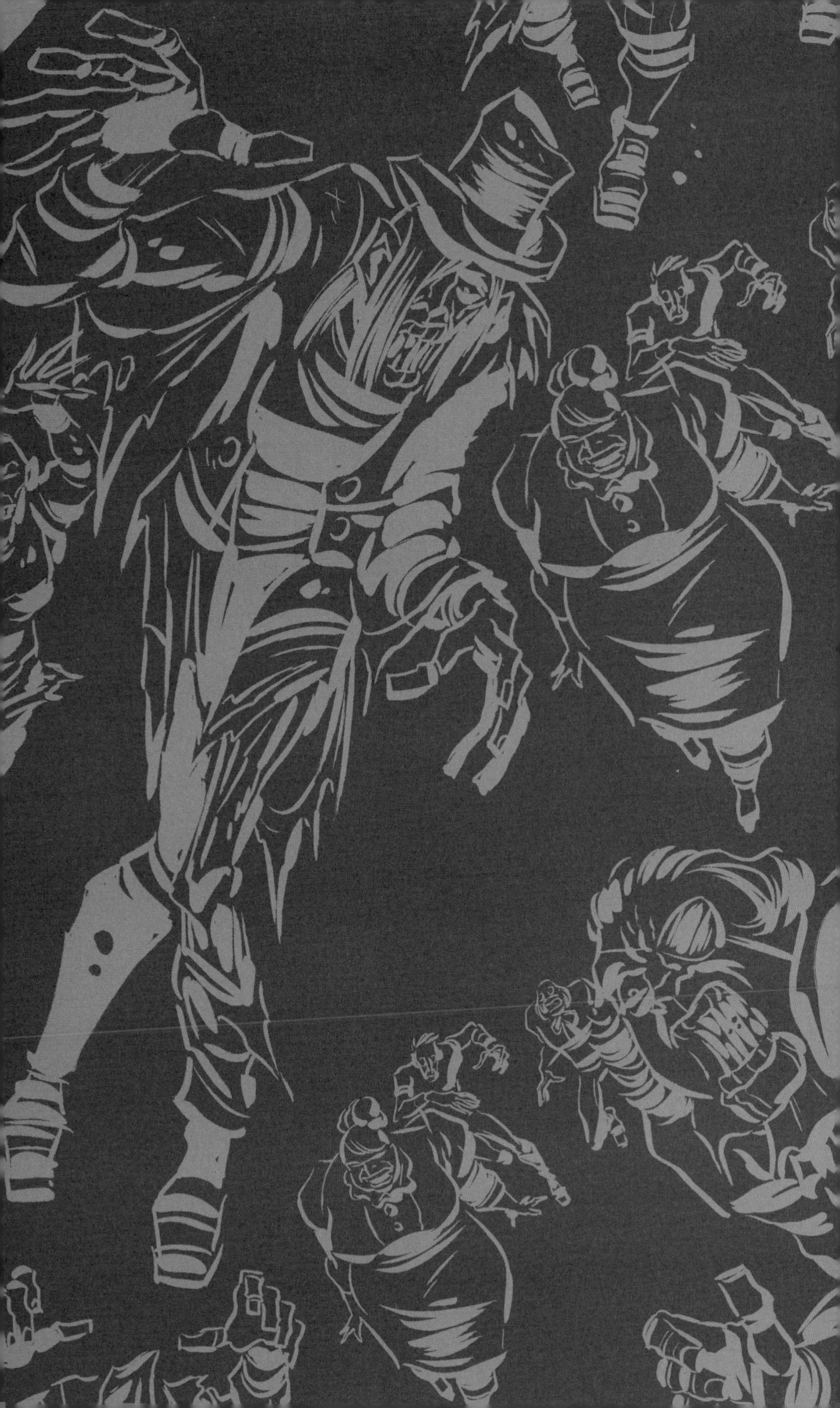

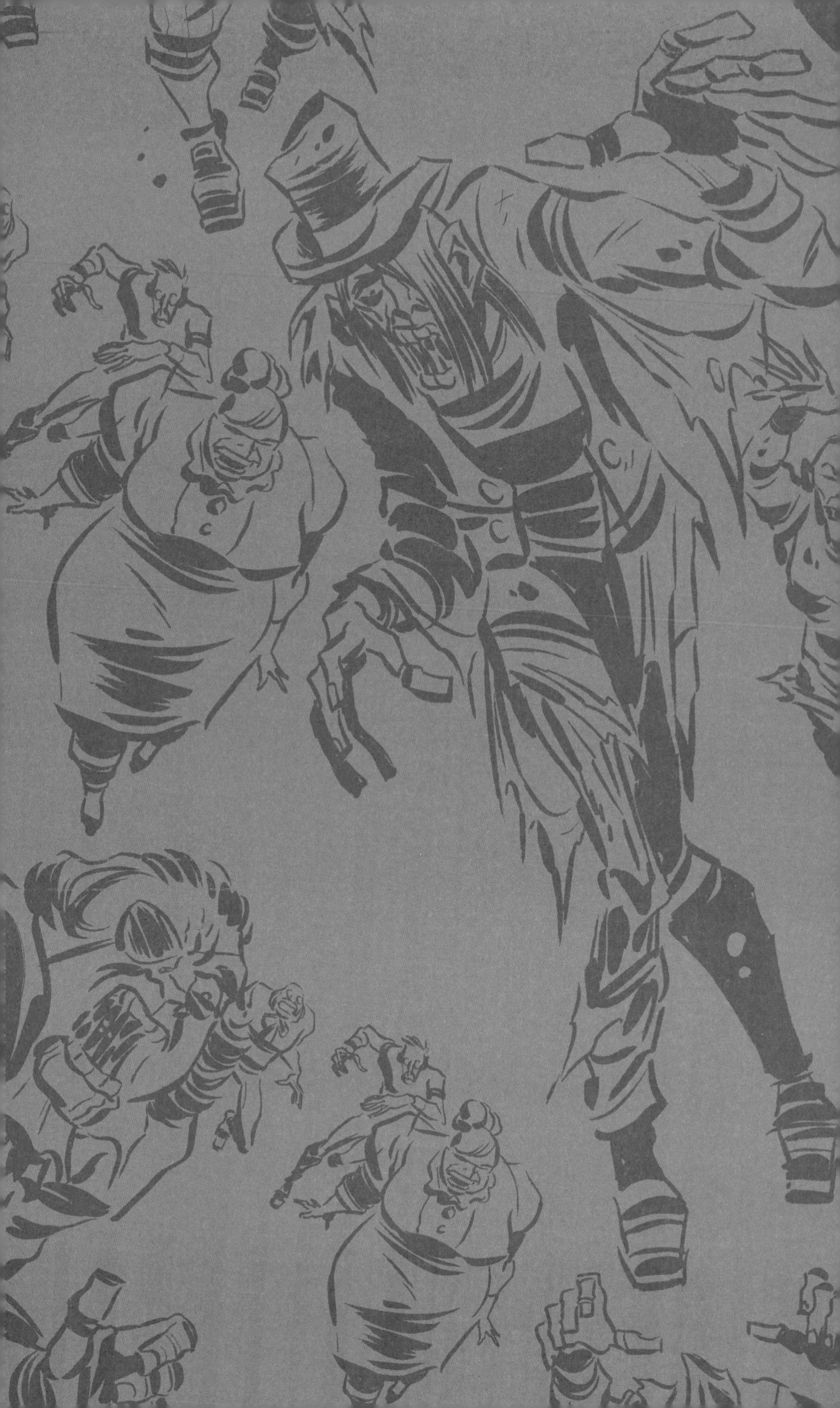